Mania and
Marjorie Diehl-Armstrong

Mania and Marjorie Diehl-Armstrong

Inside the Mind of a Female Serial Killer

Jerry Clark and Ed Palattella

ROWMAN & LITTLEFIELD
Lanham • Boulder • New York • London

Published by Rowman & Littlefield
A wholly owned subsidiary of The Rowman & Littlefield Publishing Group, Inc.
4501 Forbes Boulevard, Suite 200, Lanham, Maryland 20706
www.rowman.com

Unit A, Whitacre Mews, 26-34 Stannary Street, London SE11 4AB

British Library Cataloguing in Publication Information Available

Library of Congress Cataloging-in-Publication Data Available

ISBN 978-1-4422-6007-8 (cloth : alk. paper)

♾️™ The paper used in this publication meets the minimum requirements of American National Standard for Information Sciences—Permanence of Paper for Printed Library Materials, ANSI/NISO Z39.48-1992.

Printed in the United States of America

To
D. C. and C. P.

"Great wits are sure to madness near allied, and thin partitions do their bounds divide."
—John Dryden, *Absalom and Achitophel* (1681)

"The trouble with conspiracies is that they rot internally."
—Robert A. Heinlein, *The Moon Is a Harsh Mistress* (1966)

Contents

Acknowledgments

The travails of Marjorie Diehl-Armstrong have become almost legendary in Erie, Pennsylvania, especially at the two places where she stood trial: the Erie County Courthouse and the United States District Courthouse in Erie. The records of those and many other cases that involved Diehl-Armstrong are voluminous, and we thank all those who helped us obtain and review the files and documents. They include Susan Parmeter, Debbie Mayo, and Jennifer Dash at the federal clerk's office; and Bob Catalde, Ken Gamble, Tito Bongiorno, Kelly Malone, Karla Jeffery, Aubrea Haynes, and Paula Miller at the Erie County Courthouse. A special thanks also to Max Peaster, the law librarian at the Erie County Courthouse; and Bob Sparks, of the Nash Library at Gannon University in Erie. The Federal Bureau of Investigation provided assistance tracking down records as well. The views expressed in this book are those of the authors alone, however, and do not necessarily reflect those of the FBI. We are grateful for the work of copy editor Gary Hamel and, once again, for the work of our editor at Rowman & Littlefield, Kathryn Knigge, and for the continued guidance of our literary agent, John Talbot.

Jerry Clark: While researching this book I had numerous hours of reflection on my law enforcement career in general and my dealings with Marjorie Diehl-Armstrong in particular. I was reminded of the dedication and persistence of the outstanding agents, officers, and attorneys with whom I was privileged to work throughout my dealings with Diehl-Armstrong and the Pizza Bomber investigation. I especially want to thank my partner in the case, Jason Wick, now a retired special agent with the Bureau of Alcohol, Tobacco, Firearms, and Explosives. I also wish to express my sincere gratitude to all those who assisted in the investigation, including employees with the FBI, Pennsylvania State Police, Erie Bureau of Police, and the Erie Division of the United States Attorney's Office for the Western District of Pennsylvania, specifically Assistant United States Attorney Marshall Piccinini. I particularly want to express my deepest appreciation to Dawn Parnell and Rebecca Hart from the FBI's Erie Resident Agency for their invaluable work on the case and for their enduring friendship. I am grateful for the insights provided by my good friend the late Dennis Drotar, PhD, who was a professor in the division of behavioral medicine and clinical psychology at Cincinnati Children's Hospital Medical Center. Lastly, I would like to thank from the bottom of my heart my wife, Danielle, and children, Michael and Isabelle, for their unconditional and unwavering love, support, and patience.

Ed Palattella: The morgue of my employer, the *Erie Times-News*, was an invaluable resource in researching this book. I thank the paper's executive editor, Doug Oathout, and another top editor, Pat Howard, for their continuing interest and support. In reading all the past newspaper stories on Marjorie Diehl-Armstrong, I was reminded again of the great talents of my colleagues and friends at the *Erie Times-News*. They include Lisa Thompson, Tim Hahn, and Kevin Flowers, each of whom wrote about Diehl-Armstrong's later cases, including the Pizza Bomber case, with insight and verve. I am also fortunate to continue to enjoy friendships with now-retired *Erie Times-News* reporters John Guerriero and Jim Thompson, who covered Diehl-Armstrong's first homicide trial, in 1988, and whose articles proved so helpful for this book. And thanks, as always, to my wife, Chris, and our children, Henry and Nina, for still listening, with patience and good humor, to all my stories.

Introduction

$\mathcal{A}$t a time in her life when many people are preparing for retirement, a fifty-eight-year-old mentally unstable woman by the name of Marjorie Diehl-Armstrong was indicted in one of the most horrific bank robberies in the history of the Federal Bureau of Investigation. Her participation in that plot would have been enough, by itself, to secure her a spot as one of America's most infamous female criminals—a list that includes Bonnie Parker, Patty Hearst, Aileen Wuornos, and Susan Smith. But a series of violent and weird incidents preceded Diehl-Armstrong's most notorious crime. The pattern deepened her level of criminality and led a federal magistrate judge, in evaluating Diehl-Armstrong's entire homicidal career, to bestow upon her a dark description: "a coldly calculated criminal recidivist and serial killer."[1]

Diehl-Armstrong gained international attention starting in July 2007. A federal grand jury in her hometown of Erie, Pennsylvania, indicted her in the bizarre plot that became known as the Pizza Bomber case or the Collar Bomb case. Never before had the FBI worked such a crime. Brian Wells, a pizza deliveryman, was killed in August 2003 when a homemade bomb that was locked to his neck exploded after he robbed a bank just south of Erie. With her indictment and then her conviction, in 2010, Diehl-Armstrong became the widely photographed and televised face of the strange act of brazen outlawry. Well before then, in the largely sleepy confines of Erie, the only place she has ever lived while not incarcerated, Diehl-Armstrong instilled disbelief and fear.

Throughout her life, six men linked to her or her crimes died; five perished due to unnatural causes. The pattern started in 1984, when Diehl-Armstrong, then Marjorie Diehl, emptied a revolver into her sleeping boyfriend. Between that homicide and the bombing of Wells, four other men died. One was another boyfriend, whom Diehl-Armstrong blasted in the back with a shotgun and whose dead body she helped stuff into a freezer. Another boyfriend committed suicide. Another man died of a suspicious drug overdose. And another, Diehl-Armstrong's only husband, Richard Armstrong, whom she married in January 1991, suffered a fatal brain hemorrhage after he collapsed during a stroke and hit his head on a coffee table in the couple's living room in 1992. Each death brought more twisted celebrity to Diehl-Armstrong in Erie. Each death led many in Erie to marvel at how a certain kind of man was sure to risk danger and even death if he came to know—and, especially, if he came to love—Marjorie Diehl-Armstrong.

She is, in the words of another judge she has faced, "sociopathic."[2]

She also is, according to the federal magistrate judge and the prevailing definitions, a serial killer. She indisputably killed two men, and she was convicted of conspiring in the murder of another—Brian Wells. But Diehl-Armstrong never targeted strangers, and she never tracked or stalked her victims. Despite the level of planning inherent in the Pizza Bomber case, her slayings were more acts of calculated fury than ritualized homicides. Diehl-Armstrong, who, at sixty-eight years old, died on April 4, 2017, while serving a sentence of life plus thirty years in federal prison, was nonetheless a rarity. She was a serial killer who was also a woman.

What led her to kill?

What caused death to surround her?

Those questions have challenged us for years. Jerry Clark tried to answer them as the FBI special agent who led the investigation of the Pizza Bomber case. His background in forensic psychology helped him as he interviewed Diehl-Armstrong eight times. Ed Palattella, who reported on the Pizza Bomber case for the *Erie Times-News*, gained his own understanding of Diehl-Armstrong through his almost daily telephone conversations with her since late 2007. She has always been willing to talk—sometimes too willing.

In this chronicle of Marjorie Diehl-Armstrong's life, we aim to provide a deep understanding of her and other women like her—women who have committed serial murders. Our exploration of Diehl-Armstrong's life also examines the development of forensic psychology and psychiatry. And it looks at how the American justice system has evolved to address such issues as insanity and competency so as to be able to manage cases like Diehl-Armstrong's—cases in which mental illness is as prevalent as murder. Marjorie Diehl-Armstrong's relationship with crime is unique in American criminal history. She is as fascinating as she is deadly.

Jerry Clark
Ed Palattella
November 2016
Erie, Pennsylvania

• 1 •

Cycle of Death

Marjorie Diehl-Armstrong's Pattern of Violence

*S*he had reached verbal fury. Marjorie Diehl-Armstrong had always liked to talk, and to talk a lot, especially when she could go on and on, uninterrupted, as if on a stage. At this moment, the stage could get no bigger and the attention could get no greater.

Diehl-Armstrong was speaking into the microphone at the defense table in the middle of the most spacious courtroom at the United States District Courthouse in downtown Erie, Pennsylvania. Everyone in the packed gallery was turned toward her, which is what she liked. She was able to look at the federal judge directly, as if they were equals, which is also what she liked. The judge, Sean J. McLaughlin, had pledged, throughout her trial, to give her plenty of time to speak, and he again had shown her great patience and deference on this day, February 28, 2011—the date of her sentencing in what was known as the Pizza Bomber case or the Collar Bomb case.

Diehl-Armstrong's victim was a forty-six-year-old pizza deliveryman by the name of Brian Wells. He had been killed nearly eight years earlier when a bomb locked to his neck exploded after he robbed a bank near Erie. The case was beyond strange; the FBI had never seen anything like it. The case was so unusual and complex and deadly that the FBI elevated it to a priority, and labeled it Major Case 203. Wells's assailants had sent him on a scavenger hunt in a failed attempt for him to gather clues to deactivate the bomb before it blew up. Diehl-Armstrong had a long history of suffering from bipolar disorder and other mental illnesses. She was convicted of being an accomplice in Wells's death. She knew, as the spectators in the courtroom knew, that, at sixty-two years old, she was facing a mandatory prison sentence of life plus thirty years. Her conviction had guaranteed that punishment. But Diehl-Armstrong wanted to do whatever she could to persuade McLaughlin that she was innocent.

So she talked. And she talked.

"I'm a good, decent person," Diehl-Armstrong said. "I've got the equivalent of five college degrees, and I have a master's degree. I'm a certified teacher. I'm a music teacher. I'm a social science teacher. I worked at these jobs. I worked with the state. . . . I have a degree in sociology. I am not a bank robber. I don't have to rob banks to get money. I am a certified guidance counselor. I almost have a doctorate, less dissertation. I am certified to counsel elementary and secondary schools. I'm not crazed. . . . I am not a crazy person."[1]

"What I am trying to say," Diehl-Armstrong continued, "is I've had mental problems. I haven't made the best choices. I've made mistakes and I'm paying for them. What I've done wrong in my life, I will admit to. But I'll be damned if I'm going to take the heat for [those who] killed this guy."[2]

McLaughlin broke in. "Is there anything else that you would like to tell me?"

"I would like to say . . . ," Diehl-Armstrong said.

She started another ramble, and she declared her innocence over and over.

"Ms. Armstrong," McLaughlin said, "you've got twenty seconds to wrap up."

Diehl-Armstrong, at five feet, eight inches tall and 168 pounds, had been a forceful presence throughout her trial. Now her voice again boomed in the courtroom.

"All I'm trying to say is, Don't count me out," she said. "You know, there's an old Arkansas proverb, 'If it doesn't come out in the wash, it will come out in the rinse.' Someone get me a real lawyer; let the truth come out, please. To my dying breath let the real truth come out."

"Ms. Armstrong," McLaughlin said, "thank you very much."[3]

Diehl-Armstrong grew quiet, but she seethed as she listened to the next speaker, the assistant United States attorney who prosecuted her case, Marshall Piccinini. He detailed the evidence he had presented over the ten-day trial, which had ended with Diehl-Armstrong's conviction on November 1, 2010.

"In the end, Your Honor, there are many themes to why people become involved in criminal activity," Piccinini said. "You see regularly crimes of opportunity, crimes of passion, crimes of greed. Crimes related to drug abuse and use. But this particular case was motivated by greed and was completely characterized by evil.

"The jurors in this case saw the depths of human depravity," Piccinini said. "Not only did they see an evil plot, which in this twisted scheme

[included sending] Brian Wells on a collision course towards his death . . .
but this was an evil scheme, a plot to kill him and to jeopardize the lives of
other people in the community."[4]

Piccinini referred to Diehl-Armstrong's history of mental illness.

"She does have mental illness," he said. "But when you combine this
woman's serious mental illness with regard to her personality disorder, her
narcissism, her paranoia, her deception, her manipulativeness: You combine
that in one person with evil and this is the type of crime that results. The
combination of Marjorie Diehl and her propensity towards violence in this
particular case proved deadly."[5]

Piccinini asked that McLaughlin sentence Diehl-Armstrong to the
mandatory life plus thirty years, "to ensure that this woman will not be in a
position to kill again."[6]

Diehl-Armstrong remained quiet. The recitation of her tumultuous life
story was difficult to hear. Death was always around her. Even her only husband, Richard Armstrong, was dead; he collapsed from a stroke in 1992, less
than two years after they had married. Her relationships with men invariably
turned deadly—and in the case of Wells's, the manner of death was more
extreme than anything the FBI had ever investigated in the context of a bank
robbery. McLaughlin explained why Wells's death justified the mandatory
sentence.

"Its bizarre nature, coupled with the equally bizarre and sociopathic
personalities who have perpetrated it, have tended to obscure what this case
is really about," he said. "And that is that this defendant and her conspirators
sent a man to his certain death and, in so doing, risked injury or death to
many other people."[7]

McLaughlin referred to Diehl-Armstrong's many years of mental
dysfunction. He said other people suffer from similar mental diseases that
plagued Diehl-Armstrong, and that they did not act in cold blood "or seal a
man's fate by strapping a ticking time bomb to his neck."[8] Then McLaughlin
reached his verbal crescendo. He, not Diehl-Armstrong, had the true power
in the courtroom. He reviewed her life as she now sat in silence, almost like
a stone. Her earlier efforts at persuasion, to show the judge that she really *did
not do it*, would have never succeeded, but now their failure was complete.

"Finally," McLaughlin said, "it is worth noting that the presentence
report reflects that Ms. Armstrong was an excellent student, who graduated
twelfth out of 413 students in her high school class. She then went on to obtain a bachelor's degree in sociology. As well as a master's degree in education.
All of which begs the question as to what might have been."[9]

She received her sentence: life plus thirty years, with no parole. Marjorie Diehl-Armstrong, no matter how promising she once seemed so many years ago, was all but certain to die in prison. She left the courtroom in handcuffs, and in silence.

Prison was nothing new to Marjorie Diehl-Armstrong. She was already incarcerated when she was indicted in the Pizza Bomber case, in July 2007. She was serving a sentence of seven to twenty years in a Pennsylvania state prison for pleading guilty but mentally ill to shooting her forty-five-year-old live-in boyfriend, James Roden, in the back at the house they shared in Erie in mid-August 2003. Roden had abused her, but their relationship had appeared to reach a degree of calm before the murder. After Roden's death, Diehl-Armstrong helped her former fiancé, William A. Rothstein, stuff Roden's body into a freezer in Rothstein's garage in rural Erie County. When she stood before an Erie County judge to get sentenced for Roden's death, Diehl-Armstrong talked, as she always did, but she acted contrite rather than defiant. She apologized for Roden's death and thanked "everybody for trying to help me"[10]—a reference to her mental illness.

"I'm sorry," said Diehl-Armstrong, then fifty-five years old. "I'm not going to be in any more trouble. I know I learned my lesson. And if I get another chance in life, I'm not going to lose it and I'm going to thank God and the people that gave it to me. I'm really going to appreciate it from the bottom of my heart. And this is the truth. I'm not a bad person."[11]

Diehl-Armstrong had made similar pronouncements before. Nineteen years earlier, in July 1988, when she was known as Marjorie Diehl, she stood in a courtroom at the Erie County Courthouse for another sentencing. She had undeniably killed a man—her first known homicide victim, her boyfriend Robert Thomas, a forty-three-year-old Navy veteran of the Vietnam War. Diehl was thirty-five years old on July 30, 1984, when she shot Thomas six times as he rested on a couch in the modest house they shared in a quiet section of Erie. Diehl pleaded self-defense and claimed Thomas beat her; the contention that she was the victim of domestic abuse and mental illness would run throughout her life. Diehl spent nearly four years in prison while awaiting trial. Then she was acquitted of first-degree murder in Thomas's death.

"I've learned my lesson," she said after the verdict. "I've done my time, and I'm not going to get into any more trouble."[12]

Diehl-Armstrong lost all her appeals, including in the Pizza Bomber case, in which the federal courts turned her away again and again. In 2014, a federal magistrate judge, Martin C. Carlson, summarized Diehl-Armstrong's criminal career in harsh terms. Her myriad "crimes reflected a stunning degree of calculated cruelty,"[13] the judge wrote, and he called her "a coldly calculated criminal recidivist and serial killer who denied culpability, and possessed a high potential for future violence."[14] And as if to make sure no one, including Diehl-Armstrong, missed his point, the judge listed the reasons Diehl-Armstrong deserved no reprieve. Two of the reasons were the deaths of Jim Roden and Brian Wells.

"These facts," the judge wrote, "include her involvement in two calculated killings, murders marked by brutality, sadism, cruelty, and the morbid abuse of her victims, both living and dead."[15]

Other than prison, only one other place was home to Marjorie Diehl-Armstrong. She grew up, went to college, found jobs, and then killed in Erie, an industrial city of about one hundred thousand people in the northwestern corner of Pennsylvania, on Lake Erie and Presque Isle Bay, one of the most naturally protected harbors on the Great Lakes. Erie, known nationally for its record-setting snowfalls, is two hours equidistant from Cleveland to the west, Buffalo to the east, and Pittsburgh to the south. When Diehl-Armstrong was born, on February 26, 1949, Erie boomed as a manufacturing powerhouse, the home to plants whose well-paid blue-collar workers churned out castings and boilers and paper and washing machines and, most prominently, locomotives at the sprawling General Electric factory just to the east of town, where as many as eighteen thousand people worked in the 1940s.[16] Erie was known throughout the United States for its manufacturing prowess, and at one time, in the 1920s, it was also known as the freshwater fishing capital of the world, for the hundreds of commercial fishing boats that jammed its docks.

Erie claimed a sliver of glory in American history as well. During the War of 1812, Commodore Oliver Hazard Perry's headquarters was in Erie. While sheltered in Presque Isle Bay, he and his sailors built the ships he commanded during the defeat of the British fleet in the Battle of Lake Erie, near what is today Put-in-Bay, Ohio, on September 10, 1813. The battle flag that Perry's men hoisted that day—a bright blue banner emblazoned with "Don't Give Up the Ship," in white—was popular in Erie, and the famous phrase on the flag eventually became Erie's unofficial motto, a saying that exuded hope against desperation: However bad things get, try not to sink. Erie needed all the help it could find by the 2000s. Diehl-Armstrong heard and repeated all the pathetic nicknames for Erie, which in its glory days was known as the "Gem City," because of gorgeous Lake Erie and Presque Isle Bay. But as industry declined and the bay grew polluted (swimming in it was a hazard until the early 2000s), the stinging catchphrases proliferated. Diehl-Armstrong knew them all, and, as she got older and ended up in prison, she grew to despise the only city where she had ever lived. "Your whole town sucks," she once said. "Dreary Erie. The Mistake on the Lake."[17]

The negative sentiment took hold in the 1980s, 1990s, and 2000s—the period that coincided with Diehl-Armstrong's midlife—as Erie faced constant economic struggles. The International Paper plant, founded in 1899, closed in 2002, putting 775 people out of work.[18] GE shed thousands of jobs in Erie as it built a locomotive plant in Texas, where the workers were not unionized; by 2016, the Erie GE plant was down to about 2,900 employees. The city's rate of child poverty increased until it became one of the highest in the nation. Erie, mindful of its heritage and its past economic greatness, remained proud through the unraveling, a decline not unlike those that beset so many other Rust Belt cities, from Detroit to Cleveland to Buffalo. But many of those cities rebounded. Erie, by the late 2000s, remained mired in high unemployment, poverty, crime, and population loss, though it had also developed what remained a sparkling waterfront. Diehl-Armstrong's deterioration in many ways mirrored that of her native city. And much like Erie tended to fixate on its glorious past, Diehl-Armstrong unfailingly held herself in a high regard, no matter how damning the evidence of collapse around her.

Marjorie Eleanor Diehl was an only child. Her special place in her household allowed her, early on, to enjoy even more of the attention that she sought throughout her life. Her mother, Agnes Eleanor Wolfenden Diehl, was also an only child, though her father, Harold Diehl, known as "Hub," was one of nine children; he had two brothers and six sisters. Agnes Wolfenden and Harold Diehl wed in Erie on August 22, 1942. Harold was making locomotives at GE at that time. When he returned from World War II, he started on a career path in which he was a construction foreman and sold aluminum awnings door to door. He had fallen short of a high school diploma. His wife was much more accomplished in her education. She had a bachelor's degree from Edinboro Teachers' College, now Edinboro University of Pennsylvania, just south of Erie, and a master's degree from the University of Pittsburgh; she also did graduate work at Columbia University.[19] Agnes Diehl was teaching high school when she married, and went on to teach elementary school in the Erie School District for nearly forty years, until 1980.

The Diehls had been married six and one-half years when Marjorie was born; Agnes was thirty-two years old and Harold was thirty. They lived in the same house all their married life—a 2,016-square-foot two-family residence built in 1917 whose first owners were Marjorie Diehl's maternal grandparents, George and Eleanor Wolfenden, from whom Marjorie and her mother took their middle names. Sometimes Diehl-Armstrong was called "Ellen," after "Eleanor."[20]

The neighborhood was filled with young families who took root after World War II, during which Harold Diehl served in the United States Coast Guard in Europe, Africa, and the Middle East.[21] Agnes and Harold Diehl earned a fair amount of money over the years, which they saved and invested well. When Agnes Diehl died, at age eighty-three, in July 2000, she and her husband had accumulated an estate of $1.8 million, mostly in municipal bonds.[22] Marjorie Diehl-Armstrong regarded that fortune as her legacy, and, according to the FBI, ultimately she was willing to arrange to have someone kill for it.

Her parents' dual incomes gave Marjorie Diehl a childhood of comfort and stability. Throughout grade school and high school, she lived at the same house and attended the same schools, year after year. She went to the same grade school, McKinley Elementary, where her grandfather and her mother had gone; her mother taught at McKinley for most of her career.[23] And when she enrolled at Erie's Academy High School, in 1964, as a sophomore (which was customary at the time), Marjorie Diehl followed her parents. Her father attended Academy until dropping out, and her mother graduated from Academy before heading off to college to become a teacher.[24]

As a girl, Diehl looked up the most not to her father and mother, but to other relatives whose standing in Erie, she believed, was higher than that of her parents. She liked to talk about her cousin, John C. Diehl, an educator with the Erie School District for forty-eight years, including thirteen as superintendent of schools, from 1922 to 1935. His death, at age eighty-seven, on August 27, 1952, was the subject of a front-page story, with a banner headline, in the *Erie Daily Times*. The newspaper called him the "grand old man" of Erie education, who was "widely known as a great scholar, fine teacher, accomplished administrator, devoted civic leader and warm-hearted humanitarian."[25] John Diehl attended Oberlin College and graduated from Yale University with honors. He returned to Erie and the Erie School District and never left; the school district named Diehl Elementary School after him—a fact that Marjorie Diehl-Armstrong would relate to anyone who would listen, including jurors.

John C. Diehl's fame aside, Diehl-Armstrong as a girl identified more with her mother's family—the Wolfendens—than her father's. Her maternal grandparents lived in a house neighboring the Diehls; the backyards connected, and young Marjorie walked back and forth as she pleased. She said her maternal grandparents often babysat her, especially, she recalled, "when my father was out at the bars."[26] She adored her grandfather, George Wolfenden, an Erie police sergeant, and she considered him a surrogate father. She also admired her great-uncle, William Wolfenden, a shop worker who she said built houses with her grandfather when they were not working their regular jobs. If Diehl considered her parents fairly well off, she considered her grandparents rich, just as she yearned to be. Her Grandfather Wolfenden, she once recalled, "was a good man. . . . He was a builder of houses; this is where the money came into the family. Because he actually accrued all this wealth. He and his hard-working brother, who never married, who worked at Erie Meter Company longer than anyone ever did and saved and invested all this money and gave it all to my mother—supposedly for me, for my future because I was an only child."[27]

Her admiration for her grandparents' financial acumen instilled in her an understanding of money that turned into an obsession. At eight years old, an age when many girls of her generation played with dolls, Marjorie Diehl dreamed about money and became fixated on it. Her greed—an avarice that deepened and darkened as the years passed—could have originated in those joyful visits to her grandparents' house. Diehl liked what she saw; better yet, she believed that what she saw was destined to be all hers. She was entitled to a fortune.

"My grandparents, they handled money excellently," Diehl-Armstrong recalled. "They were wonderful people. They had a safe in their house. When I was a kid, they even showed me the money, stacked up, that they took over to Union Bank.

"They started me banking when I was a kid. I used to take their mortgage payments for them when they went out shopping or doing something. And then make or write the receipts for people. And then they would have me take the money over every Friday to the bank to deposit. They would tell me how some day that was going to be my inheritance because that's what they were building."[28]

Marjorie Diehl realized even before she was a teenager that money could make you different from other people; in her view, money could make you better. She grew up with an outsized opinion of herself as an heiress. Her neighbors were largely working class, and she considered herself above them. She got her sense of superiority, she later said, from her mother, who she said always wanted her to be at the top and apart from her peers. "I was an only child," Diehl-Armstrong once said, "and I lived an isolated life";[29] she also said she "lived in her mind."[30] Well into her fifties and sixties, when reflecting on her childhood Diehl-Armstrong returned to the same theme: Her mother loved her, but also drove her to pursue a level of perfection that many would consider unattainable. Marjorie Diehl was very much the daughter of an intellectual mother, a woman who, in the late 1930s and 1940s, was bright and bold enough to get a college degree and then do graduate work at one of the most prestigious universities in the country. Marjorie Diehl was special, as her mother was special.

"When you were raised, Marge," her lawyer asked her when she testified in the Pizza Bomber trial, "were you raised in poverty or were you raised with money?"

"I was always raised with a lot of money," Diehl-Armstrong said.

"When you went to high school, were you in the bottom of your class or the top of your class?"

"Top."

"Were you ever at the bottom of anything?" her lawyer said.

"No," Diehl-Armstrong replied.[31]

Her recollection of her childhood was fairly consistent over the years, based on trial testimony, repeated interviews, and statements she gave to psychologists and psychiatrists. Diehl, as a girl, is what would today be called overcommitted. But overcommitment and its hoped-for corollary of overachievement presented paths to a life of wealth and intellectual renown that she and her mother believed was her destiny. Though Diehl-Armstrong surely exaggerated to a degree, given her grandiosity, her childhood memories conveyed a frenzied and pressured girlhood, with music as one focus. Her father testified that she started taking piano lessons when she was five years old—a recollection that fit Diehl-Armstrong's memories.[32]

"I started studying at the Erie Conservatory when I was four," she once testified. "And I took lessons all the time. And I actually got my certificate younger than anybody—had to teach music when I was twelve years old. I was very precocious. I wanted to be a concert pianist at the time, like a child prodigy. I was playing on *Teens and Talents* TV show; I played the minor concerto when I was only thirteen years old. I did a very good job on that. . . . And I was only thirteen, so I thought that was pretty good."[33]

Diehl-Armstrong said she played cello in Erie's Junior Philharmonic as a teenager, another detail her father verified.[34] She also graduated from the Erie School of Music when she was fourteen years old.[35]

"Were you first chair, second chair?" Diehl-Armstrong's lawyer asked her about her prowess with the cello.

"First chair. First chair in my high school, junior high school, and grade school. Then I would just do solos, too, for Christmas concerts and things. Then I was a church organist, when I was about sixteen years old, and a youth choir director."

"Were you active in your church as well?"

"Yes," Diehl-Armstrong said. "I was active in Scouts. I had over one hundred merit badges. I was nominated for God and country award. I was a good person."[36]

Though Marjorie Diehl-Armstrong said she loved her parents, she also clearly resented them. Between the two of them, she often said, they inflicted a mental trauma that she believed manifested itself in her psychiatric imbalance. "My parents were fucked up," Diehl-Armstrong said in 2012, as she served her federal prison sentence of life plus thirty years. "They left a fucking mess."[37] And in what is known to be one of her earliest psychiatric exams, in 1972, when she was twenty-three, Diehl-Armstrong told a caseworker that her parents "spoiled her as a child but then 'turned mean.'"[38] In another analysis, a psychologist wrote that Diehl-Armstrong described "both her father and mother as having manic depressive periods" and she recalled "an incident where her father went at her mother with a butcher knife and she stepped in between them."[39]

Diehl-Armstrong claimed her father was an alcoholic who molested her as a girl, though she waited to make the assertion of sexual assault public in her testimony at the Pizza Bomber trial, in 2010. In the numerous interviews she had with psychologists and psychiatrists over the years, dating to as early as 1972, she never consistently accused her father of sexual assault. In 2010, on the witness stand, under oath, and trying whatever she could to win the sympathy of the jury, Diehl-Armstrong offered no hesitation before she branded her father, who was then still alive but suffering from dementia, a child molester. "He was sexually molesting me as a child and as an adolescent," she testified. "My mother always tried to be a buffer and protect me; she was a good woman."[40] Diehl-Armstrong said she never liked her father, and that, when her mother left the house and she was alone with him, she would find refuge across the backyard, at the house of her maternal grandparents and their safe stuffed with money. All that cash provided comfort, and a kind of hope, though later in life Diehl-Armstrong recalled the wealth with regret: "That money in my family was never more than a curse," she said.[41]

As much as she said she loved her mother over her father, Diehl-Armstrong considered her mother a poor influence on her as well. Looking back, she criticized what she characterized as her mother's relentless pursuit of perfection for her, as well as what she said was her parents' penchant to keep to themselves and to keep little Margie hidden as much as possible: "I was raised in the old style," she said. "Children should be seen but not heard."[42] At the same time, her mother pushed her into the public arena by enrolling her in the music classes and other events. Her mother, Diehl-Armstrong said, wanted her to be a teacher, like she was, or a medical doctor; Diehl-Armstrong once pointed out to another psychiatrist "that the first letter of Marjorie and the first letter of Diehl spelled MD."[43] She said she ultimately decided to study to become a teacher to please her mother.[44]

Long before she chose a path in adulthood, Marjorie Diehl changed. Her nascent mental illness set in. She said the transformation happened when she was twelve years old, and entering puberty. She repeatedly told psychiatrists and psychologists that she started suffering from anorexia nervosa at that age, and, at one point had to be hospitalized when her weight dropped from 135 pounds to 95 or as low as 85.[45] She blamed her father and her mother for the onset of the disorder; she said "she felt pressured by her upwardly mobile parents 'to perform,'" but used the anorexia to both succumb to and rebel against their expectations, especially her mother's.[46] She said her mother seemed to love her "only when she was playing the role of child prodigy,"[47] and she believed that her mother also despised her for perhaps stunting her mother's life and marring her mother's attractiveness. "Mother was said to be a teacher who stressed intellectual development," a psychiatrist once wrote of an interview with Diehl-Armstrong. "Mother is also said to have blamed her varicosities and abdominal stretch marks on the patient, who was born when the mother was 32 years of age. The patient wondered aloud if they had wanted a boy."[48]

Diehl-Armstrong linked sexuality to her anorexia, which she said developed just as she was maturing sexually, and earlier than most girls her age.[49] She said she considered her anorexia "as a defense against the sexual advances of males."[50] She said she had reason to be wary of boys and men. Her father, if she is to be believed, was molesting her, and she said she had "many incorrect notions" of sexuality, "such as the fact that she could get pregnant if she kissed a boy."[51] One psychologist wondered whether Diehl-Armstrong had come up with a link between anorexia and sexuality and her parents' obsession with perfection by reading psychiatric texts or if she had really experienced such problems.[52] Either way, Diehl-Armstrong throughout her life talked about the anorexia in the context of a childhood in which she finally grew "petrified of competition."[53]

She also likened her anorexia to attempted suicide. With her young life out of control, she said, she attempted to restore order to it by not eating and deciding that she would rather die. "When I was twelve," she explained, in another effort at self-diagnosis, "the conditions were getting so bad with my father sexually coming on to me and my coming into puberty and stuff, I couldn't deal with it. So I tried to starve myself to deal with the problems."[54] Looking back, she said, the sudden onset of anorexia also made sense in the context of what she considered her parents' attempts to be social strivers, to be better than their friends and neighbors—a trait that she displayed in her adulthood, with her manic levels of narcissism. In a life that would be full of extremes, anorexia represented the first time that Diehl-Armstrong went to the edge. Anorexia, she said, continuing her self-diagnosis, "frequently hits women from affluent families that have money, who are expected to be perfect and then they're afraid to come into their puberty or adulthood and all that, that was who I was. And I felt like, kind of a bird in a gilded cage. I really didn't like my life. It was almost like suicide, the doctor told me, and I had to do something. It was killing me. I was going to end up like Karen Carpenter. My heart was going to stop and I was going to be dead if I didn't do something fast."[55]

One of the psychiatrists who had the most interaction with Diehl-Armstrong vouched for her explanation that she suffered from anorexia. Robert L. Sadoff, MD, of Philadelphia, had examined Diehl six times in 1988, when he testified for the defense in her trial for the killing of her boyfriend Bob Thomas. Sadoff said Diehl told him about her anorexia as a child, and he said photos of her from that time in her life, and later, showed that she had lost a noticeable amount of weight. Sadoff, based on the photos, called Diehl "plump" rather than "overweight," but said that her appearance changed considerably. "Certainly as she got older she thinned out," Sadoff said.[56]

Mental health treatment, Diehl-Armstrong said, helped her beat anorexia, at least for a time.[57] This was the time of her life when she first had treatment for psychiatric problems,[58] when different forces mixed in the cauldron of her mind such that, as one psychologist wrote, she "has shown the seeds of severe mental illness since early childhood."[59] Age twelve, when Diehl stood between girlhood and womanhood, between innocence and experience, was a pivotal moment in her life, the moment when those seeds of dysfunction first grew into mental disorder. Finding the causes of that mental illness would elude psychiatrists and psychologists throughout Diehl-Armstrong's life, though she believed she knew for certain the reasons for her erratic behavior. She said her mental problems were manifestations of unpredictable parents, including a "schizy" mother—meaning schizophrenic—who was "either too overprotective or underprotective at different times."[60] "She blamed her mood swings," a psychologist wrote, "on 'genetics and inconsistent treatment by my parents.'"[61] At the same time, a psychiatrist once wrote, "her family history is negative for seizure disorder, mental hospitalizations or suicide."[62]

Diehl-Armstrong said her problems were not due to substance abuse. In May 1985, she told a psychologist that she did not use drugs or drink, but he also wrote that she admitted that "at various times she has taken amphetamine pills, marijuana, and pain pills. There may also have been some periods when she was abusing these drugs."[63] Despite her insistence that she drank no or little alcohol, she said she had "at least one relationship with a man when they got drunk every night."[64]

Diehl-Armstrong derived some solace that her mental illness at least had a name: manic-depressive disorder or bipolar disorder, whose signature features include alternating periods of mania and depression. One of the symptoms of her mania was her extreme sense of self-importance, which eventually turned into grandiosity and narcissism. Early on, as one psychologist wrote, Diehl-Armstrong showed "self-aggrandizing thinking in that she exaggerated the degree to which others found her attractive and the degree to which she knew important people."[65] Another symptom of her mania was what is known as pressured speech, a trait that Diehl-Armstrong routinely displayed in abundance. Whether she was on the telephone or on the street or on the witness stand, she let the words flow like a torrent, and frequently many of the words were foul. She was aggressive when she talked that way, as if she wanted to beat down the listener with words and phrases, just as she tried to do when she testified in the Pizza Bomber case in the United States District Court in Erie. She was also diagnosed as having paranoid features, to the point that she believed most everyone was out to get her; she viewed even her lawyers "almost as persecutors."[66]

Yet Diehl-Armstrong accepted her diagnosis of bipolar disorder. She seemed relieved by it. She said the psychologists and psychiatrists first told her about manic-depression in the mid-1970s, when she would have been twenty-six years old. She said read about the disorder. She said she had a revelation regarding her chronic mental woes. "Everything," she said, "fell into place."[67]

She got another diagnosis early on that she would spend the rest of her life claiming was erroneous. On August 1, 1972, a psychiatric caseworker listened to Diehl, then twenty-three years old, detail the ups and downs of her life, including what she said was her fraught relationship with her parents, particularly her father. Citing Diehl's problematic feelings toward her dad, the caseworker gave this diagnostic impression of her: "Deep seated hatred of men."[68]

Diehl-Armstrong bristled whenever someone confronted her with that finding—that she was a misandrist, a woman who despised men. Usually a psychiatrist or a psychologist asked her about her antipathy toward men, but it was the subject of courtroom discussion as well. She fumed on the witness stand in August 1984 when a prosecutor questioned her about the diagnostic impression that she had a deep-seated hatred of men. The cross-examination occurred during a pretrial hearing in the case of the death of her boyfriend Bob Thomas.

"Do you recall," the prosecutor asked her, "a discussion with the psychiatric caseworker at the time as to their diagnostic impression that you had a deep-seated hatred of men?"

"That is totally irrelevant," Diehl-Armstrong said.

The prosecutor persisted.

"And you disagree, I take it, with the conclusion that you were suffering from a deep-seated hatred of men?"

"Absolutely, and that was from a social worker who did not know what she was doing," Diehl said.[69]

She reiterated a similar position twenty-six years later, at her trial and sentencing in the Pizza Bomber case. By then she had been convicted of being part of the homicides of two other men—her boyfriend Jim Roden, shot in the back and his body stuffed in a freezer, and Brian Wells, blown up by a bomb locked around his neck. At her sentencing, an event that capped her homicidal career, Diehl-Armstrong pleaded with Judge McLaughlin to see her as she really was, rather than how she said so many others had made her out to be.

"I'm not that kind of violent, crazy person that everybody wants to perceive me as," Diehl-Armstrong said.[70]

· 2 ·

In Rare Company

Female Serial Killers in History

*M*arjorie Diehl-Armstrong's sense of superiority and intellectual authority expanded over the years until, by young adulthood, she saw herself as a genius. Her bipolar disorder and her intense narcissism fused so that she thought of herself as part of a certain class of the brilliant—individuals who, like her, suffered from bipolar disorder but were capable of achievements well beyond those of ordinary people. "You have to remember, and I am not just bragging about it," she once said of her bipolar disorder, "but it has been linked to genius. Lincoln, Churchill, Teddy Roosevelt, Van Gogh, Beethoven, Hemingway—some of the greatest artists and writers who ever lived were bipolar."[1] She also spoke of what she considered being a "functioning bipolar"[2]: "It is like Churchill. He had it, but he could also run the country."[3]

She was quick, however, to exclude herself from another class of people, though she was more suited to this group than she ever would be to the pantheon of the world's greatest creative minds. "I am not," she said, in another moment of introspection, "one of those people who goes around like Ted Bundy and does these horrible things."[4] She said she was never the aggressor, but was prey to abusive men, including her father and the two boyfriends she killed—Bob Thomas and Jim Roden. She was not "some degenerate criminal,"[5] she said, and certainly not a murderer with multiple victims.

"I am no serial killer," she once declared from prison, "and every psychiatrist who has examined me knows that. I have been a victim of this domestic shit all my life."[6]

But Diehl-Armstrong was like Ted Bundy. As the United States magistrate judge, Martin C. Carlson, repeatedly wrote in rejecting one of her appeals, Diehl-Armstrong fit the definition of a serial killer, which put her in an exclusive criminal cohort. And as a female serial killer, she was even more unique.

15

"Serial murder," according to the FBI, "is a relatively rare event, estimated to comprise less than one percent of all murders committed in any given year."[7] Using this percentage estimate, in 2015, when the FBI recorded 15,696 murders, the number of those attributed to a serial killing would have been about 157.[8] About one in six serial killers, or 16 percent, are women.[9] Most researchers agree that, no matter what the gender, a serial killer "is someone who kills three or more persons, with time elapsing between homicidal events."[10] This "cooling-off" period differentiates serial killers from mass murderers, who kill a large number of people at once, or spree murderers, who kill a large number of people over a short period of time. Serial killers are more methodical, and their slayings frequently follow patterns. For the FBI, "the time period between murders separates serial murder from mass murder,"[11] and the bureau has developed its own definition of serial murder, in terms of numbers. The FBI, as of 2005, defined serial murder as "the unlawful killing of two or more victims by the same offender(s), in separate events."[12]

The FBI's definition was broader than what Congress developed seven years earlier, in 1998, in the Protection of Children from Predators Act. It strengthened federal penalties for a variety of crimes against children, and allowed the federal government to take over jurisdiction of investigations of serial killers: "The Attorney General and the Director of the Federal Bureau of Investigation may investigate serial killings in violation of the laws of a State or political subdivision, if such investigation is requested by the head of a law enforcement agency with investigative or prosecutorial jurisdiction over the offense."[13] As for serial killing, the act stated, "The term 'serial killings' means a series of three or more killings, not less than one of which was committed within the United States, having common characteristics such as to suggest the reasonable possibility that the crimes were committed by the same actor or actors."[14] As the FBI noted, the act provided a legislative definition of serial murder primarily for purposes of jurisdiction: "It was not intended to be a generic definition for serial murder."[15]

Forensic criminologist Eric W. Hickey, who has extensively studied serial killers, offers a broad definition, one focused less on precise numbers than on the pattern of killing and the commonality of victims:

> In essence, *serial murderers* should include any offenders, male or female, who kill over time. Most researchers agree that serial killers have a minimum of three or four victims. Usually there is a pattern in their killing that can be associated with the types of victims selected or the method or the motives for the killing. This includes murderers who, on a repeated basis, kill within the confines of their own home, such as a woman who poisons several husbands, children, or elderly people in order to collect insurance.

In addition, serial murders include those men and women who operate within the confines of a city or a state or even travel through several states as they seek out their victims. Consequently, some victims have a personal relationship with their killers and others do not, and some victims are killed for pleasure and some merely for gain. Of greatest importance from a research perspective is the linkage of common factors among the victims.[16]

Taking the various definitions together, a serial killer can be defined as a man or a woman who kills at least two or three people in separate incidents, with a cooling-off period of at least a week.[17] The killings also often share common characteristics or methods, "to suggest the same offender committed the murders."[18]

No matter how insightful the findings of Hickey and other criminologists, their research can be secondary to a source that has perhaps most influenced Americans' views of serial killers: the movies. The number of films about serial killers has exploded in recent decades. More than 270 went to the big screen in the 2000s, compared with 150 in the 1990s, 23 in the 1980s, 20 in the 1970s, 12 in the 1960s, and 4 in the 1950s.[19] The increase in the number of movies reflects the increase and notoriety of serial killers. The case of Ted Bundy, convicted in 1979, executed in 1989, and known to have killed as many as fourteen women in the 1970s, invariably helped boost the number of cinematic depictions of serial killers. So did the cases of John Wayne Gacy, "The Killer Clown," convicted in 1980 and executed in 1994 for the deaths of thirty-three mostly teenage boys in the Chicago area; "The Green River Killer," Gary Leon Ridgeway, who pleaded guilty in 2003 to murdering forty-eight women in Washington state in the 1980s and 1990s; and Jeffrey Dahmer, who was convicted in 1992 in Milwaukee, Wisconsin, of dismembering seventeen men and boys, some of whose body parts he ate or stored in his freezer. In Hollywood, where a good story usually features a villain and a hero, films about serial killers contain both, to the extreme: the careful, obsessive, and sexually twisted serial killer is the human destroyer who must be stopped; the world-weary and wily FBI agent or police detective is the last hope to catch the killer and end the carnage.

The success of the formula peaked in 1991, with the release of *The Silence of the Lambs*, the only horror film to win the Academy Award for best picture. It also took the Oscar for best adapted screenplay (Ted Tally), director (Jonathan Demme), actor (Anthony Hopkins), and actress (Jodie Foster). The film's main characters have become cultural icons: Foster's

Clarice Starling, the FBI trainee assigned to help catch a serial killer known as Buffalo Bill; and Hopkins's Hannibal Lecter, a serial killer to whom Starling turns for guidance in finding her quarry. The movie, based on the 1988 novel by Thomas Harris, portrays Lecter as immensely intelligent, vicious, cannibalistic—and debonair. He is the serial killer as modern-day Lucifer: a psychopath whose charisma and elegance nearly mask his depravity. "Hannibal," *New York Times* critic Vincent Canby wrote, "is one movie killer who is demonstrably as brilliant and wicked as he is reported to be."[20]

Anthony Hopkins's Hannibal Lecter has a female counterpart, to a degree. She is Aileen Wuornos, a real-life serial killer from Florida whose troubled existence unfolds in the 2003 film *Monster*. Charlize Theron won the Academy Award for best actress for her portrayal of Wuornos, a prostitute-turned serial killer who fatally shot seven men along highways in Florida in 1989 and 1990. She was convicted in 1992 and executed by lethal injection in 2002, when she was forty-six years old. Wuornos attracted intense media attention long before *Monster* posthumously introduced her to a wider audience. She was a woman, and a serial killer—a combination that, in 1989 and 1990, was so foreign in popular culture and among law enforcement that the FBI called Wuornos America's "first female serial killer."[21] The title was erroneous. "Oh, no she's not," Eric Hickey recalled telling the FBI about its first-ever designation for Wuornos. "I go way back to the 1800s."[22]

The recognition that women were capable of serial murder goes back much farther, to the ancient Greeks and the tales they told to make sense of the world. The various versions of the myth of Medea, the sorceress and doomed wife of Jason, the leader of the Argonauts and searcher of the Golden Fleece, are replete with murder. Medea, out of love for Jason and later out of revenge, kills eight people, directly or indirectly, including her children.[23] But Medea is also portrayed not as a cold-blooded killer but as a complicated person whose animosity toward her unfaithful husband can be considered justified. For many critics, Medea, particularly as Euripides portrays her in his masterpiece, *Medea*, represents a signal heroine in "proto-feminism."[24]

Greed, revenge, power, and heartbreak mostly motivate Medea. But she is a tragic figure—one of the most tragic and complex figures in Greek literature, immortalized in *Medea*, which Euripides wrote in 431 BCE. His Medea is strong, deadly, and manipulative, yet also sympathetic, a woman whose anger at Jason is understandable. She kills her brother, betrays her father, and abandons her homeland to help Jason steal the Golden Fleece and achieve fame, but he casts her aside for a younger princess. Murder is Medea's only defense, for her and her children. She kills two of their sons so that a furious

Jason will not punish her by enslaving them. And in killing their sons, Medea punishes Jason. Medea proclaims the reasoning behind the murderous rage of her final serial killings, of her children, in *Medea*:

> For though a woman is timid in everything else, and weak, and terrified at the sight of a sword: still, when things go wrong in this thing of love, no heart is as fearless as a woman's; no heart is so filled with the thought of blood.[25]

Medea ends with Medea flying into the sky on a chariot pulled by dragons. Her dead children are at her side.

Hundreds of years after Euripides wrote *Medea*, two powerful women were real-life serial killers in ancient Rome, and they once worked together to poison an emperor. One of the women was royalty: Agrippina the Younger (15–59 CE), the "empress of poison," who was a lover to her brother, Emperor Caligula; a wife of her uncle, Emperor Claudius; and the mother of Emperor Nero. Agrippina was also the daughter of a Roman commander, Germanicus; a great-granddaughter of Mark Antony; and a granddaughter of Caesar Augustus.[26]

Agrippina killed primarily to advance her career and to secure power for her son, Nero. When he became emperor, she reached the height of her authority: she was known as Augusta, or an empress, and had her visage stamped on Roman coinage—an honor reserved for men and women elevated to "godlike status."[27] Agrippina's contemporary and co-killer was Locusta (believed to have died in 69 CE), a native of Gaul who settled in Rome, where she turned into the preeminent poisoner of the age—an age when poison, derived mainly from mushrooms, herbs, and other plants, was a preferred method of murder, particularly in royal households. Unlike Agrippina, Locusta mainly killed for hire.

Agripinna's household was filled with death, sex, and intrigue among brothers and sisters and other relatives. Roman historians said she conspired in a number of deaths, including that of one of Caligula's wives, who was forced to commit suicide, and Agrippina's sister-in-law. Agrippina's most brazen killing occurred in 54 CE, when, according to the historian Tacitus, she had a servant serve the sixty-four-year-old Claudius, her husband, mushrooms laced with poison—a poison that Tacitus reported Agrippina got from Locusta: "What was needed was something subtle that would upset the emperor's faculties but produce a deferred fatal effect. An expert in such matters was selected—Locusta, recently sentenced for poisoning but with a long career of imperial service ahead of her. By her talents, a preparation was supplied."[28] Claudius's death allowed Nero, who was Claudius's adopted son, to take the throne instead of Brittanicus, who was Claudius's biological son and Agrippina's stepson.

The murders continued. Agrippina, upset with Nero over one of his romantic affairs, started to favor Brittanicus, and suggested he would be a better emperor. Nero had Locusta fatally poison Brittanicus. The first effort at poisoning failed, and Nero had Locusta tortured; she concocted a second mixture, "from well-tried poisons," and it worked.[29] A grateful Nero is said to have rewarded Locusta with a villa, and he established a school for her in Rome, where she taught about poisons. Nero also is said to have hired Locusta to poison his mother. Agrippina survived, though Nero later had her executed. Locusta, wealthy from her poisoning commissions, lost influence after Nero killed himself in 68 CE. The new emperor, Galba, had her executed in 69 CE. According to the Roman historian Cassius Dio, "Lucusta [*sic*] the poison merchant, and some others who had been active in Nero's day, he [Galba] ordered to be carried in chains all over the city and afterwards to receive punishment."[30] Locusta, whom one emperor hired to kill, lost her life at the hands of another.

Agrippina and Locusta often murdered for causes, including a desire for power and control. They were serial killers with political agendas, who acted more like serial assassins than serial killers who murdered largely for the thrill. The crimes of Agrippina and other "imperial serial killers," including the likes of Locusta, "lack the sexual dimension we associate with modern serial killers," according to journalist Peter Vronsky, who has compiled a history of female serial killers. "The first female who classically fits the bill of the modern serial killer," Vronsky has also written, "is Elizabeth Báthory—the female Dracula."[31] Also, from Vronsky: "Elizabeth Báthory is special in that she is the only female sexual sadistic serial killer without a dominant male partner—to this day, four hundred years later. We have never had another quite like her."[32]

Báthory, a countess, was born into aristocracy in 1560 in the Kingdom of Hungary, and married a count at fifteen; they had four children before the count died when Báthory was forty-three. Marriage was not the source of Báthory's power. Her own family controlled Transylvania, home of the fictional Count Dracula, whose creation she is said to have influenced. Her castle still stands in Čachtice, in western Slovakia. Over thirty-five years, until her arrest, at age fifty, in 1610, Báthory, known as the Blood Countess, is believed to have killed hundreds of young women and girls, many of them servants. Legend holds that she bathed in her victims' blood to retain her youthful complexion. Though Báthory is not believed to have drawn such bloody baths (none of the court records in her case contain such allegations), the rise of such a legend is understandable—in truth, according to records from her trial, she beat her victims so badly that she was covered in their blood, as if she had bathed in it.[33]

Báthory, highly educated and wealthy, appears to have killed out of wantonness and cruelty, and because she could, again and again. The authorities declined to investigate why scores of girls had failed to return from Báthory's castle until the missing girls were nobles, rather than peasants. Whatever the social class of the victims, Báthory treated them the same—she beat and tortured them to death, often by burning their genitals with a candle, biting their shoulders and breasts, and pouring cold water on their naked bodies as they were left to die in the snow. Báthory had accomplices—her top servants helped with the murders—but she was in control of her castle and in control of those who lived and died. With the statements of Báthory's top servants as evidence, the Hungarian Parliament charged Báthory with killing as many as fifty-one girls over sixteen years. The number was likely much higher. One witness testified at trial that she found, in Báthory's chest of drawers, a register that listed the names of 650 of her victims.

Báthory's case never went to a public trial. But based on the evidence, the Hungarian king's lord in her region, Prince George Thurzo, Báthory's cousin, ordered her in 1611 to spend the rest of her life walled in an apartment in Čhactice Castle. The Hungarian Parliament ordered her name never be uttered in "polite society."[34] Four of her servants were tried and convicted, and three were executed. Báthory was found dead in her castle in 1614, at the age of fifty-four.

Báthory died without explaining her crimes, which were so plentiful and horrific as to seem unreal today, as if Elizabeth Báthory were a mythic murderer, such as Medea, or a fictional character, such as Dracula. Some have argued the case against Báthory was exaggerated and political, and based on "a family plot to seize her wealth."[35] But Báthory was a real person, and evidence of her slayings included the dead bodies found throughout her castle and the documented statements of witnesses who were consistent in their testimony. As one of her most thorough biographers has written: "While history has embroidered portions of the Countess' infamy, she was still, however, torturing and killing servant girls."[36] As to why Báthory killed, witnesses in the case against her suggested "diabolical impulses."[37] Others believe she experienced epileptic seizures and fits of rage as a child, and that members of her family might have suffered from mental illness, possibly from inbreeding.[38] Why

Báthory killed remains in dispute, as does the number of her victims. No matter how many girls and young women Báthory killed, her inhumanity set her apart, even among serial killers.

Elizabeth Báthory's case for decades remained a secret to the populace in Hungary. The case against her was never made fully public when she was arrested, and the Hungarian Parliament's order of silence about her case also kept her crimes off limits for public discussion. Because of these prohibitions, Báthory "would have remained merely an anonymous monster had not a Jesuit scholar, Father Laszlo Turoczy, discovered the trial records in 1720, about one hundred years after her death. Turoczy restored the legendary female vampire to human form with a name, identity, history, and detailed description of her crimes in a book published only in Latin."[39] Báthory's story, though made public, remained filled with legend until the 1980s, when an American scholar, Raymond T. McNally, got access to the original trial documents. Then her life and crimes became even more widely circulated.

Without the discovery of the trial records over the centuries, Elizabeth Báthory might still exist in the haze between history and fiction, if she were known to exist at all. The slow dissemination of her story shows how much of the information about female serial killers, including their number, is limited to how much their contemporaries disclosed about them. Other female killers might have struck in the seventeenth century and earlier, but perhaps the authorities in their cases covered up the prosecutions, as they did in the case of Báthory. Such secrets were much harder to conceal in the 1800s, as the rise of newspapers coincided with the massive growth of cities during the Industrial Revolution. As more and more people packed into London and other urban areas, criminals, including serial killers, had more available victims than they did when the population was largely rural. And when a serial killer claimed victims in the cities, the newspapers were sure to report about the deaths. As Peter Vronsky has written, "By the time Jack the Ripper made his appearance in 1888, the press was primed for and experienced in its coverage of horrendous crimes."[40]

The reporting of female serial killers had become more frequent in the decades before Jack the Ripper first appeared in the press. The number of female serial killers exploded between 1843 and 1852 in England, when nine female serial killers were known to have been executed. The rise of the female serial killer coincided with the "Hungry '40s," an era of deep depression in Great Britain.[41] Poisoning was the most common method of murder, and arsenic the most common poison—it was easily available at pharmacies or chemists in the 1800s for use as a cosmetic; women took it in small doses to improve their complexions. And arsenic was easy to dissolve in coffee and other hot liquids. In using arsenic to murder, female serial killers turned to what was most available to them; if arsenic helped a woman become more beautiful in a man's eyes, it was also effective in killing that man. Arsenic was so potent a weapon for English women that the British Parliament in 1851 passed the Sale of Arsenic Act, which restricted the sale and use of the poison.[42]

But arsenic was still available. Mary Ann Cotton, a nurse and Sunday school teacher who lived in a mining village in Durham County, in northeastern England, extracted arsenic from rat poison, whose sale remained unregulated in Great Britain. She fatally poisoned as many as twenty-one victims between 1864 and 1872. They included eight of her biological children, seven stepchildren, a lover, three husbands, and her mother.[43] Cotton, who was executed in 1873, when she was forty years old, was "the most prolific British serial killer before Harold Shipman"—one of the most prolific serial killers in history, a physician known as "Doctor Death," who authorities believe killed at least 215 of his patients between 1975 and 1998 by lethal injection of the painkiller diamorphine, also known as medical heroin.[44]

Mary Ann Cotton killed primarily to collect insurance. Her murders reflected the poverty of the mining communities where she grew up and later worked as a nurse. The symptoms of arsenic poisoning—such as diarrhea and vomiting—were also prevalent in general among the poor and undernourished. "The incompetence and heavy workload of local physicians, the poor nutrition of the urban working class, and imperfect record-keeping all helped the killings to go unchallenged," according to a detailed study of Cotton's deadly career. "Meanwhile, Mary Ann's experience as a nurse gave her perfect access—and she undoubtedly relished monitoring the painful, protracted deaths of her victims."[45]

Cotton's killings stopped after she poisoned her seven-year-old stepson in 1872. Investigators first suspected death by natural causes, but the police probed further and the newspapers—their quest for a sensational crime story on full alert—reported on Cotton's deadly past. Her infamy was such that a nursery rhyme circulated after her execution, by hanging:

> Sing, sing, oh what can I sing?
> Mary Ann Cotton is tied up with string.
> Where, where? Up in the air,
> sellin' black puddens a penny a pair.[46]

The profusion of her murders gave Mary Ann Cotton, like Elizabeth Báthory, nearly mythical status.

Female serial killers also struck in the United States in the mid- and late 1800s, and arsenic was frequently their poison of choice, too. Unlike Britain, the United States had no laws regulating arsenic's availability and use, which made it even more available in the United States. One female serial killer, Lydia Sherman, was known as the "Derby poisoner," because of the town in Connecticut where she lived and killed, with arsenic. Police believed she killed three husbands and several children—some accounts put the number of her victims at as many as ten—though she was convicted, in 1871, only of killing her third husband, Horatio N. Sherman, in a second-degree murder. She mixed arsenic in hot cider, her husband's favorite drink. A suspicious doctor ordered an autopsy, and a toxicology expert at Yale College determined that Horatio Sherman had arsenic in his system when he died. The police charged his wife.[47]

Lydia Sherman killed for insurance money, and to relieve herself of husbands and children who had become burdensome. Serial murder allowed Lydia Sherman to achieve a sense of freedom when she felt unduly tethered to a spouse or to the hearth. The first husband she killed, Edward S. Struck, was a disgraced policeman in suburban New York City who was discharged from his job in a dispute over a fight at a saloon in which a detective was killed. Unable to work, he became too much trouble for his wife, who decided to kill him after a friend suggested "she could get rid of the man by poison," according to a contemporary newspaper account. "She took kindly to the idea, and she gave him arsenic in his food, and she also, with the same poison, killed their youngest two children, so that they should also not be burdens to her, and should not have, as she says, to grow up to life's cares."[48] Lydia Sherman, then Lydia Struck, moved to Litchfield, Connecticut, where she married another man, Dennis Hurlburt. She poisoned him because "she did not get along particularly satisfactorily to herself with him."[49] Lydia Sherman's final stop was Derby, where she served her third and final husband his hot toddy of death. She also killed their two small children with arsenic. She got it from a familiar source: rat poison.

Lydia Sherman was sentenced in 1872 to life in prison, where she died, at age fifty-eight, in 1878. She was a black widow—a label for a female serial killer that police would attach to so many of her successors in multiple murder.

A twentieth-century equivalent of Lydia Sherman was Nannie Doss, known as the "Giggling Grandma," who started killing at age thirty and did not stop for twenty years, in 1954, in Tulsa, Oklahoma. Her victims were four of her five husbands (the first survived), two children, her mother, two sisters, a grandson, and a nephew. She killed by poisoning her victims with liquid rat poison, and she killed primarily for insurance money and because one husband after another upset her.[50] One cheated on her, and she said another drank too much, though she appeared to need no excuse to kill. "The media dubbed her the 'Giggling Grandma' because Nannie laughed and smiled while admitting to police that she had killed four of her five husbands."[51] They were Robert F. Harrelson (liquid rat poison in corn whiskey), Arlie J. Lanning (poisoned amid accusations of infidelity), Richard C. Morton (poisoned for cheating), and Samuel Doss (killed with arsenic-laced stewed prunes).[52]

After Samuel Doss's death, police pressed Nannie Doss once an autopsy showed he had large quantities of arsenic in his system. The police questioned Nannie Doss and she finally confessed to killing ten people. Doss was a forty-nine-year-old babysitter and housekeeper who devoured romance novels and told police that she was "searching for the perfect mate, the real romance of life."[53] Doss pleaded guilty to murdering her last husband and in 1955 was sentenced to life in prison, where she died of leukemia ten years later.[54]

Doss died a celebrity; her fame originated in the number of her victims and her attitude to them and to her life. She continued to read romance novels in prison, and wrote her memoirs for *Life* magazine. While incarcerated, she also kept a sense of humor and lighthearted outlook—characteristics that were evident when she smiled for the cameras as she left the courthouse in Tulsa after receiving a life sentence. Doss alluded to her poisonings of the past when she joked with a reporter from the *Tulsa World* who visited her in prison, where she was the second-oldest inmate. "When they get shorthanded in the kitchen here, I always offer to help out," she told the reporter, "but they never do let me."[55]

Aileen Carol Wuornos's method of murder betrayed none of the patience of her predecessors, such as Nannie Doss, who poisoned their victims to death slowly but surely. Wuornos was the rare female serial killer who used a gun—a .22-caliber pistol that she fired into seven male victims, mostly in the chest, though she shot one in the head. Their deaths were intensely violent and quick. No serial killer, male or female, can ever be said to have killed without anger or malice. But Aileen Wuornos killed with extraordinary rage—toward men.

She had reason to be furious. By the time she committed her roadside murders in central Florida between December 1989 and November 1990, when she was thirty-three and thirty-four years old and a prostitute, Wuornos had survived a past almost beyond comprehension in its horror.

She was born to teenage parents in 1956 in suburban Detroit. Her father, a repeat sex offender, killed himself while in prison and had no part in her life. Her mother abandoned Wuornos and her older brother when Wuornos was three years old; the two went to live with their maternal grandparents, who adopted them. When she was thirteen years old, Wuornos learned that her grandparents were not her real parents and that her aunts and uncles were not her siblings, as she had thought. In this regard, as Peter Vronsky has written, Wuornos's childhood was similar to that of Ted Bundy, who learned in adolescence that his father was really his grandfather and his mother was really his sister.[56]

Wuornos was seen in family photos as an attractive child, but she was severely burned in the face when she and her brother were playing with lighter fluid when she was six years old. Her grandfather sexually abused her, and at age fourteen she became sexually active with neighborhood boys, was raped, and became pregnant; she gave her baby boy up for adoption. Wuornos would later state that she was raped at least five times before her eighteenth birthday. According to one summary of her life: "By the age of fifteen, Wuornos had been rejected by her grandfather, her grandmother was dead, and she was a ward of the court. In 1971, at that young age, she began a life of petty crime, prostitution, and drifting that eventually led to a year of serial killing in Florida."[57]

By the time she was twenty-two years old, Wuornos had tried to kill herself at least six times. At age twenty, she had hitchhiked to Florida, where she scratched out a living as a hustler and prostitute. She married a wealthy seventy-year-old yachtsman, though the relationship lasted only a month after the two accused each other of abuse. Throughout the 1980s, while still in Florida, Wuornos was charged with a number of crimes, including what was the most serious before she murdered—armed robbery of a convenience store in Edgewater, for which she was convicted and served thirteen months in prison. In June 1986, Wuornos started a four-year intimate relationship with a woman she met in a bar. Wuornos and the woman, Tyria Moore, lived together and were occasionally in trouble with the law together. Wuornos by 1989 had a number of aliases: Susan Lynn Blahovec, Lee Blahovec, Lori Kristine Grody, and Cammie Marsh Greene.

Aileen Wuornos's first murder victim was found dead in December 1989 in a wooded area near Daytona. He was Richard Mallory, a fifty-one-year-old electrician who had picked up Wuornos for sex. She shot him three times in the chest. The other murders followed in an orderly succession. Each victim, police said, was a john: David Spears, a forty-three-year-old equipment operator, shot six times, May 1990; Charles Carskaddon, a forty-year-old rodeo worker, shot nine times, June 1990; Peter Siems, a sixty-five-year-old missionary, shot, July 1990; Troy Buress, a fifty-year-old truck driver, shot twice, August 1990; Dick Humphreys, a fifty-six-year-old child-abuse investigator, shot seven times, September 1990; Walter Antonio, a sixty-year-old truck driver and reserve police officer, shot three times in the back and once in the head, November 1990.[58]

Wuornos robbed many of her victims and stole their cars, which left behind a trail of evidence investigators used to catch her. In November 1990, police connected Wuornos and Moore to an accident involving a car they had stolen from Wuornos's victim Peter Siems in July 1990. In December 1990, Wuornos, sometimes using an alias, pawned items that she had stolen from victims Richard Spears and Richard Mallory. In January 1991, police arrested Wuornos at a bar in Ormond Beach, Florida, called the Last Stop. Tyria Moore, who was involved in none of the murders, agreed to cooperate; in recorded phone conversations, Moore urged Wuornos to confess. Wuornos eventually admitted to all seven murders, including that of Siems, whose body was never found.

Wuornos argued self-defense at her trial, in Volusia County in January 1992, for the murder of Mallory, her first victim. Wuornos claimed Mallory beat, raped, and sodomized her, though testimony from Moore undercut Wuornos's testimony. The trial also did not include evidence that Mallory was a convicted rapist, which could have bolstered Wuornos's credibility. Following her arrest and before her trial, Wuornos had told police that she shot all the victims in self-defense: "I mean, I had to kill them," she said. "Or it's like retaliation, too. It's like, you bastards, you are going to hurt me."[59]

Wuornos's trial lasted two weeks, and the jury deliberated for two hours before convicting her of first-degree murder on January 27, 1992. The jury two days later recommended the death penalty. Wuornos, known as "the highway hooker" and "damsel of death,"[60] went on to plead guilty in the deaths of six of the other victims, except for Siems, whose murder she admitted to out of court. She got a total of six death sentences.

After her conviction in Mallory's death, Wuornos shouted at the jury: "I'm innocent! I was raped! I hope you get raped!"[61] But as her appeals went on for a decade, she eventually recanted her claims that the victims raped and sodomized her and that she killed in self-defense. "I robbed them, and I killed them as cold as ice, and I would do it again, and I know I would kill another person because I've hated humans for a long time," Wuornos said in a prison interview.[62] In letters to the Florida Supreme Court in 2001, Wuornos wrote she wanted to make peace with God, and that she wanted to drop her appeals and get executed. "There are six cases which had all been unanimously decided for in Death, and of which I firmly agreed in with their final decision, since I'm one who seriously hates human life and would kill again," Wuornos wrote in one letter. In another, she wrote that she had "come clean . . . so would prefer to cut with the chase then and get on with an execution—of which I've been sentenced under 6 times. Taxpayers money has been squandered and the families have suffered enough."[63]

Questions persisted about Wuornos's sanity during her appeals, though Florida governor Jeb Bush lifted a stay on her execution after three psychiatrists who interviewed Wuornos found that she understood the reason for her pending death. Aileen Carol Wuornos was executed by lethal injection at the Florida State Prison near Starke, southwest of Jacksonville, at 9:47 a.m. on October 9, 2002. She was the tenth woman in the United States executed since the United States Supreme Court reinstated the death penalty in 1976.

In her last words, Wuornos said she had given up her fate to "the Rock," or Jesus, and she referred to a popular movie about brave forces from Earth that repel an alien invasion. "I'd just like to say I'm sailing with the Rock and I'll be back like *Independence Day* with Jesus, June 6, like the movie, big mothership and all," Wuornos said. "I'll be back."[64] Members of the victims' families said they had no regrets that Wuornos was gone. "It's sad to see anyone die," one said, "but I'm not sad she died."[65]

• 3 •

Killing Like a Man

Angels of Death, Black Widows, and Damsels of Doom

Nine months before Aileen Wuornos was executed, an opera about her life premiered in San Francisco. *Wuornos* was one of several artistic works, including the 2003 film *Monster*, that she inspired. The opera, like the movie, portrayed Wuornos as undeniably violent but also worthy of understanding—a tragic figure, like Medea.

The opera's composer, Carla Lucero, also raised the question of why Wuornos, as a female serial killer, should seem so unusual. If Wuornos were a man, Lucero suggested, her crimes, though still horrendous, would have been considered more normal. "Men are expected to lash out, to be violent, to defend themselves, to retaliate," Lucero wrote in a synopsis of the opera. "Is it so shocking that a woman, horribly abused as a child and later as an adult, killed in self-defense and then had knee-jerk reactions to threats of violence to her person time and again? Men returning from war call it shell-shock. Yet women have been in the trenches for centuries. Aileen Wuornos's actions are not to be applauded, though there is a message loud and clear: Abuse is cyclical."[1] Lucero also wrote of another lesson from Wuornos's life: "Unrequited fury will inevitably become unbearable."[2]

Lucero's need to compare Wuornos's behavior to a man's proved that, to many, Wuornos—though introduced to mainstream America through the movies, the media, and even an opera—remained an exception. She was not seen as the latest in a long line of female serial killers, dating to the 1800s in the United States, and as far back as ancient Rome, but as a murderous freak who, thankfully, had no counterparts, then or now. Even the *New York Times* editorialized in 1991 that, Wuornos aside, women most definitely could not be serial killers. Such mayhem was the province of men. Certainly, wrote the *Times*, women had been known to kill multiple victims, but those women

29

were not serial killers, because they killed only "when there was something to be gained—either money or retribution."[3] But killing for the sake of killing? The *Times* not only defined a serial killer by that concept, but said it only applied to men, and never women. "What the press, psychologists and the F.B.I. mean by 'serial killer' is a man—a man who kills because he likes to," the *Times* wrote.[4]

The *Times*'s editorial nonetheless accurately described the sentiment that had kept American popular culture from recognizing that women could be serial killers, too. Women are said to be the caregivers, the keepers of the hearth, the members of the fairer sex, who are somehow disinclined to kill and especially disinclined to kill and kill again. "They're much more apt to wring their hands than other people's necks,"[5] the *Times* wrote. As Eric W. Hickey, who wrote one of the first articles on female serial killers, in the mid-1980s, said, "We have a stereotype of women [as serial killers]—when they do it, we think they are more evil than men."[6] Or, in the words of Marissa A. Harrison, an evolutionary psychologist at the Pennsylvania State University at Harrisburg, "I think society is in denial that women are capable of such hideousness."[7] Marjorie Diehl-Armstrong understood the bias. Though she never offered an opinion on gender and serial killers, she linked certain crimes—such as murder using an explosive device—to masculinity, and tried to use the correlation as a defense. She said the bombing death of Brian Wells was a crime that only a man could execute, and she said she didn't rob banks.[8] "A woman doesn't do this crime," she said of Wells's death.[9] "I don't ever think I know a woman who would do this. It is a guy's crime."[10]

Such stereotypes, for a time, infected the study of serial killers with sexism. While women were accepted to be capable of multiple killings, they were not considered serial killers unless they killed like a man, such as in the case of Aileen Wuornos. Even a retired FBI behavioral profiler is once said to have stated, at a conference in 1998, that "there are no female serial killers."[11] Marjorie Diehl-Armstrong believed that theory as well. In November 2014, when she was awaiting prosecution in the Pizza Bomber case, in which she was connected to her third homicide victim, she declared: "I am not a serial fucking killer. As far as I know, no woman has been a serial killer."[12]

This has never been the reality; what has changed is the recognition that a woman can be a serial killer on her own terms, without having to achieve some kind of male standard. Women can be just as brutal as men, but in different ways. As Hickey has found, "the real issue is method."[13] Female serial killers, such as Nannie Doss, frequently poison their victims, a means of murder that is much less violent than gunfire but certainly no less effective. No matter how they kill, women are capable of serial murder, and, in the words of Hickey, "To say that a woman cannot be a 'true' serial killer unless she acts like a male is myopic."[14]

Such thinking is also risky. It establishes the mind-set that can let a woman get away with murder—a mind-set that can encourage reluctance, on behalf of law enforcement, to investigate a woman as a serial killer or to investigate a murder committed by a woman as something other than self-defense or an isolated crime of passion.[15] Because female serial killers often use more secretive methods to murder their victims, such as poisoning, suffocation, and staged accidents,[16] investigators can be more inclined to misclassify homicides as accidental deaths. For Amanda Farrell, a professor at Marymount University who, like Hickey and Harrison, has studied female serial killers in detail, "These misclassifications, combined with the hesitancy to accuse a woman, particularly if the victim was someone close to her, of murder can stall the investigation before it begins, leading to the loss of valuable evidence and information."[17]

In Sacramento, California, in 1988, Eric Hickey consulted with the FBI on a case of a woman who ran a boarding house where police found the remains of seven bodies. The police suspected the operator of the boarding house, a sixty-year-old woman by the name of Dorothea Puente, had poisoned the residents, who were elderly and disabled, to steal their Social Security checks. The FBI agents declined to call Puente's case that of a serial killer. "Of course, it was," Hickey recalled. "They just didn't recognize it then. Women were not considered to be predators that way."[18] Puente was accused of murdering nine people between 1982 and 1988; was found guilty in three of the deaths in 1993; and was serving two life sentences when she died in prison in 2011, when she was eighty-two years old. One of her first victims died in 1982 from an apparent overdose of codeine and Tylenol. The boarder, Puente said, was depressed because her husband had died of cancer. Police initially treated the death as a suicide.[19]

The police likely would not have made such an error if the victim had died violently, such as from a gunshot wound, or had been sexually molested before or after death. Investigators immediately would have suspected a homicide and, if the death fit a pattern, suspected a man as the serial killer, rather than a woman. With few exceptions, male serial killers employ much more violent methods than do women, and, unlike female serial killers, they will more frequently sexually molest their victims before or after death. "We rarely, if ever, hear of a female 'Jack the Ripper,'" Hickey has written. "Women who kill serially generally use poisons to dispose of their victims and are not associated with the sexual attacks, tortures, and violence of their male counterparts."[20] Female serial killers, as many researchers have found, tend to be "quiet killers" whose less violent methods of murder might be said to conform with their feminine and traditionally less violent natures. By poisoning their victims or suffocating them or staging their deaths, female serial killers prefer "not to allow their aggression to manifest in visible violence or brutality. It is unlikely you would find a woman sexually assaulting a corpse or engaging in cannibalistic or vampiric activities"[21] (with some exceptions, such as Elizabeth Báthory).

Researchers have used Freudian analysis to explain why men and women tend to kill so differently, and they have used evolutionary theory: Men are generally thought to kill for sex, while women are generally thought to kill for resources, such as money. "Women's motives for serial murder," Hickey has found, "appear to center on financial security, revenge, enjoyment, and sexual stimulation."[22] Murder, whether serial or otherwise, can represent an extreme and unlawful expression of basic human drives. The male, able to produce unlimited amounts of sperm, seeks "multiple sexual opportunities," while the female, able to produce a limited amount of eggs, seeks "a stable, committed partner with sufficient resources."[23] These subconscious urges, combined with society's stereotypes of feminine and masculine behavior, can also engender empathy or understanding for a female serial killer—reactions that most communities would be far less likely to express for a male serial killer, especially one who sexually violates his victims. In the case of a woman such as Aileen Wuornos, victimized and oppressed throughout her life, her murders, though serial, can seem justified, as in the opera that bears her name. Why would a woman kill and kill again unless she was provoked or so desperate that murder, even serial murder, would seem her only way out?

The nicknames bestowed on female killers over the years reflect the disparity between how society views them compared to male killers. While male killers are known as Jack the Ripper, the Night Stalker, and the Boston Strangler, female serial killers have been known by monikers that soften their images: Giggling Grandma, Sister Amy, Belle of Indiana, Duchess of Death, Old Shoe Box Annie, Beautiful Blonde Killer, Black Widow, Death Angel, the Highway Hooker, Damsel of Death.

No matter what their nicknames, motives, drives, or methods, female serial killers represent a challenging class of criminal to study. Group-based research, rather than research that focuses on a single female serial killer, is limited; much of the most detailed analyses has occurred over the past several decades. The lack of research before then is most likely due to the misconception that women were not capable of serial murder. Studying a group of female serial killers was unthinkable before the late 1980s and early 1990s because such a group was not thought to exist. Eric Hickey pioneered the field in 1991, when he published a comprehensive study that examined the case histories of sixty-four female serial killers. Twenty-four years later, in 2015, Marissa Harrison and colleagues examined the case histories of sixty-four female serial killers (the identical numbers are a coincidence) to help update the scholarly understanding of women who kill repeatedly.

Harrison et al.'s work offers a general statistical profile of female serial killers, based on their analysis of the sixty-four women, who killed between 1821 and 2008. The majority of them were white (88.7 percent), married (54.2 percent), middle class (55.3 percent), and with a mean age of thirty-two, though "at the time of their first killings, they ranged in age from 16 to 65, evincing considerable variation."[24] Most of the women in Harrison's study had college or professional degrees (34.6 percent), though 15.4 percent were high school graduates and another 30.8 percent were high school dropouts. Information on intellectual capability was limited to a quarter of the sixty-four women; among those, half were believed to have average intelligence, 12.5 percent high intelligence, and 28.6 percent were believed to have intellectual disabilities or deficiencies. Six of the women, or 9.4 percent, were found to have suffered severe childhood illnesses, such as head trauma or scarlet fever.[25]

Psychological trauma was prevalent among the sixty-four women. Based on the available information, 31.5 percent were physically or sexually abused, 23.4 percent suffered from drug or alcohol abuse, and 39.1 percent suffered from severe mental illness, including two women who were diagnosed with schizophrenia, two with antisocial personality disorder, and two with major depressive disorder.[26] Though nearly 40 percent of Harrison et al.'s subjects suffered from mental illness, and 12.4 percent were institutionalized,[27] none was found to be legally insane—a designation that covers only 2 to 3 percent of all serial killers.[28] Most of the women in the study killed victims they knew—victims who were aware of the killer's mental and physical infirmities. While female serial killers, like their male counterparts, have been known to stalk strangers before killing them, the majority of women Harrison and her colleagues studied, 62.5 percent, knew their victims. A total of 43.8 percent killed their biological children, while another 29.7 percent killed their husbands, fiancés, or boyfriends.[29]

The victims of female serial killers, in most instances, are passive—they do not engage in behavior that helps bring about their death. Harrison et al., Hickey, and other researchers have found that many of the victims are children and others also had little to do with instigating their deaths. "Female offenders almost exclusively killed victims who were categorized as low-facilitation homicides (the victims played a small role, if any, in their own deaths)."[30] Also among these helpless victims are the elderly and residents of nursing homes—victims whom female serial killers typically poison through drug overdoses and other means. One female serial killer, Jane Toppan, a nurse in Boston, is known to have killed thirty-one hospital patients and was suspected of killing as many as seventy more between 1887 and 1901. Her method of killing was a lethal injection of morphine.[31] At her trial, Toppan, who was found not guilty by reason of insanity, said: "This is my ambition— to have killed more people—more helpless people—than any man or woman has ever killed."[32] Toppan was a well-regarded nurse (though she was obsessed with autopsies). Like many female serial killers, Toppan was, until she was charged, seen as normal: "Your next-door neighbor."[33] But a disturbed next-door neighbor nonetheless, one of any number of serial murderers who, upon closer examination, "appear to be unhappy, unsuccessful individuals who choose to make their mark on society through violent means."[34]

Jane Toppan is what researchers of female serial killers call an angel of death—a woman, such as a nurse or a mother, who is in a nurturing occupation and generally kills helpless victims, including patients in her care. Other categories of female serial killers are sexual predators, revenge killers, profit or crime killers, team killers, killers of questionable sanity, and unsolved murderers.[35] The category of angel of death is also included in a larger class of female serial killers—the power seeker. The other three classes, or typologies, are hedonistic, or those women, such as black widows, who kill for money, comfort, or the thrill; visionaries, who kill at the command of visions and other hallucinations; and missionaries, or those who murder "to rid the world of 'undesirables.'"[36]

The members of these typologies and categories for serial killers have different personalities and different motives, but they share many traits— women and men both. "The women," Hickey has written, "tended to be insincere, amoral, impulsive, prone to exercise manipulative charisma and superficial charm, without conscience, and with little insight, because they failed to learn from their mistakes."[37] These traits—whether a male or female serial killer exhibits them—are generally attributed to psychopaths. As the FBI defines it, psychopathy is "manifested in people who use a mixture of charm, manipulation, intimidation, and occasionally violence to control others, in order to satisfy their own selfish needs."[38]

To measure an individual's level of psychopathy, behaviorists, investigators, and others use the *Psychopathy Check List Revised*, which Robert Hare, a Canadian criminal psychologist, developed in the 1980s and early 1990s. The check list is a tool to gauge the level of psychopathy in four areas: interpersonal, affective, lifestyle, and antisocial. The FBI, in its 2005 manual *Serial Murder*, provides thorough summaries of the traits that typically fall under each category.

> The *interpersonal* traits include glibness, superficial charm, a grandiose sense of self-worth, pathological lying, and the manipulation of others. The *affective* traits include a lack of remorse and/or guilt, shallow affect, a lack of empathy, and failure to accept responsibility. The *lifestyle* behaviors include stimulation-seeking behavior, impulsivity, irresponsibility, parasitic orientation, and a lack of realistic life goals. The *anti-social* behaviors include poor behavioral controls, early childhood behavior problems, juvenile delinquency, revocation of conditional release, and criminal versatility. The combination of these individual personality traits, interpersonal styles, and socially deviant lifestyles are the framework of psychopathy and can manifest themselves differently in individual psychopaths.[39]

Psychopaths share many personality traits with sociopaths, though the two are different in many ways. Both sociopathy and psychopathy are antisocial personality disorders, and psychopaths and sociopaths have no remorse and no regard for the rights of others. But sociopaths tend to be more nervous, agitated, and outwardly disturbed, and live on the "fringes of society," while psychopaths are apt to be charming, manipulative, more highly educated, and better able to form long-standing relationships.[40] Sociopaths who are serial killers tend to operate on impulse and with little planning. Psychopaths are more methodical in their killing, and often have contingency plans. "Unlike their sociopathic counterparts, psychopathic criminals are cool, calm, and meticulous."[41]

Not all sociopaths and psychopaths are serial killers and not all serial killers are sociopaths or psychopaths. Psychopathy, according to the FBI, does not alone explain a serial killer's motives. But serial killers who are psychopaths have no value for human life and often treat killing as a game, particularly when a serial killer stalks his or her victims. For a serial killer, victims can be like trophies.

A serial killer's psychopathic traits also represent his or her vulnerabilities—a theme that runs through *The Silence of the Lambs* and other fictional psychological thrillers about serial killers. Psychopaths often have distinct criminal behaviors that can provide clues to link serial killings. Investigators often can take advantage of a serial killer's psychopathic traits to catch a serial killer or to get a serial killer to admit to crimes in an interview. As the FBI has observed: "Psychopaths are *not* sensitive to altruistic interview themes, such as sympathy for their victims or remorse/guilt over their crimes. They do possess certain personality traits that can be exploited, particularly their inherent narcissism, selfishness, and vanity. Specific themes in past successful interviews of psychopathic serial killers focused on praising their intelligence, cleverness, and skill in evading capture."[42] Like many people, psychopathic serial killers enjoy talking about themselves, and they like to hear that they are the best at what they do—even if their career involves killing.

Among female serial killers, Marjorie Diehl-Armstrong is a hybrid. Her personality included attributes of both a sociopath and a psychopath: impulsive yet methodical, haphazard but also careful, seriously mentally disturbed in some instances but clearly sane in others. Like a sociopath, she had few friends who were regulars in society, but like a psychopath she was highly intelligent and well educated. As for typologies, according to the evidence against her: she was a hedonistic black widow who killed for money, but also a missionary murderer who killed to cleanse the world of men she thought beneath her. She can also be considered a revenge killer and an angel of death: she killed to get back at her boyfriends, but she killed them when, according to the police, they were in a helpless state—when they were on a couch or when they were sleeping.

Above all, no matter whom she killed or why, Diehl-Armstrong saw herself as a brilliant victim, a smart and worldly woman who was trapped in situations beyond her control. She was never the problem. She had the skills needed to excel in life. Her problem was men, and specifically the men she said were attracted to her. They were abusive imbeciles who would have amounted to nothing without her. And what did she get in return? Trouble and wretchedness.

Of her problematic relationships with men, she said, "I killed abusive boyfriends who tried to kill me in my own home."[43]

"I am always between dumb and dumber and a rock and a hard place," she liked to say.[44] Another of her favorite lines was, "I'm the pickle in the middle with hell on all sides."[45]

This narcissism and grandiosity are among the many attributes of Diehl-Armstrong's psychopathy. Eric Hickey, in an analysis of Diehl-Armstrong, said she would rank "fairly high" on the scale of Robert Hare's *Psychopathy Check List Revised*. Hickey said Diehl-Armstrong's case is similar to that of Aileen Wuornos and that Diehl-Armstrong was highly unusual among female serial killers, as Wuornos also was highly unusual. Diehl-Armstrong, like Wuornos, had an antipathy toward men; and Diehl-Armstrong, when she worked alone, also chose a method of murder—gunfire—that is more typically common among male serial killers. When Diehl-Armstrong worked with others, in the Pizza Bomber case, the method—a bombing—was just as violent. (Among the sixty-four female serial killers Harrison studied, half used poison, 10.9 percent used guns, and none used explosives.[46])

Hickey's descriptions of Wuornos can apply to Diehl-Armstrong: "She was physically strong and could become very aggressive when provoked. She killed like a male, except for the fact that most of her victims were shot in the torso, which is more typical of female killers; males are prone to shoot into the victim's head."[47] Hickey also wrote: "Aileen Wuornos was not the first female serial killer . . . but rather an anomaly. Wuornos was an atypical female serial killer. We have almost no documentation of anyone similar to Wuornos, and there is nothing to suggest we will see more like her in the foreseeable future."[48]

Marjorie Diehl-Armstrong, Hickey said, is an exception. "She acts on her own and has no regard for human life." When she was working alone, she was "not working under the guise or spell of another person," he said. "That moves her into a special category—like Aileen Wuornos."[49] "She is more the outlier than the mainstream," Hickey said of Diehl-Armstrong. "It is a very tragic case."[50]

• 4 •

A Cluttered Mind

Marjorie Diehl's Hoarding and Other Obsessions

𝒜 crowd surrounded Marjorie Diehl's rented house in a solid middle-class Erie neighborhood on a tree-lined street called Sunset Boulevard. Neighbors and onlookers were stunned at what Erie police and officials with the Erie County Health Department were pulling out of the 672-square-foot bungalow on August 2, 1984.

Three days earlier, on July 30, 1984, police had found the dead body of Diehl's boyfriend Bob Thomas—her first known homicide victim—shot six times and sprawled on the couple's living room couch. Investigators had returned to the scene to secure evidence and to survey the inside of the house on August 2, 1984. The task was close to insurmountable. Marjorie Diehl, thirty-five years old and on Social Security disability for mental illness, was not only a murder suspect.

She was also a hoarder.

Stuff filled her house from the basement to the attic. The four-room place was virtually uninhabitable. The authorities' inventory of the belongings ran for pages. One back bedroom had no furniture; a huge pile occupied the room: clothing on top, as many as six hundred wire hangers in the middle, and books and magazines and papers and garbage at the bottom.[1] Police described the periodicals as "war magazines," with titles such as *Soldier of Fortune, New Breed, Eagle,* and *Warriors.*[2] Police found a book called *The Shooter's Bible.*[3] Photocopies of scholarly articles on mental illness were scattered throughout the house as well, confirming the suspicions of psychiatrists and psychologists that Diehl had read up on her mental disorders and had a thorough understanding of them. The titles included "Psychoses in Adult Mental Defectives, Manic Depressive Psychosis," "A Survey of the Patients in a Large Mental Hospital," "Medical and Social Needs of Patients in Hospitals for the Mentally Subnormal," "Mental Deficiency and Manic-Depressive Insanity," "Schizophrenic and Paranoid Psychoses," and "Behavior Therapy Versus Psychoanalysis."[4] And among the newspaper clippings Diehl saved were those about the Saturday night special handgun and a man convicted of attempted murder more than a year earlier, in May 1983.[5]

As voluminous as they were, the papers and documents made up the house's secondary clutter. Most prominent—to the eyes and the nose—was the food, mainly government surplus food, stored in cupboards and closets and in the attic, where the temperature had reached as high as ninety-five degrees.[6] Most of the food was rotting, and the stench was overwhelming.[7] Diehl had collected the food by visiting food pantries for the needy three to five times a week for the past four months, often with signed notes from her friends stating that she was authorized to pick up food for them.[8] In one instance, she claimed she was the mother of three children, ten, eight, and seven years old.[9] "It is very easy to double dip. It is a shame, but it happens," the executive director of the Erie Community Food Bank, which supplied the food pantries, said as the police were clearing Diehl's house.[10]

And double dip Diehl did. The widespread availability of surplus government cheese started two and one-half years earlier, on December 22, 1981, when President Ronald Reagan signed a farm bill that authorized states to distribute the food to the poor through nonprofit organizations. The cheese, to the embarrassment of the free-market-touting Reagan administration, had stockpiled because farmers could make more money by selling their cheese to the government at government-set support prices than they could by selling it in stores.[11] The nationwide cheese stockpile was still growing when Reagan signed the farm bill, but in December 1981 the surplus amounted to 560 million pounds of cheese—"more than two pounds of cheese for every person in the United States," according to one report.[12] Diehl over the years made sure she got her share.

In July 1984, Erie County valued her food hoard at $9,890—the equivalent of $22,944 in 2016.[13] A county official's final inventory listed 389 pounds of USDA butter, which had been refrigerated, and 727 pounds of cheese, which had not.[14] Opened pastries and pies were strewn throughout the kitchen along with moldy bread that had turned green and "was stacked up in the refrigerator and freezer," an Erie police detective said.[15] "Rats were having a heyday" in the house, one city official reported.[16] Diehl also had inside the house, according to a partial list of the official inventory: 111 five-pound boxes of dried milk, 37 dozen eggs, 111 cans of tuna, 231 cans of vegetables, 61 cans of fruit, 55 packages of frozen meat and vegetables, 33 five-pound bags of flour, 36 five-pound bags of cornmeal, 180 boxes of macaroni and cheese, 44 boxes of spaghetti, 50 boxes of cornflakes, 44 boxes of pancake mix, 15 bags of matzo crackers, 93 jars of honey, 11 boxes of instant potatoes, 26 cans of beef stew, 58 bags of egg noodles, 9 pork chops, 29 boxes of Fruitful Bran, 6 boxes of Choco Crunch, 4 boxes of Cap' n Crunch, 5 pieces of spoiled sausage, a box of Team Flakes, a container of Tang, one bottle of A.1. Steak Sauce, and a bag of shrimp.[17]

The police and health authorities dumped four tons of food into a garbage truck, which disposed of it. (No reports mentioned Diehl having pets in the house.) Erie's director of police operations, Arthur Berardi, asked the county Health Department to inventory the food, and he ordered the truck to haul it away because it posed a health hazard. The packed house was so odd that Berardi left his office at City Hall to visit the scene. "There was so darn much stuff," Berardi said. "They were stacked in the attic and on the ledges."[18] Said a police officer at the scene: "It was unreal, like a supermarket. There's butter in the refrigerator, cheese and hundreds of other items all over the place."[19]

No one in Erie had ever seen anything like Marjorie Diehl's residence on Sunset Boulevard, but it would not be the only house that she would ruin by packing it with stuff and food in her criminal career. Even worse would be another house in Erie, where she would shoot her boyfriend Jim Roden in the back in mid-August 2003, about the same time she was helping to plan the Pizza Bomber plot. Much of what filled that house would be trash that Diehl-Armstrong was known to have picked up from the street on garbage night. Her former fiancé, Bill Rothstein, would tell the police that Diehl-Armstrong said she was compensating for her parents scrimping on toys for her when she was a child. With few playthings as a girl, she now "picks up all this crap and stuff," Rothstein said, including, once, a dollhouse that was missing a side.[20]

Diehl-Armstrong later in life saw herself as a collector and as something of a connoisseur of fine items. She said she never owned junk; she owned only quality things. When questioned about her belongings at the Pizza Bomber trial, in October 2010, Diehl-Armstrong looked at photographs of the interior of one of her many houses where she had stayed throughout her life—but not the Sunset Boulevard residence—and testified about what she had stored there. Her spirits lifted as she described all the stuff in a manner that reflected her pathological grandiosity: "I had a lot of furs that were gifted to me, minks of all colors: white, yellow, every color. And then I had a black seal skin and all kind of rabbit coats. I had lots of diamonds and a lot of precious jewels."[21]

"Were they cheap or expensive?" her lawyer said.

"They were all real and they were all expensive," Diehl-Armstrong said.

"Were they the worst or the best?"

"They were the best."[22]

Her lawyer showed her another photograph. He asked her to describe the coats pictured in it.

"I had some other coats that were like Persian lamb," Diehl-Armstrong testified. "And I had leather coats and suede coats, blue suede; burgundy leather with lamb's wool around the wrist and stuff. Dress coats and stuff."

"Were they the best or the worst?" her lawyer said.

"They were top-of-the-line items," Diehl-Armstrong said. "I had good stuff."

"Cheap or expensive?"

"Expensive."

"So you were a woman of means?" Diehl-Armstrong's lawyer said.

"Definitely," Diehl-Armstrong said. "But I was not a money-hungry type person that was a status seeker. I just happened to acquire a lot of valuable items. Although I have quite a Bohemian streak in me . . . I don't define myself that way. In other words, I'm not into conspicuous consumption; but it just so happened, I was gifted with a lot of things that were very valuable. I was also gifted with some antiques by a boyfriend that gave me all his mother's crystal and her fine china cabinet that was handed down for years. I just acquired a lot of stuff."[23]

The closest Diehl-Armstrong came to adopting the label of "hoarder" was when she referred to herself as "like a pack rat" in 1988, when she was on trial for the death of Bob Thomas.[24] She estimated police took 157,000 items from the house, including her college psychology textbooks and the articles on mental illness she said she had read for class.[25]

"I saved everything," Diehl testified. "You know what the condition of my house was like. I saved everything. When I say everything, I saved all my school books. I saved all of my tests. I saved all of that stuff. I was like a pack rat, if you want to know the truth."[26]

She acknowledged that the condition of her house on Sunset Boulevard was a sign of her and Thomas's mental instability. "There's emotional and logical things that you do for gut-reaction reasons and things you do for intellectual reasons and these are two separate issues," Diehl testified. "My emotions were messed up. You could tell that from the house, the cheese line. We were messed up and were on the wrong track. . . . To me, it was indications that we were sick."[27]

The psychiatrists and psychologists who examined Diehl-Armstrong considered her acquisition and storage of so much stuff as clear evidence of hoarding—one of the most visible symptoms of her mental illness. In many ways, Diehl-Armstrong fit the psychological profile of a hoarder, as outlined by two of the pioneers in the study of the condition, Randy O. Frost and Gail Steketee. Diehl-Armstrong consistently displayed activity consistent with disorders associated with hoarding: obsessive-compulsive disorder (OCD) and impulse control disorder (ICD). "Classic OCD symptoms are associated with anxiety," Frost and Steketee have written. "The sequence begins with an unwanted intrusive thought (e.g., 'My hands are contaminated from touching the doorknob'), followed by compulsive behavior designed to relieve the stress created by the intrusive thought (e.g., extensive hand washing or cleaning)."[28] While Frost and Steketee recognize possible links between OCD and hoarding, they contend that hoarding resembles more of an ICD, which is "characterized by the inability to resist an urge or impulse even though the behavior is dangerous and harmful."[29]

Diehl-Armstrong's compulsive behavior was also on display in an obsession she had with her teeth, whose whiteness and straightness she discussed often. She said she needed her teeth repaired because of injuries she suffered in an auto accident as an adult, but, for whatever reason, her dental hygiene and the look of her teeth became topics of constant discussion for her.[30] The ultimate compliment for Diehl-Armstrong, especially from men, was that she had "nice teeth" and "that million-dollar smile."[31] Her teeth were central to her concerns about her physical appearance. "The patient continues to exhibit excessive and compulsive behavior regarding cleanliness and personal hygiene," a psychologist wrote of Diehl in 1987, when she was in a Pennsylvania state prison system awaiting trial in Thomas's death. "For example, the patient brushes her teeth three full cycles before stopping, i.e. she applies toothpaste and brushes 32 times, rinses and then reapplies toothpaste until the ritual is complete."[32]

Diehl-Armstrong's ICD—her inability to control her impulses that resulted in harm to her—has been on display throughout her life, from her hoarding to her choice of men, many of whom had violent pasts. Her hoarding has never ceased: Whenever she has had the space and the means, Diehl-Armstrong has acquired and collected thousands of items, despite the risk to her personal health from rotting food or stacks of stuff that could collapse on her. Her houses were so packed that she could only get through them through narrow passageways, known as "goat paths."[33] She sculpted the tunnel-like routes, some as narrow as two feet wide, through the debris.[34] Diehl-Armstrong hoarded even in prison, where surplus items are hard to find and any unusual or disruptive behavior can lead to sanctions from the guards. Her hoarding and other strange behavior caught the attention of a psychiatrist who visited Diehl as many as sixty-four times when she was in prison awaiting trial in the Thomas case; while in prison, Diehl was getting outside items from nuns who visited her regularly. The prison staff, the psychiatrist wrote, "indicated that it has been necessary to monitor what the patient keeps in her cell, as she tends to horde [*sic*] items, varying from prison stationery to free booties and nightgowns, which she gets from the nuns who, apparently, periodically provide them."[35] The psychiatrist, David B. Paul, also wrote that "the patient was described as not using sanitary napkins when menstruating, at least with perceived regularity, and a need was seen to oversee her personal hygiene."[36] Others would report that, while in prison awaiting trial in the Thomas case, she filled garbage bags with items, including newspaper clippings, that she had collected in her cell.[37]

The hoarding and other behavior showed that Diehl-Armstrong had lost her ability to think clearly—that her judgment, due to her mental illness, had become almost irrevocably impaired. She had lost her ability to reason, in certain instances, and acted on impulse, particularly in how she stuffed her house with food and junk. Another of her longtime psychiatrists, Robert L. Sadoff, testified about her lack of judgment in light of all the food pulled out of her house on Sunset Boulevard. The hoarding, Sadoff said in 1988, was symptomatic of Diehl's bipolar disorder. "In the person with bipolar disorder," Sadoff said, "when they get up in the manic phase, they are way up there to the point that they are not in touch with reality. We call them psychotic. Psychotic means not in touch with reality. So people do bizarre things."[38]

Diehl's lawyer then asked Sadoff, a forensic psychiatrist, whether bipolar disorder included an impairment of judgment. "Without question," Sadoff said. "This is the hallmark of the illness, that a person in a manic phase says and does things that are so off the wall and you would look at them and say, 'This person is impaired in their judgment.'"[39]

The lawyer showed Sadoff photos of Diehl's house on Sunset Boulevard. The lawyer listed all the food that had been piled up in the house—the more than seven hundred pounds of cheese and the nearly four hundred pounds of butter, among the other items, many of which were kept in an attic stifling from the summer heat.

"These foodstuffs, for all practical purposes, were rancid and had to be destroyed," the lawyer, Leonard G. Ambrose III, said to Sadoff. "By all practical purposes, does that indicate, based upon what you note, any impairment of judgment?"

"Yes, absolute impairment of judgment," Sadoff said. "One doesn't hoard stuff like that and let it rot in that way if one has good judgment. That is a clear indication of her impaired judgment."[40]

Hoarding perhaps gave Diehl-Armstrong a sense of control—she was in charge of collecting all the items, keeping them, and imbuing them with whatever significance she believed they deserved. A desire for control and security are reasons for hoarding.[41] Another reason is desire for perfectionism, a quest well known to Diehl-Armstrong, who said she felt a constant need to please her mother. Hoarders are often highly intelligent people, like Diehl-Armstrong, and so are those who suffer, as Diehl-Armstrong did, from anorexia, another disorder linked to an unhealthy need to be perfect and a desire for control.[42] Diehl, concerned about her weight, surrounded herself with food so plentiful and perishable that she could never have eaten it all. As Randy O. Frost, Gail Steketee, and their colleague David F. Tolin have written of the connection between perfectionism and hoarding:

> It's hard for many people to understand how perfectionism and compulsive hoarding can go together. After all, when most of us think of a "perfectionist," we think of someone whose home is immaculately clean, with everything in place, and so on. But for some people, perfectionism works in a slightly different way. They become so afraid of making the wrong decision—for example, that they will accidentally throw away something useful—that the prospect of making decisions gives rise to strong feelings of anxiety and worry. As a result, the person tends to avoid the decision-making process altogether. The basic operating principle seems to be, "If I can't be sure of doing it exactly right, I'd better not do it at all." Paradoxically, therefore, the person's perfectionist beliefs contribute to his or her home becoming the model of *im*perfection.[43]

The same could be said about Diehl-Armstrong's life. In seeking perfection, and burdened with mental illness, she became a mess, a paragon of imperfection to the extreme. She became a woman who, in the words of a federal prosecutor, was characterized by evil and consumed by greed; a woman who, in the words of a federal magistrate judge, was a serial killer. Not only did Diehl-Armstrong hoard food. She also hoarded money. And she hoarded men. Her obsessions, like her mental illness, ultimately fully took hold. But they were held in check for several years, between when she was a teenager and a new college graduate trying to set out on her own.

Marjorie Diehl-Armstrong credited her maternal grandparents—her beloved Wolfendens, with the friendly house and the safe filled with cash—from rescuing her from her early mental illness so that she could once again function in regular society, even if just for a time. At age fourteen, and still at risk of starving herself, she went to live with the Wolfendens. The medical professionals, she said, were prepared to take severe steps when they decided that moving her in with her grandparents, and away from her parents, would only benefit her and help treat her anorexia. Otherwise, she said, she would have ended up in a hospital. "They were getting ready to force feed me," Diehl-Armstrong recalled, "but I had to go live with my grandparents because the doctor said it was a mental thing and that my parents' environment was causing it."[44] Her grandfather, she said, cried as he pleaded with her. "I still remember," she said, "my grandfather told me you got to eat because I don't want to see you dead."[45]

She recalled her stay with her grandparents as something like a fairy tale. If her parents—her supposedly alcoholic and abusive father and her domineering mother—were like evil stepparents, then the Wolfendens were like her fairy godparents, who understood her and protected her and released her from her gilded cage. "At age 14," one of her psychiatrists noted, "she lived for a while with her maternal grandparents, whom she characterized as using the 'soft sell' approach rather than the direct pressure which was her parents' method."[46] She said she thanked God "that I had some decent grandparents that took care of me,"[47] and she characterized her Grandfather Wolfenden as something of her ideal male. "She sees her grandfather as one of the few positive figures in her childhood and indicates that she has had good relationships with men who remind her of her grandfather," a psychologist wrote in 1985, when Diehl was thirty-six years old and awaiting trial in the Thomas case.[48] And by 2007 and 2008, when she was awaiting trial in the Pizza Bomber case, for the bombing death of Brian Wells, Diehl-Armstrong referred to her grandparents as proof that she could never have been involved in such a crime, or any crime. She knew better, she said, because her "grandfather was a police officer."[49] And she knew that she was able to stay in control, and stay out of trouble, because she was able to follow her grandmother's advice to be careful about letting her life get out of hand: "My grandma always used to say, 'Don't overload your plate.'"[50]

Marjorie Diehl appeared to have reached a degree of mental normalcy as a teenager and young adult. She was still driven, as shown by her playing cello in the Junior Philharmonic, playing organ at what she said was her family's Lutheran church, and participating in all kinds of clubs and activities, including Brownies and Girl Scouts, and being a majorette.[51] But she also provided no reports to her psychiatrist and psychologists that she needed treatment when she was in high school and college, where, by all accounts, she excelled academically. Her high school yearbook photos reveal a well-groomed and attractive young woman who looked no different than most of the other girls in her graduating class—the Class of 1967 at Erie's public Academy High School, which was founded in 1919 and whose first principal was Diehl's cousin, John C. Diehl. Academy drew many students from the wealthy Glenwood area of Erie, but its student body was also made up of many students from working-class families like Marjorie Diehl's. One of Diehl's classmates would go on to be elected an Erie County judge and then a judge on one of Pennsylvania's appellate courts. And, in a coincidence that Diehl-Armstrong never let anyone forget, the Erie County district attorney who prosecuted her for Jim Roden's death, a shrewd lawyer by the name of Bradley Foulk, was two years ahead of Diehl at Academy. Foulk was a perpetually poor student, while Diehl was a straight-A student throughout grade school and high school.[52]

Her immersion in music continued at Academy, where she participated in the orchestra and an annual student talent show called Academy-on-Parade. She was also, according to the student yearbook, a hall monitor and was in the speech club and the French club. Her senior yearbook portrait shows her smiling with her black hair stylish in a pixie-like bouffant. She is wearing a pearl necklace, with a low-cut graduation gown exposing her shoulders. Diehl appears happy as she looks directly at the camera with bright eyes. She fits in with the other students, especially the girls. She appears to be contented—with herself and her place at Academy, where, she said, "I did real well. I was a commencement speaker. I was up in the upper percent of my class."[53] Throughout her life she considered her achievements in high school noteworthy, another example of how she was destined for an exceptional adulthood. As late as February 2016, when she was sixty-seven years old and serving the federal prison sentence of life plus thirty years in the Pizza Bomber case, she still spoke of her years in high school with wistfulness and pride. "I have a nice voice," she said. "That is why they picked me as a commencement speaker."[54] She also looked healthy in high school. She was no longer anorexic. As Sadoff said when he examined a picture from Diehl's high school graduation, she "looks like she was pretty average at this point."[55]

Diehl-Armstrong's intellectual acumen was never in doubt, in high school and then in college and graduate school. Her estimated verbal IQ was in the bright-normal range (110 to 119) to the superior range (120–129),[56] and other psychological testing put her intellectual level in the superior range.[57] She also maintained that she had a photographic memory and total recall, and testing showed that her recall was indeed in the superior range.[58] But she said her mental illness heightened her memory when she was manic and dulled it when she was depressed. Her explanation pointed to a larger truth about her intellectual functioning: she did extremely well in the classroom and other more sterile and controlled environments, but struggled in more regular settings. "This level of intellectual functioning is being measured in a way that is 'conflict free,'" one psychologist wrote. "That is, though she may show good memory and judgment on intellectual tasks where her emotions do not interfere, those situations where she is emotionally involved can produce confusion, poor judgment, and inadequate memory."[59]

Another psychologist found that Diehl, despite her intellectual achievements and obvious intelligence, suffered from poor self-esteem and was generally helpless to succeed on her own. "In general, the patient is seen as a rather dependent individual who in spite of her educational background relies on others very heavily for support and direction in her life," according to the psychologist's report, from 1987, when Diehl was awaiting trial in the Thomas case. The psychologist continued:

> The interpersonal relationships with significant others appear to be strained and there is some question as to whether she has ever maintained a meaningful adult relationship. She has many perfectionist strivings which stem from her overwhelming need to please others in order to gain acceptance. Although she may ostensibly appear aloof and distant her behavior is largely motivated out of insecurity and poor self image. The expectations which she and others have held for her have seldom been achieved and she therefore carries with her the identity of being a failure. Associated with this apparent lack of success in life is a strong sense of guilt and remorse.[60]

Diehl's physical appearance in college masked, to a degree, the emotional turmoil that she must have been experiencing. She graduated from Academy High School, she said, as an award-winner: she took home four scholarships, various musical awards, and won four state essay contests.[61] While living at home with her parents, she went on to attend what was then called Mercyhurst College, now Mercyhurst University, which the Roman Catholic Sisters of Mercy founded in Erie in 1926. The campus was less than two miles from the Diehls' house. Mercyhurst started admitting men in 1969, two years after Diehl enrolled, in 1967. She graduated in 1970, a year early, with bachelor's degrees in sociology and social work and no firm career plans, though she later desired to become a teacher, like her mother. Her initial focus, she said, was "helping people."[62] She liked to say she was the first person at Mercyhurst to finish with an honors degree in three years rather than four. And she said her course concentrations at Mercyhurst were in pre-law and pre-med, and that she later took the LSAT, the law school entrance exam, and "scored in the upper percentile."[63] She wore fashionable clothes while at Mercyhurst, based on her yearbook and other college photos, and wore her hair in a longer bouffant. Her clothes showed off a slim figure—a figure that Robert Sadoff came to believe was too thin. "She's extremely thin in this picture, much more so than when she graduated from high school," Sadoff once said, referring to a photograph of Diehl in college. "This would be consistent with the anorexia."[64]

Diehl-Armstrong, by her own admission, remained a virgin in college.[65] She said she kept to herself, but also considered herself highly attractive, based on what she said men told her. She said during the Pizza Bomber trial that men were always interested in her, and that she did not have to go out of her way to find men. But she also said she was reserved. "I was kind of weird in high school," she said, though she said she did go to the prom.[66] "I was more of an egghead," she said. "I'm an intellectual type. I like to read and study, and I'm a lone wolf. I like to practice my music and do weird things. So that doesn't necessarily mean I'm good for a relationship. But they would be intrigued by intelligence or turned on by certain things like that, and I would have plenty of people coming on to me and stuff."[67]

Looks clearly were important to Diehl-Armstrong, and she said she was bothered by the amount of weight she gained later in life, when she was in prison. "When I was young I was a model. I was good looking," she also said during the Pizza Bomber trial. "When I was young, I was pretty doggone good looking and a model and all, if I do say so myself, not to be bragging about it or anything."[68] She said she took a level-headed approach to beauty, recalling an aphorism she said her only husband liked to tell her, "Beauty is only skin deep and a lot of them ought to be skinned." "So I don't put a lot of importance on judging a book by its cover or by what a person looks like," Diehl-Armstrong then said, explaining what her husband meant. "It's in the heart that counts with me or what a person is all about."[69] Yet she also boasted that she could charm and bed almost any man she wanted. "Sex," she said, "has never been a worry to me."[70]

When she graduated from college in 1970, Diehl was twenty-one years old—a pivotal age for her. She was twenty-one when she left her house and went out on her own. Just as twelve was a threshold age for her—and age when she started puberty—so was age twenty-one—the age when she was independent as an adult for the first time in her life. And just as she suffered anorexia during adolescence, Diehl began to suffer from major mental illness as a young adult, in the years after she had left behind her parents' residence. Once Diehl turned twenty-one, her father once said, she was "on her own."[71]

He also told the police that, once his daughter turned twenty-one, she be-came "her own person" and rarely visited her parents.[72] Diehl described her twenty-first year as another of the "transitional points in my life."[73]

Diehl said she signed up with an employment agency and worked at various secretarial jobs when she was twenty-one and in the years shortly thereafter. When she was twenty-one she also met an eccentric handy-man, electrician, and substitute teacher: Bill Rothstein—the man who, in the mid-2000s, would be accused of working with Diehl-Armstrong in the Pizza Bomber case and helping her stuff the dead body of her boyfriend Jim Roden into a freezer. Diehl-Armstrong recalled her first meeting with Rothstein with precision. Rothstein was twenty-six years old in 1970, and she remembered him as something of a catch: his parents owned Erie's Rola Bottling Company, the home of the local soft drink Rola Cola. Diehl-Armstrong said one of her friends, worried that she was "too much of a bookworm," introduced her to Bill Rothstein because the friend thought that he and Diehl would be a good match.[74] The friend was correct. The two went roller skating on their first date, and Diehl-Armstrong recalled that she immediately swooned over Rothstein, who was six feet, two inches tall, six inches taller than Diehl. "He was built perfectly," Diehl-Armstrong said, "like a young Elvis."[75]

The two were nearly inseparable for a time. They both went to col-lege—he studied electrical engineering at the University of Toledo, in Ohio, but never graduated—and they both liked to talk and hold themselves out as superior intellects. By now, Diehl had become immersed in a lifelong interest in astrology and voodoo, and Rothstein, like Diehl, also believed in karma and liked numerology. He would often talk about planning the best time for a date, a time when the planets aligned. While he helped his par-ents run the Rola Cola plant, she worked in the plant's deli with Rothstein's mother, selling bagels and lox for the Rothsteins, who were Jewish.[76] Diehl and Rothstein got engaged in 1970. The year was easy for Diehl to remem-ber, because, she said, "that was the year the movie came out"—*Love Story*, their favorite movie, in which Ryan O'Neill played Oliver Barrett IV, and Ali McGraw played his soul mate, Jennifer Cavilleri, who was dying of cancer.[77] Diehl said Rothstein proposed to her by giving her twelve long-stemmed red roses, the album soundtrack to *Love Story*, and a diamond ring from New York City. "It was a perfect ring," Diehl-Armstrong recalled, "it was a full carat flawless."[78]

The marriage never occurred. Diehl and Rothstein lived together at his parents' house, but they failed to make the engagement work. She claimed some of the tension grew out of Rothstein "trying to convert me to Judaism and all this."[79] Diehl-Armstrong decades later placed some of the blame on herself. When she turned twenty-one years old, she said, she started experiencing mental problems and also developed what she described as a fear of commitment. "I started to have difficulties," she recalled. "But Bill wanted to get engaged, and other people wanted to get engaged, but I could not make that commitment. I was scared to death of making that commitment because what I had seen in my parent's marriage. I was very commitment phobic."[80]

After she split with Rothstein, Diehl met someone new shortly thereafter, in 1971. She started dating Bob Thomas, who would become her first homicide victim in 1984. Thomas was twenty-nine or thirty years old when they met at a dance at a downtown Erie bar. They dated for six or seven months, Diehl said, and saw each other several times a week. She said Thomas was the first man she had sex with.[81] Thomas was separated from his wife, whom he had been accused of beating, and he was a Navy veteran of the Vietnam War with mental problems of his own. Psychiatric records showed he suffered from posttraumatic stress disorder and schizophrenia with paranoid behavior: "three potentially explosive or violent illnesses," as Sadoff testified at Diehl's trial.[82] By October of 1971, Diehl and Thomas had stopped seeing each other. And by 1972, Diehl had started seeking mental health treatment.[83]

Diehl gave various explanations for why, at twenty-three years old, she sought outpatient psychiatric care. She went to Erie's Hamot Hospital. She once said she needed therapy because of her fear of commitment, to figure out why "I wasn't able to trust people, why I was paranoid about this stuff and what was wrong with me."[84] She also said she visited Hamot, where she was an outpatient, because, while working as a secretary, "I was having trouble with my job and I was nervous and I was having a lot of anxiety."[85] In another explanation, Diehl said she sought treatment "to get enrichment for my life. I was not told to go. I believe in psychotherapy to learn about yourself. So I went in and I was told that I had nothing wrong with me at the time. This was in the medical report. He [the psychiatrist] said maybe passive-aggressive personality disorders, but as far as that, I find nothing wrong . . . with you."[86] And in another explanation, Diehl connected her desire for mental health treatment to her difficulties with men. "I told them I wanted to find the right marriage partner," Diehl-Armstrong said, referring to the mental health professionals. "I was having problems with relationships and I wanted to seek analysis to, more or less voluntarily, to help me overcome my neurotic tendencies that might be hampering me finding the right marriage partner."[87]

The notes from Diehl's first meeting at Hamot, on August 1, 1972, show that she complained of problems with her parents, including her "alcoholic father," problems holding down a job, and problems with men: "You can't trust men," she said. "They all lie."[88] The psychiatric caseworker listed the diagnostic impression that would continue to anger Diehl years later, during the Thomas trial: "a deep-seated hatred of men . . . [with] passive aggressive personality traits."[89] A psychiatrist at Hamot diagnosed her with "bipolar disorder with passive aggressive personality with hysterical features."[90] She was not placed on medication, according to the records and her testimony.[91]

Diehl at this point was able to cope with her mental illness and work various secretarial jobs. She also worked, in 1973, in the office of an Erie counseling center for alcoholics, where she also met with clients. She felt qualified for the job because of her bachelor's degree in social work, but she said she could not get a job as a counselor unless she had a master's degree. In 1973 she started attending Erie's Gannon College, now Gannon University, also a Roman Catholic institution, and graduated in 1975 with a master's degree in education with a focus on guidance and counseling,[92] and with twenty-one credits toward a doctorate in education. She said she was also certified to be a guidance counselor for elementary and high school students, and was certified to teach social studies to high school students.[93] She went on to teach American history as a substitute in the suburban Millcreek Township School District[94] and taught private music lessons, but she was unable to get a job at the Erie School District, the largest school district in the region and the district where her mother the teacher was on her way to becoming something of an institution. Diehl blamed her failure to get a job at the Erie School District on her mother: "I tried [the] Erie district, but, despite the fact my mother was [there] for years and secured positions for everybody, she refused to help me get a position even though she promised she would help me if I became a counselor. And I did and she still wouldn't help me, so I was unable to secure a position."[95]

Diehl continued to live on her own. She rented an apartment in downtown Erie, in a fourteen-unit building that included lawyers' offices. Her landlord was a lawyer, Larry D'Ambrosio, who would become her personal attorney for much of her life, and a key counselor to her in the Pizza Bomber case.[96] While living in the apartment building, suffering from an unmedicated bipolar disorder and fearful of crime in downtown Erie, Diehl bought her first gun—a .25-caliber Browning automatic handgun she purchased at a local sports store in her name. She also bought a carrying case. She said she never fired the gun, and that only her boyfriend at that time—not Bob Thomas—loaded it. "I purchased it for protection," she said.[97]

Diehl had a number of male acquaintances, and she was never known to complain about a lack of sexual activity. When she was in a manic phase, Diehl once told a psychiatrist, she needed "an excessive amount of sex," and said that when those situations developed, "she falls for people she regrets later."[98] Diehl, twenty-six years old in 1975, was unable to find a job in her chosen field—teaching—and was unable to keep whatever job she could find. She worked for several months in 1975 as a social worker at the Erie County welfare office, a civil-service job in which she made $3.50 an hour, or $1.50 more than the federal minimum wage.[99] Months after she lost that job, she sought psychiatric help because "I couldn't function in my job," she said. "I was let go and I had a breakdown. I was not able to get out of bed."[100] She believed that her mental disabilities were preventing her from working.

The professional who became her regular psychiatrist, Robert B. Callahan, MD, first met with Diehl on May 5, 1976. He found that she "had multiple depressive symptoms and was considered to be totally incapacitated for employment," but also determined that her prospects were good for a return to "gainful employment" with psychotherapy and medication.[101] Callahan diagnosed Diehl as suffering from manic-depressive disorder, depressive type, and the related cyclothymic disorder, in which a person has cyclical episodes of depression and excitement. Callahan treated Diehl in a total of thirty-eight weekly and biweekly sessions for fourteen months, until July 29, 1977. He listened as she talked compulsively about her troubled and pressured childhood, including her anorexia and her inability to live up to her mother's expectations. Callahan noted Diehl's "superior attitude," but said she would also become "severely depressed," "with severe identification problems and likewise severe covert authority problems."[102]

Callahan prescribed Diehl the antidepressant Tofranil, the first known prescribed medication she took for her mental illness. Diehl "was displaying severe interpersonal relationships with family, friends and even casual acquaintances," Callahan wrote, and often failed to take the medication as directed, mainly because of what she said were "frequent somatic complaints [or complaints about physical problems], dizziness, nausea, headaches, chest pain, flu symptoms."[103] Callahan wrote of his patient and her difficulties: "She frequently cuts down on dosage or stopped medications entirely against the recommendations of this physician. She rejected any attempts to use suggested medications on a trial basis to see if they would be more beneficial than the Tofranil."[104]

When Diehl's treatments with Callahan ended, he believed her mental state could go either way in the years ahead, depending on how Diehl handled her care. Callahan wrote:

During the 14 months I saw this patient, I felt at times she was gaining some insight into her emotional problems and that her prognosis was good for functioning in a competitive job market, but I did point out to her that I felt she had set her goals too high. At other times, I was of the opinion that even if she was successful in finding employment, her frequent "ups and downs," her disorganized behavior, her personality affect and frequent physical complaints would result in termination rather quickly and she would regress into a severe depressive state.

In summary, I did feel that I had been moderately successful with this patient, that when therapy was terminated she definitely knew that she would be in need of further treatment and would seek help.[105]

For the first time since 1975, Marjorie Diehl worked a steady job in 1980. What she did nearly sent her to prison.

Diehl was working as a counselor for a nonprofit she created, the Erie Women's Center, which arranged for abortions in Buffalo, New York, and which Diehl considered more of a fertility clinic.[106] Erie police on April 23, 1980, charged her with criminal conspiracy and attempted theft by deception. Police said the referrals Diehl made to the clinic were her sole means of income. In a convoluted case, police accused her of falsely telling a woman on April 18, 1980, that, based on testing of the woman's urine sample, the woman was pregnant and could have an abortion. Diehl, the police said, made an appointment for the woman for the next day, and said the abortion would cost $150. The police charged Diehl in a sting. The woman with whom she met was an undercover police officer, and the urine sample she gave to Diehl was that of a male police lieutenant.[107]

Diehl said she did nothing wrong. She acknowledged that she met with the woman on behalf of the Erie Women's Center at the Erie County Library, in downtown Erie.[108] Diehl said the clinic had two offices for referrals in Erie, but that she and the woman decided to meet at the library because the clinic also "wanted a central meeting place, privacy, wanted a place for people if they wanted material on health-related matters. It seemed like a logical place and, in my mind, not a sleazy place like a bar or restroom where things could be heard and private things, confidentiality, could be violated."[109] Diehl said nothing was sinister about the meeting with the woman. She said her lawyer and landlord, Larry D'Ambrosio, would vouch for her. She said the urine sample was meant to be part of an overall pregnancy screening, rather than the only part of the test, and she did not analyze the urine sample in any case. She said urine tests can be unreliable, and that males can test positive for pregnancy if a man has taken medication or has had testicular cancer "or other extreme conditions."[110]

Diehl mainly blamed the police and the Erie County District Attorney's Office. She said she had been falsely arrested. "It was entrapment," she said. "It was an election year, Right to Life movement, and it was an abortion issue. And the district attorney is new and he is a political animal in this situation. He wanted to take advantage of it."[111]

She also said working at the clinic conflicted at times with her personal beliefs. "I have never been in favor of women's lib, per se," she later testified. "I'm an old-fashioned type of woman in a lot of ways and I like to be treated like a lady. I am not a women's lib type. I do believe women have every right to equal pay and freedom of choice."[112]

The case ended with a beneficial arrangement for Diehl. The District Attorney's Office accepted her into a program called Accelerated Rehabilitative Disposition (ARD), for nonviolent, first-time offenders. ARD defendants are not required to plead guilty, and they get sentences of probation rather than prison. ARD defendants also get no criminal record for their case if they successfully complete their probation, which Diehl did. A county judge on November 11, 1980, sentenced her to two years of probation, to include sixty hours of community service. Diehl performed her hours at the state-run Pennsylvania Soldiers' and Sailors' Home in Erie.[113] The judge discharged her from ARD on November 30, 1982.

"Marjorie was an excellent volunteer, helping out with office work, activities and field trips," a volunteer coordinator wrote to the head of the ARD program. "They were very pleased with Marjorie and said she's the best volunteer they've had in some time."[114]

She still was unable to work. After the criminal case led to her departure from the abortion clinic, Diehl never again held full-time employment. She continued to seek psychiatric treatment in the early 1980s, but with different psychiatrists; Callahan, with whom she had met for eighteen months, moved away, so Diehl started seeing psychiatrists affiliated with another Erie hospital, Saint Vincent Medical Center.[115] She complained of gaining weight and of an alcoholic father and domineering mother. In one examination, on August 6, 1981, she was diagnosed with cyclothymic disorder with manic episodes and "fluctuations w/ depression and hyperactive states"; she remained on Tofranil.[116] In a follow-up exam, in September 1981, the evaluator noted that Diehl's mood was "very, very up," and that she spoke of being "very unsure of myself; constantly worried about what is going to happen."[117] The evaluator wrote that Diehl's speech was "nearly non-ending," and that Diehl explained that she had anorexia as a child and had trouble with her parents (but no mention of sexual abuse). "She has trouble with her relationships w/

men, feeling that younger men are 'too shallow,'" the evaluator wrote. Diehl said she was still taking Tofranil. The diagnostic impression was cyclothymic disorder, with a recommendation of continued therapy and medication.[118]

Diehl continued to go to the psychiatrists to get mental help, but also to achieve a goal that had come to nearly consume her: to get a diagnosis that would show her mental condition was a permanent disability that made her unable to work and thus made her eligible for Social Security Supplemental Income disability benefits. To get the benefits, she asked for help from her treating psychiatrist at the time, Paul Francis, MD. She wrote to him on December 15, 1981, complaining that she was unable to get disability benefits based on her claim that she had temporomandibular joint disorder (TMJ). She wrote that being on regular welfare was humiliating, and that getting disability benefits for a "permanent disability" was what she deserved. Diehl wrote to Francis:

> Please fill out the enclosed form and return it to me as soon as possible. . . . I submitted the letter documenting the severe TMJ . . . problem, but was notified this was not enough. Bureaucratic requirements need to mention "permanent disability." Obviously, they ignored the dentist's use of "permanent disability." I have spent a lot of time and money over the last year or so trying to get the small amount which I feel I deserve. I am really frustrated. After all I can't even get a small rebate much less any disability from social security. . . .
>
> Being on welfare is degrading and doesn't really reflect my problems. Will you help me by documenting as best you can that I have a "permanent disability" psychologically? . . . I am having a lot of anxiety. My financial situation would be improved if I was to receive this little compensation, I would be much better off psychologically.[119]

Decades later, those statements would come back to trigger increased scrutiny of Diehl-Armstrong's mental state.

Dr. Francis issued his findings on December 22, 1981. He diagnosed Diehl with dysthymic disorder, or persistent depression, and mixed personality disorder, which could include narcissism and antisocial behavior. Francis stopped short of diagnosing Diehl with bipolar disorder—which features persistent depression and persistent mania—but he concluded her mental condition made her unfit for employment. "Persistent depression and associated symptoms over 10 years," Francis wrote of Diehl, then thirty-two years old. "Long-standing difficulties with interpersonal relationships and severe impairments in social and occupational functioning. Personality style manifested by rigidity and hostility."[120] Francis wrote of her job prospects: "Prognosis is considered to be poor because of the chronicity of the problem and the failure to benefit in a sustained fashion from psychiatric therapy in the past. In my opinion she would be completely unable to hold down any type of work in the competitive job market."[121]

The evaluation failed to help Diehl with the Social Security Administration. Francis needed to provide a more detailed report to move the case along, but he declined. He was unwilling to schedule a follow-up appointment with Diehl because of "her history of missed appointments and failure to comply with treatment recommendations."[122] Diehl still tried to get disability benefits. She met with other psychiatrists, but complained about them, as she had with Francis, because she still was unable to get a diagnosis she believed would get her benefits for a permanent disability. She said one of the psychiatrists "had failed to fill out a disability evaluation form in a manner that would qualify her for disability and public housing."[123]

Diehl finally got enough information to apply for disability benefits. The government first denied the application on January 27, 1983, and continued to do so throughout the rest of the year. In a denial dated April 19, 1983, the disability claims examiner noted that Diehl's eligibility for disability benefits, based on her earnings, ran out on June 30, 1976, shortly after Diehl received her first psychiatric treatment from Callahan on May 5, 1976. The examiner wrote that the lack of treatment in 1976 meant that Diehl could have continued to work. "You did not have any treating medical sources prior to 1976," the examiner wrote. "Thus, the conditions would not have prevented you from working as of June 30, 1976, when your eligibility expired."[124] The examiner also wrote that "evidence in file reveals a manic disorder," but noted that Diehl said she sought no treatment earlier in 1976 because "she didn't trust physicians."[125] The examiner concluded: "The medical evidence indicates claimant's impairment causes no significant loss of work-related functions prior to June 30, 1976. Therefore, claim is denied as impairment not severe prior to the date of last insured."[126]

Diehl appealed. She showed her trademark persistence in seeking more records and filing for more information. In later years she would display this persistence by writing repeated and long handwritten letters to lawyers and judges and journalists. In the case of her disability claim, Diehl (who was supposed to be unable to function), did not write the letters to the government and physicians herself. She relied on a legal-aid lawyer as well as her erstwhile boyfriend and self-described paralegal, Edwin A. Carey, a World War II Army veteran who was originally from Pittsburgh and had worked at the Hammermill paper plant in Erie. Carey, who turned sixty-four in 1983, wrote handwritten letters on Diehl's behalf, according to the case files. Diehl remained on Tofranil, although the case records also show that she sometimes failed to take her medication regularly. She was prescribed the mood-stabilizing drug lithium carbonate, but said she stopped taking it because it gave her seizures.[127]

Diehl won her appeal for disability benefits on January 31, 1984. An administrative law judge wrote that she was disabled as of May 5, 1976, when she first saw Callahan, and that the medical evidence established that she has "severe manic depressive disorder and cyclothymic disorder."[128] The judge wrote that he based his decision on medical records, Diehl's testimony at a benefits hearing, and the testimony of a vocational expert, who said that Diehl was unemployable. Diehl, the judge wrote, testified about her poor work history and her mental health problems: "The claimant testified she was first treated for emotional problems as a child when she had anorexia nervosa. She finally went to a doctor who told her she had a personality disorder and had trouble getting along with people. She has memory problems. She has no hobbies and spends most of her time getting herself ready to cope with everyday living. She lives in an apartment but does not go out often. She finds most people are irritating."[129]

The administrative law judge, Robert M. Ague Jr., used an expansive definition of disability for Diehl's benefit. He found that, from the medical evidence, her mental problems—severe manic-depression and cyclothymic disorder—failed to meet the definition of a "listed impairment" under the law. But he awarded her disability benefits, citing what he found to be Diehl's "severe depression," despite medication; her compulsive talking; and her disorganization and "severe difficulty in interpersonal relationships." Ague continued in his decision:

> She has regressed into severe depressive states as a result of termination of employment.
> Her history indicates she has responded poorly to treatment and she has been functioning poorly as far as day to day activities are concerned. In view of her high level of anxiety, agitation, depression, and impaired judgment, she has fallen into markedly restricted activities with a guarded prognosis.[130]

The evidence, Ague wrote, showed that Diehl was "under a disability." "Her capacity to work at all levels is significantly compromised," he wrote, "and the remaining work which she could be functionally . . . capable of performing, considered in combination with her age, her education and her work experience, directs that she cannot be expected to make a vocational adjustment to work which exists in significant numbers in the national economy."[131] Ague ordered the benefits retroactive to May 5, 1976, the date of Diehl's first meeting with Callahan. At thirty-four years of age, Marjorie Diehl was, by the government's definition, so mentally ill as to be disabled and unfit for any employment. By the time of the Pizza Bomber case, her disability benefits would be $580 a month.[132]

Diehl had made several major changes by the time she was awarded the disability benefits in January 1984. In the late summer of 1983, she had moved from the downtown apartment building into the bungalow on Sunset Boulevard, where she lived alone and used a federal housing subsidy to help pay her rent. Her landlord was Edwin Carey, her paralegal, who had bought the house for $28,900 on August 3, 1983. Also, by the time she was awarded the benefits, Diehl had rekindled her relationship with Bob Thomas, whom she had last dated in October 1971. They started seeing each other again in early 1984.

Diehl had encountered Thomas a number of times before then, in the late 1970s and early 1980s. She would run into him at the post office, where she had a box, and she would see him at a local amusement park, Waldameer, where she said Thomas drove a miniature train part-time.[133] In 1979, she said, Thomas told her that his wife had divorced him, and that he was available. "Every time I used to run into him, he used to ask me to go out with him," she said.[134]

They got together again one day in early February 1984. Diehl recalled that the two met as they were waiting on a line to get government cheese. Thomas was living in another area of the city, with a male friend who had also served in Vietnam. After getting their cheese, Diehl and Thomas left together in Diehl's 1970 Ford Gran Torino 500. Diehl drove to her rented house on Sunset Boulevard. Thomas stayed overnight, and they had sex. They kept seeing each other afterward. Diehl said she loved him.[135]

Diehl and Thomas did a lot together. They often waited together on cheese lines. While on line, in public, Thomas occasionally beat Diehl, according to witnesses.[136] Diehl also said Thomas beat her while on line.[137] The accounts of the beatings later would become evidence at Marjorie Diehl's trial for the homicide of Bob Thomas.

• 5 •

Dictionary of Disorder

Defining Mental Illness

*M*arjorie Diehl's hoarding was, for her lawyers in the Bob Thomas case, irrefutable evidence of her psychosis. The Erie County District Attorney's Office was not nearly as sure. While the prosecution did nothing to dispute that Diehl was a hoarder, it would disagree with the underlying idea that she was mentally ill. The challenge was broad. The District Attorney's Office questioned the efficacy of psychiatry in general—its ability to really figure out what is going on in the human mind. The defense's ambassador for psychiatry was Robert L. Sadoff, who had diagnosed Diehl so many times. He explained at her trial that her hoarding was symptomatic of her manic-depressive illness and that it signaled a serious impairment of her judgment. Sadoff said psychiatric analysis had helped prove that Diehl was mentally unstable.

The prosecutor was not as convinced. An exchange between him and Sadoff captured their differences—and encapsulated the basic differing views about the effectiveness of psychiatry.

"There's an awful lot we don't know about human behavior; would that be a fair statement?" the prosecutor said to Sadoff at trial, in May 1988.

"That's a fair statement," Sadoff said.[1]

The prosecutor, John A. Bozza, an assistant district attorney, asked whether Diehl's mental illness had a physiological component. He was questioning, in front of the jury, whether Sadoff's diagnosis that Diehl suffered from manic-depression had any validity or was flawed because it was based more on observation than on pure science.

"When we talk about certain personality disorders, we are really talking about descriptions of behavior, are we not, at least to some degree?" Bozza said.

"To some degree, we are, yes," Sadoff said.

61

"I mean, when we say that someone is manic depressive," Bozza said, "we are really describing how they behave on occasion, is that not correct?"

"It is part of what we are doing, yes," Sadoff said. "Not the whole thing."

"Well," Bozza said, "when you talked about Marjorie Diehl, you indicated that she had been diagnosed for a long period of time as manic depressive."

"Yes."

"I believe you indicated that she had conveyed in some way the symptoms of this illness?"

"Yes, she did," Sadoff said.

"Now, those symptoms were behavioral in nature, were they not?" Bozza said.

"Yes, they were."

"They were things that people could see?"

"Yes."

"Things actually that people could hear, correct?"

"Yes."

"Because they are verbal—verbalization behaviors, also, are they not?"

"Yes," Sadoff said. "That's correct. I would accept that."

"Now," Bozza said, "we don't know in Marjorie's case whether or not there is something physically wrong with her, do we?"

"You mean apart from the fact that she has manic-depressive illness?" Sadoff said.

"We don't know what the physical features of manic-depressive illnesses are?" Bozza said.

"We have not uncovered all of the physiological components," Sadoff said. "We have not."

"You haven't done any physiological tests on Marjorie, have you?"

"No, I have not," Sadoff said.

"This wouldn't be like uncovering a virus or a bacteria, would it?" Bozza said.

"It would not," Sadoff said.

"Really," Bozza said. "The impressions of this particular disorder are very subjective, are they not?"

"On whose part?" Sadoff said.

"On any psychiatrist's part."

"Well, if you have an agreement among a number of psychiatrists about the symptoms that we have observed over the years in patients who fit a certain category," Sadoff said, "I think it becomes more objective than it does subjective."[2]

Bozza asked Sadoff about Robert Callahan's diagnosis, in 1976, twelve years earlier, that Diehl suffers from manic-depressive illness.

"Was that not a subjective interpretation?" Bozza said.

"On his part?" Sadoff said.

"Yes," Bozza said.

"At that time," Sadoff said, "that would be subjective for him with respect to her based on the agreed symptoms of thousands of other psychiatrists who have seen patients in the same way and subjectively arrived at the same conclusions."

"I understand that," Bozza said. "But there was no objective—a test available to him to determine that she had manic-depressive illness?"

"There's no manic-depressive virus or bacteria," Sadoff said.

"No depressive virus," Bozza said.

"No."

"Nothing to be tested?" Bozza said. "Physiologically to be tested to see if anyone has the disease?"

"At this stage of the game?" Sadoff said.

"At this stage of the game or in 1975," Bozza said. (He misspoke here, meaning to say 1976, the year of Robert Callahan's diagnosis.)

"Right," Sadoff said.

"So in a sense, really, psychiatry," Bozza said, "is it fair to say, is somewhat less scientific than some of the other branches of medicine?"

"If you put it in those terms," Sadoff said, "yes, I would agree with you."[3]

Bozza continued to discuss what he suggested were psychiatry's deficiencies and advances. During the examination, Sadoff had a book with him on the witness stand. It was the most important volume in modern psychiatry: the third and latest edition of the *Diagnostic and Statistical Manual of Mental Disorders*, the bible that mental health professionals use as they diagnose those with mental illness.

Bozza said to Sadoff: "Psychiatry, Doctor, in all deference to you and all of the fine work that others like you I am sure do, has certain limitations, does it not, with regard to human behavior?"

"I would be the first to admit that," Sadoff said.

"For example,' Bozza said, "do we know, generally, why people behave the way we do?"

"In some cases, generally, we do," Sadoff said.

"OK."

"In some cases, specifically, we may not," Sadoff said.

"So we are not at that point in psychiatry of being what you might say is an absolute scientific," Bozza said.

"I would never claim that," Sadoff said. "I don't think psychiatry would be absolutely scientific. As long as we can be certain within a reasonable medical certainty, that would be enough for me."

"We have improved," Bozza said. "I think psychiatry has improved in the last twenty years."

"I think we are coming to improve, a dynamic flow towards improvement," Sadoff said.

"But there are lots of mysteries about human behavior?" Bozza said.

"That's what makes life so interesting," Sadoff said.[4]

The prosecution's contention—that psychiatry is more subjective than objective, more a compiling of behaviors than a scientific enterprise—extended well before and beyond the trial of Marjorie Diehl, a troubled woman on trial for murder in a Rust Belt city in northwestern Pennsylvania in the 1980s. The tension between psychiatry and science has existed for thousands of years. But each generation has continued to find that the observation of behavior still remains, in many ways, the key pathway to trying to understand the psyche and the mental illness that can undermine it. As Sadoff said, those observations, made of countless patients over so many years, have created a catalog of dysfunction that has become a foundation for psychiatry and its quest for more scientific certitude. Central to that process, to that compilation of unusual human behavior, is the tome that was at Sadoff's side on the witness stand: the *Diagnostic and Statistical Manual of Mental Disorders*, or the *DSM*. It is a book built on thousands of years of experience, observation, and theorizing over what constitutes mental illness.

Madness, for the ancient Greeks, was a matter of imbalance. The physician Hippocrates traced physical and mental ailments to the four humors: blood, yellow bile, black bile, and phlegm. The humors roughly corresponded with the four natural elements: air, fire, earth, and water. As each of the natural elements comprised the world's physical surroundings, the four humors stood alone or combined to form human temperaments; the humors represented not just phlegm, blood, and bile, "but vital forces."[5] Phlegmatic, from phlegm, was related to water and connoted tolerance and reasonableness; melancholic, from black bile, was related to the earth and connoted depression and moodiness; choleric, from yellow bile, was related to fire and connoted passion or, in the extreme, aggression or mania; and sanguine, from blood, was related to the air and connoted liveliness and sociability. A proper balance of the humors produced a person who was of sound mind and body, whose mental and physical health thrived.

Hippocrates (460–377 BC E) linked mental illness to an imbalance of the humors, such as black bile, or *melania chole*, an overabundance of which he said created melancholy or depression. Though black bile is absent from nature—the gall bladder, in contrast, really does produce yellow bile—Hippocrates and his predecessors, such as Empedocles (495–430 BCE), insisted black bile was indeed genuine—a belief that recognized that depression and other forms of mental illness were seen as real in ancient society. As Andrew Solomon has noted in *The Noonday Demon*, his extensive history of depression, Hippocrates was innovative in connecting mental illness to the brain, even as he also linked mental illness to imbalances of the humors. "It is the brain which makes us mad or delirious, inspires us with dread and fear, whether by night or by day, brings sleeplessness, inopportune mistakes, aimless anxieties, absentmindedness, and acts that are contrary to habit," Hippocrates wrote. "These things that we suffer all come from the brain when it is not healthy, but becomes abnormally hot, cold, moist, or dry."[6]

Thousands of years of hindsight reveal humoral theory's obvious flaws, such as a reliance on a bodily fluid—black bile—that does not exist. Yet the theory was remarkably prescient. Hippocrates and his contemporaries were correct in surmising that an imbalance of sorts leads to mental illness. In another example of his foresight, Hippocrates believed depression—and the excess of black bile—resulted from a mixture of "internal and external factors," and that some mental trauma could be traced even to prenatal development.[7] Homer, in the *Iliad* and the *Odyssey* (circa mid-eighth century BCE), has madness and depression doom even the strongest warriors, such as the Greek hero Ajax—another recognition of mental illness as intrinsic human trait. Socrates (circa 470–399 BCE) and Plato (circa 428–347 BCE) largely downplayed what Solomon calls Hippocrates's "organic" approach to madness and depression; the two great thinkers considered mental illness more a psychic than a physical ailment, a type of woe that philosophers rather than physicians could better understand.[8] Plato traced the origins of madness to childhood, among other sources, but, like Hippocrates, he grounded his overall understanding of mental illness to imbalances, whether due to internal or external turmoil.

Seventy years after the death of Hippocrates, Aristotle (384–322 BCE) shared this view, as he too accepted the idea that a proper mixture of the four humors produced equanimity in spirit and body. While he never discounted the ill effects of depression, melancholy, and madness, Aristotle helped originate a concept that persists to this day: that depression is often a characteristic—some might argue a requisite characteristic—of great artists. When Marjorie Diehl-Armstrong asserted that her bipolar disorder—a dysfunction rooted in depression—placed her among such eminences as Hemingway and Lincoln, she was espousing a belief that Aristotle had articulated three hundred years before the dawn of the Common Era: "All those who have attained excellence in philosophy, in poetry, in art, and in politics, even Socrates and Plato, had a melancholic habitus; indeed some suffered even from melancholic disease."[9] Aristotle, even more bluntly, also said, in a well-known maxim attributed to him, "No great mind has ever existed without a touch of madness."

The Roman physician Galen, perhaps the greatest doctor after Hippocrates, expanded on humoral theory to explain depression. Galen (129–199 BCE) developed nine temperaments, including melancholy, which he believed to be an intrinsic part of the human psyche. Melancholy was a trait Galen said originated in the self, though he also attributed it to an excess of black bile. He prescribed opium, mandrake, and herbal remedies to relieve depression.[10] Galen's emphasis on the four humors, combined with his discoveries regarding the circulatory system, also contributed to the popularity of bloodletting, the highly invasive procedure meant to relieve physical and mental problems. Bloodletting and the use of purgatives and laxatives, common among the ancient Greeks and Romans, were thought to adjust the levels of blood and the other three humors, including the mysterious black bile, to recalibrate the body to a healthier and more balanced state. "Both mental and physical disorders were considered by Galen to be caused by an excess (*plethora*) of one of the four humors."[11] The famous quotation from the Roman poet Horace (65–8 BCE), "*Est modus in rebus*," or "There is a mean in all things," captured the Roman and Greek axiom that an even-tempered life is a productive life.

Humoral theory and bloodletting persisted well into the 1800s, as physicians and then psychiatrists continued to struggle to find the causes of physical diseases and mental infirmities. The conception of mental illness nonetheless had changed long before then. In the Middle Ages, believers considered mental illness the consequence of Lucifer's constant struggle with God and Christ. By the Renaissance, as superstition ceded to science, physicians looked to direct observation to help explain mental illness, including depression, the saturnine disorder attributed, in astrological terms, to those born under the sign of Saturn. By the 1700s and the Enlightenment, "mad-doctors," and "lunatic-doctors" concentrated on treating the mentally ill in private and public asylums in England. The most famous of these institutions, "Bedlam," or the Bethlem Royal Hospital, operated as a hospital starting in 1329, and "bedlam" eventually became synonymous with mental disorders. Also during the 1700s in Britain, doctors who worked in insane asylums started classifying mental illness, creating a rudimentary system that psychiatrists expanded over the centuries. As autopsies became more common, physicians and others studied the bodies of the dead for empirical evidence of mental illness.

What became psychiatry originated in the 1800s, as physicians in France and Britain studied mental illness in medical schools. Those who treated the mentally ill became known as "alienists," after the French physician Philippe Pinel published his treatise on *l'alienation mental*, or "mental alienation,"[12] in 1801; it was translated into English five years later as *A Treatise on Insanity*. "Of all the afflictions to which most humans are subject," Pinel wrote, "the loss of reason is at once the most calamitous and interesting."[13] Physicians who specialized in mental illness became known as psychiatrists by the 1840s, "the pivotal decade in the history of the profession."[14] Later, in the 1880s, psychiatry further took hold in Europe, as Robert Koch, in Germany, and Louis Pasteur, in France, discovered germ theory as the cause of physical diseases. The breakthroughs in medicine gave alienists reason to hope: "If scientific understanding and cure were possible for the suffering of the body, then why not for the suffering of the mind?"[15]

The recognition of psychiatry as a separate branch of medicine spread to the United States, whose major contribution to the field had been the publication, in 1812, of *Medical Inquiries and Observations upon the Diseases of the Mind*, by Benjamin Rush, a Philadelphia physician who studied insanity at the Pennsylvania Hospital. Rush served as surgeon general of the Continental Army and signed the Declaration of Independence as a founding father of the United States. He is also known as the founder of American psychiatry. He was an insightful physician who, like his peers, still practiced bloodletting, just as Hippocrates and Galen had done. He also advocated purging the body through the use of mercurous chloride, or calomel, popularly known as mercury.

Many of Rush's entries in *Medical Inquiries and Observations upon the Diseases of the Mind* are speculation; Rush observed that "Single persons are more predisposed to madness than married people,"[16] and that masturbation, or onanism, can cause madness, particularly in young men.[17] But Rush also observed, with more of a foundation, the relationship between madness and genius. Echoing Aristotle, he wrote:

> Persons of strong and active minds are said to be more predisposed to madness than persons of an opposite character. [The poet John] Dryden has given a currency to this opinion, by asserting "great wit and madness to be nearly allied." Where this is the case, it is the effect of an active imagination and strong passions predominating over the understanding. But the

cases are few, in which a vigorous intellect, elevated above the dominion of the subordinate faculties of the mind, has been perverted by madness from mental causes. Where the disease has been induced by intense study, I think I have observed it most frequently to occur in persons of weak understandings, who were incapable of comprehending the subjects of their studies. Certain occupations predispose to madness more than others. Pinel says, poets, painters, sculptors and musicians, are most subject to it, and that he never knew an instance of it in a chemist, a naturalist, a mathematician, or a natural philosopher.[18]

Rush died in 1813 in Philadelphia. Thirty-one years later, also in Philadelphia, thirteen superintendents of mental asylums met to form the Association of Medical Superintendents of American Institutions for the Insane, the first organization of its kind in the United States. In 1892, it became the American Medico-Psychological Association, and it was renamed the American Psychiatric Association (APA) in 1921. The APA (whose seal features a profile of Rush) soon would lead the push to classify mental illness, as Rush had attempted to do. The association's work manifested itself in the most important psychiatric textbook ever produced in the United States—the *DSM*, whose publisher is the APA. The *DSM*, by detailing categories and subcategories of hundreds of mental abnormalities, provided psychiatrists, at last, with their own catalog, their own dictionary of disorder.[19]

The *DSM* affected Marjorie Diehl-Armstrong's life more than perhaps any other book. The psychologists and psychiatrists who examined her used it to put a name to her mental troubles in her many criminal cases. And, relying on scientific advances, particularly those in the late twentieth century, the professionals who examined Diehl-Armstrong were able to look to a growing body of biological and genetic studies to try to determine the origins of her mental illness. Bipolar disorder and schizophrenia, for example, are now believed to have genetic, biological, and environmental causes, though the interplay between the three, as well as the details of the genetic damage, remains elusive. Despite the encouraging scientific work, "the madness that haunts us still evades our grasp," the psychologist Leonard George has written. "Millions around the world succumb, and few recover fully."[20]

Defining a disorder differs from being able to fully explain it. Debate continues over whether the *DSM*, for all its heft (the current edition, the *DSM-5*, published in 2013, is 947 pages and lists 157 disorders), has truly delivered psychiatry from "the approach that was at once its salvation and its scourge: a classification of diseases based on description and observation but with no account of what caused them."[21] The *DSM* greatly helps professionals identify and label mental illness, and it represents the authoritative text for insurance coverage. Yet the *DSM* offers no unifying explanation for why mental illness occurs—a reflection of the persistent and perhaps eternal difficulty of unlocking the mysteries of the human mind. Marjorie Diehl-Armstrong's multiple psychiatric diagnoses illustrate the puzzle: though professionals, to varying degrees, have been able to specify what mental diseases afflicted her, and to prescribe powerful drugs to address those diseases, they have never been able to pinpoint the sources of her instability—biological, genetic, or otherwise. Many clues and possibilities exist for her behavior. But in her case, as in so many others, the *what* comes with solid answers. The *why* does not.

Today's scientific research has made a breakthrough increasingly possible. Psychoanalysis, which Sigmund Freud pioneered in the 1890s, has fallen short—its effectiveness is now highly disputed—and that failure helped to turn psychiatry even more toward an empiricism that focuses both on the mental and the biological. In this regard, the humoral theory of Hippocrates and Galen has survived, in a more sophisticated fashion, as psychiatrists seek a "holistic" approach to examining mental illness: "We suffer not just as ill bodies or as ill minds but as ill persons."[22]

The naming process—the province of the *DSM*, with its pages and pages of defining the *what* in pursuit of the *why*—remains critical nonetheless. "Give a name to suffering, perhaps the most immediate reminder of our insignificance and powerlessness, and suddenly it bears the trace of the human," psychotherapist Gary Greenberg has written in his history of the development of the *DSM*. "It becomes part of our story. It is redeemed."[23] For better or for worse, the *DSM* continues to stand as psychiatry's bible, its definitions meant to illuminate cases such as Marjorie Diehl-Armstrong's.

The first edition of the *Diagnostic and Statistical Manual of Mental Disorders*, which the APA published in 1952, was rooted in science. Its forerunner was a textbook by German psychiatrist Emil Kraepelin, often considered the father of modern psychiatry because of his emphasis on scientific analysis; his belief that mental illness had biological and genetic origins; and his insistence on rigorous classification of mental illness. Kraepelin, who spent some of his formative professional years examining patients in an Estonian asylum, advocated for psychiatry as a branch of medicine, and his major works sought to classify mental illness as a medical doctor would classify physical diseases. In 1883, he published his *Compendium der Psychiatrie: Zum Gebrauche für Studirende und Aertze* (*Compendium of Psychiatry: For the Use of Students and Physicians*), which became *Ein Lehrbuch der Psychiatrie* (*A Textbook: Foundations of Psychiatry and Neuroscience*).

The sixth edition of the *Psychiatrie*, published in 1899, was among Kraepelin's most influential contributions. It "reordered the psychiatric cosmos for the next century by grouping most of the insanities into two large categories, dementia praecox (or premature dementia) and manic-depressive illness."[24] Dementia praecox, later to become known as schizophrenia (from the Greek "to split" and "the mind"), led to severe mental deterioration, including delusions and hallucinations, that Kraepelin found to be all but permanently debilitating. Manic-depressive illness, which would come to encompass bipolar disorder, was "the non-deteriorating and sometimes remitting form of serious psychotic disturbance,"[25] whose major symptoms included swings between severe depression and mania. Kraepelin diagnosed both dementia praecox and manic-depressive illness as brain disorders. Before his analysis, those with mental illness had, for the previous four hundred years, been grouped under one category: insane, from the Latin *insanus*, meaning unsound mind.[26]

Kraepelin's clear-eyed taxonomy of mental illness is now considered a bedrock of psychiatry. It initially waned in popularity for a time, as Freud's psychoanalysis captivated the profession. But the American Psychiatric Association and its predecessors looked to Kraepelin, rather than Freud, as they formulated their own classification system for mental illness. As Gary Greenberg has written, one of the first challenges for such a classification system, known as a psychiatric nosology, came in 1917, in an address that Thomas W. Salmon, a prominent psychiatrist with the United States Public Health Service, delivered to the American Medico-Psychological Association in Buffalo, New York. "The present classification of mental disease is chaotic," Salmon said. "This condition of affairs discredits the science of psychiatry and reflects unfavorably on our association."[27] He called for "a classification of twenty different mental diseases 'that would meet the scientific demands of the day.'"[28]

The impetus for Salmon's classification system came, in part, from the United States Census Bureau, which in 1840 started to count individuals who were "insane." The bureau, however, lacked any categories for mental illness. Taking the lead from Salmon, who took his lead from Kraepelin, the American Medico-Psychological Association in 1918 published the *Statistical Manual for the Use of Institutions for the Insane*. The association collaborated on the forty-one page *Statistical Manual* with the Bureau of Statistics of the National Committee for Mental Hygiene, in New York City; Salmon, who helped write the *Statistical Manual*, was the committee's medical director.

The *Statistical Manual* was a success, in that the Census Bureau adopted its system to help classify the mentally ill. The *Statistical Manual* took an unvarnished approach—it was designed, the authors wrote, as a handbook for mental institutions as they used forms to compile their annual statistics. The handbook's definitions were meant to help professionals catalog mental illnesses rather than diagnose patients. "The manual and duplicate forms will be furnished free to all cooperating institutions," the authors wrote, "and it is earnestly hoped that they will generally be adopted, so that a national system of statistics of mental disease may become an actuality."[29]

Though it was a survey rather than a diagnostic tool, the *Statistical Manual* offered insight into the understanding of mental illness at that time. It listed twenty-two disorders, each with its own set of definitions and explanatory notes. One disorder, psychosis with Huntington's chorea, or a neurological disease, was described as having symptoms that include "mental inertia and an emotional change, either apathy or silliness or a depressive irritable reaction with a tendency to passionate outbursts."[30] Its cause: "hereditary in nature."[31] Descriptions of other disorders featured no causes; the disorders seemed more like manifestations of other problems. The disorder known as involution melancholia, for example, included "the slowly developing depressions of *middle life and later years* which come on with worry, insomnia, uneasiness, anxiety and agitation, showing usually the unreality and sensory complex, but little or no difficulty in thinking. The tendency is for the course to be a prolonged one."[32]

Among the longest descriptions were those for the two disorders that Kraepelin had studied so intensely: dementia praecox ("the term 'schizophrenia' is now used by many writers," the *Statistical Manual* said[33]), and manic-depressive psychosis. Of the two, the definition for dementia praecox was less precise, though the authors said it could include a number of characteristics, such as "a seclusive type of personality," and "a gradual blunting of the emotions, indifference or silliness with serious defects of judgment and often hypochondriacal complaints, suspicions or ideas of reference."[34] In describing manic-depressive psychosis, the *Statistical Manual* was more detailed. It set forth an analysis that would generally fit those to come:

> This group comprises the essentially affective benign psychoses, mental disorders which fundamentally are marked by emotional oscillations and a tendency to recurrence. Various psychotic trends, delusions, illusions and hallucinations, clouded states, stupor, etc., may be added. To be distinguished are:
> The *manic* reaction with its feeling of well-being (or irascibility), flight of ideas or over- activity.

The *depressive* reaction with its feeling of mental and physical insufficiency, a despondent, sad or hopeless mood and in severe depressions, retardation and inhibition; in some cases the mood is one of uneasiness and anxiety, accompanied by restlessness.

The *mixed* reaction, a combination of manic and depressive symptoms.[35]

World War II increased the need for psychiatric tools that were more sophisticated and comprehensive than the *Statistical Manual*. Thousands of soldiers returned home with mental and physical trauma; treating them required more categories for disorders and even more uniformity of classification. The New York Academy of Medicine had called for such standardization as early as 1927, and six years later, the American Medical Association, with the help of the APA, published *A Standard Classified Nomenclature of Disease*. It listed twenty-four disorders, and like the *Statistical Manual*, was indebted to Kraepelin and his scientific approach to mental illness.[36]

During World War II, however, standardization for the evaluation and classification of mental disorders still was largely absent. The U.S. Army and Navy had their guides, and the United States Veterans Administration had its own, in addition to *A Standard Classified Nomenclature of Disease* as well as the *Statistical Manual*. Psychiatrists found the *Statistical Manual* particularly lacking as they tried to understand the mental problems of so many returning soldiers and their other patients: "Its basic terms didn't even come close to describing what psychiatrists were seeing in the clinic."[37] Led by George Raines, chairman of its committee on nomenclature, the APA set aside plans for revamping the *Statistical Manual* and instead created an entirely new publication: the first edition of the *Diagnostic and Statistical Manual of Mental Disorders*, which came out in 1952 and ran to 132 pages.

The federal government by then had fully taken control of compiling statistics for mental illness; such work was a task of the National Institute of Mental Health, founded in 1949. The APA and its psychiatrists were able to focus more on diagnoses; the APA tailored the first *Diagnostic and Statistical Manual* for that endeavor. It listed and defined 106 disorders; psychiatrists diagnosed patients to determine which definition fit. According to the APA: The *DSM-I* "was the first official manual of mental disorders to focus on clinical utility for classification. Definitions were relatively simple and consisted of brief prototypical descriptions."[38] The *DSM-I* became the universally accepted textbook of psychiatry, a book that set forth taxonomy of mental disorders and their treatment.

The *DSM-I* and its successors would include the broad categories of mental disorders that would apply, in varying degrees, to the case of Marjorie

Diehl-Armstrong. The *DSM* listed psychoses, or severe mental disorders in which the patient is often out of touch with reality and suffers from delusions and hallucinations; neuroses, or less severe disorders in which anxiety is a prevalent symptom; and personality disorders, in which the patient acts in socially unacceptable and destructive ways. The specific disorders in the broad categories came under steady review, as the APA revised the *DSM* to reflect changes in society and advances in the understanding of mental illness. The *DSM-II*, published in 1968, listed 182 disorders.

It differed prominently from the *DSM-I* in that it eliminated the possibility that mental disorders could be a reaction to something, rather than illnesses that simply existed. As one critic has written, this one change was momentous, and made diagnosing mental illness less grounded in science than under the *DSM-I* by "severing cause from effect" and abandoning "the rigorous proofs of the scientific method."[39] From now on, according to this analysis, "in the absence of cause and effect, a mental illness would be anything the psychiatric profession chose to call a mental illness."[40] Among the other more important developments in the *DSM-II* was that it "encouraged users to record multiple psychiatric diagnoses (listed in order of importance) and associated physical conditions."[41] Twelve years later, such an emphasis on multiple layers of diagnoses would become a hallmark of the *DSM-III*, published in 1980.

The third edition was, at the time, the longest *DSM* (494 pages) and the most comprehensive (265 disorders). The definitions were more detailed. The *DSM-III*, according to the APA, "was the first effort by a medical specialty to provide a comprehensive and detailed diagnostic manual in which all disorders were defined by specific criteria so that the methods for making a psychiatric diagnosis were relatively clear."[42] What also stood out was the *DSM-III*'s expansion of the multilayered approach of the *DSM-II*. The *DSM-III* introduced "a multiaxial classification system" with five axes, one or more of which could be part of the diagnosis of a mental illness.[43] The five, according to the APA, are: "I. Clinical syndromes and 'conditions not attributable to a mental disorder that are the focus of attention and treatment'; II. Personality disorders and specific developmental disorders; III. Physical disorders; IV. Severity of psychosocial stressors; and V. Highest levels of adaptive functioning in the last year."[44] The multiaxial system, though later phased out for a single axis system, would help in the evaluations of Marjorie Diehl-Armstrong.

Each edition of the *DSM* reflected changes in society. Each edition added or deleted disorders. One change that brought the most attention was the APA's elimination of homosexuality as a psychiatric disorder in 1973; the *DSM-III*, published three years later, no longer included it, though other types of disorders related to homosexuality had entries.[45] "Sexual orientation disturbance" first replaced "homosexuality"; the APA revised the entry to "ego-dystonic homosexuality" before dropping references to homosexuality in 1987.[46] The change, though slow, showed how the *DSM*, at its best, could be a fluid and progressive document.

At its worst, the *DSM* could still be subjective, a textbook filled with speculation rather than empirical evidence. The imprecision exists because of a problem that goes back to the ancients: the mind, particularly a troubled mind, is a mystery. "This is not cardiology or nephrology, where the basic diseases are well known," one critic of the *DSM*, psychiatric historian Edward Shorter, has said. "In psychiatry no one knows the causes of anything, so classification can be driven by all sorts of factors—political, social and financial. What you have in the end is this process of sorting the deck of symptoms into syndromes, and the outcome all depends on how the cards fall."[47]

Similar criticism greeted the development of the *DSM-IV*, published in 1994 with 297 disorders and 886 pages. One satirist captured the trepidation that had come to accompany each new edition of the *DSM*.

> The *DSM-IV* is on its way! The *Diagnostic and Statistic Manual of Mental Disorders*, a comprehensive index of mental illnesses published by the American Psychiatric Association, will creep into the hearts and offices of mental health professionals next month when its fourth edition rolls off the presses.
>
> What is found therein? The special 27-member task force responsible for researching and writing the *DSM-IV* has retained many of the listings from the index's revised third edition, including notoriously tragic mental illnesses like Caffeine Intoxication ("more than two to three cups of brewed coffee" leading to symptoms like "restlessness," "nervousness," "excitement," "insomnia" and the like) and Nicotine Withdrawal ("Abrupt cessation of nicotine use" followed by "dysphoric or depressed mood," "insomnia," "anxiety," "restlessness" and the like). Among the new mental illnesses that the index suggests are rampaging the country is Inhalant-Induced Anxiety Disorder.[48]

Another writer characterized the *DSM-IV* as psychiatrists' latest futile but lucrative attempt to pigeonhole human behavior to such a degree that everyone could be considered to suffer from some type of mental illness. "Here, on a staggering scale," argued this commentator, "are gathered together all the known disturbances of humankind, the illnesses of the mind and spirit that cry out for the therapeutic touch of—are you ready for this?—the very people who wrote the book."[49]

The APA's own sober analysis characterized the *DSM-IV* as fulfilling a need "that has been clear throughout the history of medicine": a need to classify and categorize mental disorders.[50] "The utility and credibility of *DSM-IV* require that it focus on clinical, research, and educational purposes and be supported by an extensive empirical foundation," its editors wrote. "Our highest priority has been to provide a helpful guide to clinical practice."[51] The editors of the *DSM-5*, published nineteen years later, addressed their critics more directly: "Why be concerned with *DSM*?" they wrote. "Why indeed. Simply put, *DSM* provides a common language to those among us who conduct research on and/or treat individuals with psychiatric disorders. Perhaps one of its most important missions is to help insure consistency in the definition of mental disorders for clinicians in the United States and elsewhere."[52]

More than a decade before the release of the *DSM-5*, the APA in 2000 published a text revision of the *DSM-IV*, called the *DSM-IV-TR*. The revision corrected errors and added new information, but left intact the diagnostic criteria of the *DSM-IV*. The findings in the *DSM-IV* are what professionals would use to diagnose Marjorie Diehl-Armstrong following her indictment in the Pizza Bomber case in 2007. With all its faults and all its advantages, the *DSM-IV* would be the one guidebook that the psychiatrists, and the courts, would have to rely on to examine Diehl-Armstrong's mental instability. The *DSM-IV* would help classify her imbalance—even if, as Robert Sadoff intimated on the witness stand, it would never be able to fully explain why that imbalance had come to plague her as she was brought to court, again and again, for the deaths of men, starting with the killing of Bob Thomas.

• 6 •

Death of a Boyfriend

A Fatal Shooting, a Suicide, and a Question of Stability

𝓜arjorie Diehl had met the woman in late July 1984, on a cheese line. They met a week before Diehl fatally shot Bob Thomas. Diehl, thirty-five years old, and the woman, Donna Mikolajczyk, who was fifty, made a quick connection. Diehl came to like Mikolajczyk, who had just been released from the State Correctional Institution at Muncy, in central Pennsylvania. The prison stay interested Diehl. She listened to Mikolajczyk even more when Mikolajczyk started talking about how her boyfriend beat her and sexually abused her. Diehl thought she knew precisely what Mikolajczyk was talking about.[1]

"Yes, I am the same way," Diehl recalled telling Mikolajczyk." I'm scared of my boyfriend and he beats me, too, and he sexually abuses me, too."[2]

The two also spoke about how Diehl wanted to sell some of the surplus butter and cheese they had been getting at a food bank in inner-city Erie. Lots of people made such illegal transactions, which created a black market for government foodstuffs.[3] For one reason or another—for assistance in selling surplus food or for advice on how to cope in an abusive relationship—Mikolajczyk told Diehl that day on the cheese line to contact her if she ever needed help. Mikolajczyk wrote her address on a scrap of paper.

Diehl soon visited Mikolajczyk's house. She stopped by at about one o'clock in the afternoon on July 30, 1984. Diehl said she needed help.

"Donna, I need a friend," Diehl said. "I have a psychic feeling about you. We're into astrology. Could you keep your mouth shut for a lot of money?" She said she had shot her boyfriend to death, and she wanted to get rid of his body. She offered Mikolajczyk $25,000 if she would lend a hand. Mikolajczyk thought Diehl was joking until Diehl pulled out more than $18,000 in cash.[4]

Diehl had $18,401.80 in a zippered blue bank bag in her gray purse and another $925 in food stamps. She was also toting two yellow plastic grocery bags bursting with stuff, as if she had become a hoarder on the move or a hoarder ready to go on the lam. One bag contained, among other things, keys, a rod for cleaning a gun, a glass ashtray, a comb, barrettes, scissors, a letter holder, a case for holding eye contacts, contact solution, and a pair of hands painted gold.[5] The other bag was heavier. It contained, in addition to the cash, items such as tubes of lipstick; other containers of makeup; small change purses; a Canadian dime; an Erie police accident report; magazines; a newspaper; five pens; Diehl's Social Security card; Thomas's Social Security card; her identification card for getting surplus food; papers related to her landlord and erstwhile boyfriend, Edwin Carey; receipts, including the receipt for the .38-caliber Smith & Wesson revolver she used to kill Thomas and that she bought at a downtown Erie sports store five days earlier, on July 25; a business card for a local lawyer; two sets of keys; a gold watch; and a black telephone that Diehl had unplugged from her rented house on Sunset Boulevard, where Thomas had been staying with her.[6]

The phone had been near Thomas's dead body, which, hit with six bullets, was still bleeding on the couch in the living room in the house. Diehl told Mikolajczyk she was worried that Thomas might still be alive, would wake up, and call for help. So Diehl brought the phone with her.[7] She also brought the gun. Inside one of the bags was a box that contained the revolver Diehl had used on Thomas about eight hours earlier. Six spent bullet casings were still in the gun. Diehl had not called the police.

Shortly after killing him, she had changed out of her nightgown into a purple sweater and blue jeans, packed the grocery bags, and got in her car, a blue 1974 Gremlin with a white stripe.[8] Diehl later said she had thought about killing herself, but she collected her thoughts, grabbed the gun and the bullets and the other belongings, and drove to her parents' house. She was thinking about running away.[9]

Diehl had seen her parents only sporadically over the last fourteen years, after she had moved out of their house at age twenty-one. Her parents, she thought, would be willing to help. She pulled the Gremlin into the driveway and knocked on the back door of the house. Her parents, both in their early seventies, stood at the door and listened, trying to figure out what their only child was trying to say. Marjorie Diehl later said she only told her parents that "something happened," but did not tell them that she had killed Bob Thomas. They both had high blood pressure, and she was worried that full disclosure would cause both of them to suffer strokes.[10] Diehl never got the refuge she wanted.

Diehl left the house and drove to a bank. If she was going to run away, she needed money, and she had access to it. Even before going to the bank, she had about $12,300 in cash, which her lawyers in the Thomas case later said she had received in a settlement over a car accident,[11] though they were evasive about all the facts.[12]

Diehl got the rest of the money when, after killing Thomas, she went to the bank and cashed a check for $5,656.37 in back Social Security disability benefits.[13] She placed all her cash, now more than $18,000, in the zippered banker's bag and drove to a downtown radiator shop, where, still thinking she might want to run away, she paid $58.19 for repairs to a hole in her Gremlin's radiator.[14] While she waited for the car, Diehl walked across the street to a shopping mall, where she used a pay phone to call her parents. They were not home. She went into a bathroom and vomited. Opening her purse to find a comb, she came across the piece of paper on which Donna Mikolajczyk had written her name and address when the two were on the cheese line.[15] By coincidence, Mikolajczyk lived about a block from the shopping mall. Diehl got into her newly repaired Gremlin and drove over.

Diehl told Mikolajczyk that she had killed Thomas and that she needed help getting rid of the body. Diehl said she was justified in the slaying. She explained that he had come at her that morning. "I had to kill him," Diehl said she told Mikolajczyk.[16] The remarks stunned Mikolajczyk.

"At first, I didn't believe her, but she said the man had treated her terribly," Mikolajczyk said the night of Diehl's arrest. "He had beaten her and she had finally shot him. She said she didn't mean to do it, but he slapped her and just kept coming at her, pushing her. You should hear the things he did to her. And he was always looking at younger women, she said, even kids. Personally, I think she deserves a badge."[17]

Mikolajczyk said Diehl convinced her she was serious about getting rid of Thomas's body when she pulled out the cash.

"But then I believed her. When she showed me the money," Mikolajczyk said. "She had $18,000 in cash. I don't know where she got it. But she said her family was well-to-do. She would give me $25,000 if I would help her."[18]

The two talked for hours about what to do with Thomas's body. Unclear, according to testimony and interviews, was who offered the ideas first. But Diehl and Mikolajczyk agreed the conversation happened.

"I told her she couldn't bury it because that would be too much work and there still would be bones if someone ever found it," Mikolajczyk said. "I said you could not dump it off the pier because of the Coast Guard. And people would see you if you burned it."[19]

Mikolajczyk and Diehl walked to the shopping mall so Mikolajczyk, now frightened, could use the pay phone. She called her sister, Susan Lasky, who drove over. Mikolajczyk and Diehl got in Lasky's car, and Diehl repeated her offer: that she would pay $25,000 for help in disposing of Bob Thomas's body. Diehl insisted that she get rid of the body to prevent police from linking her to the bullets investigators would find inside the corpse and around the house.

"The gun is registered and they'll find the bullets and trace it to me," Diehl said.[20]

"Did you do it?" Lasky said.

"Yes, I did," Diehl said.[21]

Lasky was repulsed.

"Get the hell out of this car," she told Diehl. "I wouldn't do anything like that for $25,000 or $150,000."[22]

Diehl would not get out of the car. She seemed confused to Mikolajczyk, who thought Diehl needed a friend. To her, Diehl was acting hurt, "like a beaten puppy."[23]

Mikolajczyk and Lasky persuaded Diehl to get out of the car by telling her they would meet her later at a bar. The sisters telephoned their mother, who called the police. Mikolajczyk and Lasky gave descriptions of Diehl and her car. By six o'clock that evening, the police had found Diehl, not far from Mikolajczyk's house—a woman in the blue Gremlin with the white stripe and carrying two yellow plastic grocery bags filled with a gun, bullets, a phone, and other stuff; plus more than $18,000 in cash.

The detectives read Diehl her rights at the Erie police station. She told them she shot Thomas at about seven thirty that morning.

"He threatened me," she said. "I have a mental disability. He's paranoid-schizophrenic. He came on me with the Vietnam shit, post-traumatic syndrome. I got manic and scared, and that was all. I told him last week I was getting a gun. . . . I told him I had the gun when he came after me. I freaked out.

"We were in the living room. I was sitting there. He told me, 'My hands are lethal weapons. I learned it in Vietnam,' and he came at me. I told him I got the gun; leave me alone. And he said, 'Ha, ha, ha. I'll take the gun away from you.' So I figured, Well, I'm not going to give you the chance. I figured he'd kill me.

"I just fired the gun, and he fell back on to the couch. That's where he was when I left."[24]

Diehl continued to talk while she was in the holding cell at the police station. She said Mikolajczyk, not her, wanted to dispose of Thomas's body.

She said she was afraid of Thomas, and that it was just a matter of time before he killed her, so she shot him.

"It would have been better if I had just wounded him," she said.[25]

Diehl said she had never seen a dead man before, and that Thomas's body was the grossest thing she had ever witnessed. She said she had warned him that she had a gun, and she said she was not a good shot. Diehl said "she hoped against hope" that Thomas was not dead.[26] By then, the police, using a key obtained from Diehl and after getting a search warrant, had already visited her house on Sunset Boulevard. Edwin Carey, Diehl's landlord, let the police in. The officers and detectives found Thomas's bloody body on the living room couch, amid the junk and rotting food.

"It might be noted," Erie County Coroner Merle Wood wrote in his report on the homicide, "that the kitchen area was in complete disarray with food mostly in boxes, lying on the sink area and kitchen table. The cupboards were completely full of food. In addition, two refrigerators & a cooler were full of food, mostly which was butter."[27]

Wood ruled that Thomas had died at 7:13 a.m. on July 30, 1984, and that the cause of death was a laceration of the aorta due to a gunshot wound to the chest. Thomas, wearing pants and a short-sleeve shirt with the buttons open, had been shot six times. The bullets were fired at a close enough range that, according to Wood's report, "Powder burns were visible around four holes in the shirt, one which was over the left pocket, two on the left shoulder & one in the upper left arm."[28] Thomas also had a gunshot wound behind the left ear and another to his left wrist. Thomas's body, the coroner wrote, was "lying on his right side on the couch with his feet on the floor & his head . . . lying on the arm rest. The lower portion of his body was covered by a plaid throw."[29] Investigators recovered three slugs from Thomas's body and another three from the house, including two from behind the sofa. The police also recovered a box of .38-caliber shells, less six rounds.

Diehl was still prescribed the antidepressant Tofranil when she was arrested. Her prescriptions would change over the next several years, as medical professionals tried to set a course so she could reach a degree of mental stability to stand trial. Diehl and her defense team initially contemplated but never pursued an argument that she was legally insane—that, though she indisputably killed Thomas, she was nonetheless not guilty because she had no idea of right or wrong when she pulled the trigger.[30] Her lawyers instead argued that she was mentally incompetent to stand trial—that, because of her bipolar disorder, narcissism, paranoia, and other mental problems, she was unable to cooperate with her lawyers and assist in her defense. Diehl, her lawyers quickly found, was obstreperous and believed she was smarter than they and everyone else. "You're so full of shit your eyes should be brown," she once told one of her lawyers.[31]

While awaiting trial in the Thomas case, Diehl also started a practice that she would continue throughout her other cases, including her prosecution in the Pizza Bomber case. She constantly wrote letters to the judge—in the Thomas case, Erie County Judge Roger M. Fischer. She used the handwritten missives, in which her scrawl covered nearly every spot on the page, to rail against her attorneys, proclaim her innocence, and plead for an opportunity to reenter society. "I am not crazy or dangerous," she wrote in one letter to Fischer. "I have a serious nervous condition but need a chance. . . . I want to lead a decent life. I have no criminal record and was never an alcoholic or a drug addict. Old friends, neighbors, and clergy support me."[32]

At first, Diehl had the benefit of preparing her defense in the Thomas case while she was out of prison. Over the objections of the Erie County District Attorney's Office, Fischer on August 27, 1984, ordered Diehl released from the Erie County Prison on $10,000 bail, or 10 percent of the full bond amount of $100,000. Harold Diehl posted the bail, and he had pledged at a bond hearing three days earlier that he and his wife would monitor their only child while she was free and awaiting trial for murder. Harold Diehl was in tears when he told Fischer that he would take Diehl in when she was released. "She would be living in the same room that she always had when she lived with us," Harold Diehl testified.[33] Marjorie Diehl also testified at the hearing; the judge and the prosecution and defense got their first insights into Diehl's treatment history and her present mental state. This was the hearing when Diehl reacted with anger when the prosecutor—trying to show that she would be a danger to the community if she were released on bail—confronted her with the social worker's diagnostic impression, in 1972, that she had "a deep-seated hatred of men."

Diehl enjoyed her freedom for only a brief period. On December 4, 1984, Judge Fischer signed a bench warrant at the request of the prosecution to revoke Diehl's bail and keep her in prison while she awaited trial. The impetus was an accusation that Diehl four days earlier had solicited a state prison escapee to kill two people who refused to testify as character witnesses for Diehl in her soon-to-be scheduled trial for Thomas's death.[34] Detectives with the District Attorney's Office taped phone conversations between Diehl and the supposed hit man, though Diehl said the recordings showed that the man, and not she, brought up the idea of hurting the potential witnesses. Diehl said she was innocent of the plot and accused the purported hit man of coming up with the scheme and framing her. The man helped himself little by contradicting himself at Diehl's bond revocation hearing, at which he also testified he had withheld information from the Erie police and the District Attorney's Office in their investigation of the plot.[35] Diehl said the man could not be trusted.

She shouted when the man testified at the hearing. "I can't sit here and take any more of this. Give him a lie detector test."[36]

Diehl was never charged in what the police said was the murder-for-hire plot, though Fischer on January 3, 1985, revoked her bond and ordered her held at the Erie County Prison to await trial. Diehl's prosecution appeared to be imminent. Fischer scheduled jury selection to start on February 27, 1985, and he made arrangements for the lawyers to pick jurors from a pool of people from outside Erie County. The pretrial publicity, Fischer ruled, was too pervasive for Diehl to get a fair trial before a jury selected from Erie County.

Diehl's trial would not occur for more than three years. Her case changed course when she changed lawyers. On February 13, 1985, she dropped her two court-appointed lawyers (she got them because she said she had no money, contending all her cash was tied up as evidence) for two lawyers her parents retained. The initial payments were $20,000, for the lead counsel, a meticulous attorney named Leonard G. Ambrose III, and $4,000 for his co-counsel, Michelle Hawk. By the end of Diehl's case, her parents would pay a total of $60,000 in attorneys' fees and other costs, such as expert fees, for her defense.[37] Ambrose and Hawk would make sure the money was well spent.

While Diehl waited at the Erie County Prison for her case to take shape, another man close to her died. Diehl had no role in the death of Edwin Carey, her paralegal, landlord, and sometime boyfriend, though the authorities made a link between her case and Carey's suicide on April 3, 1985. He hanged himself inside the house on Sunset Boulevard, where he had been living since Diehl was arrested nearly a year before. Carey, who was black, was sixty-five years old.

Carey suffered from throat cancer, according to the coroner's report, and he had undergone a laryngostomy, in which surgeons created an artificial hole in his larynx. Doctors at the Erie Veterans Administration Medical Center had told him he would need further surgery.[38] One of Carey's close friends had called police on April 4, 1985, when Carey did not answer his door. The friend told police that he was concerned because Carey had been despondent and had mentioned suicide. The police went inside and found Carey's body in the darkened bungalow. "The house was completely secured and he had pulled down all of the shades and blinds so that it would be impossible to look into the house," according to the coroner's report. "The police had found two handwritten notes in the living room which contained apologies to his family for his actions. We found other handwriting done by Mr. Carey that matched the writing on the suicide notes."[39]

Merle Wood, the Erie County coroner, then referred in his report to one of the best-known murder defendants in the county at that time. "Mr. Carey," Wood wrote, "is the owner of this home and had rented the home to Marjorie Diehl, who allegedly killed her boyfriend Robert D. Thomas in this house [on July 30, 1984]." Wood also wrote that Carey's close friend "explained that Mr. Carey has been extremely distressed since this murder. He has been the object of much harassment."[40]

Diehl-Armstrong remembered Carey fondly throughout her life. A month after his death, while she spoke to a psychologist at the Erie County Prison, she recounted how she was dating Carey at the same time she was seeing Bob Thomas. "Ed recently died through suicide which upset her greatly," the psychologist wrote.[41] More than twenty years later, when on trial in the Pizza Bomber case, she recalled Carey as a "terrific" self-made man who was worthy of her. "Mr. Carey was a very good man," she said. "I was with him for many years. Edward Alexis Carey. He was a mortician. And he was a very successful man. He was also supervisor of the whole yard at Hammermill Paper Company. He worked there for many years. He also had his own gas station, TV repair shop, and a restaurant."[42] She later described Carey in chivalric terms, speaking about his moral uprightness and devotion to her, and likened Carey to her husband, Richard Armstrong, who died in 1992, "they were like saints to me," she said.[43]

Leonard Ambrose had made his reputation as one of the most sought-after defense lawyers in Erie County by his careful presentation and his relentless probing in the courtroom. He also had a deep interest in psychology and psychiatry, which made him an ideal defense lawyer for Marjorie Diehl. His first move was to ask Fischer to declare Diehl incompetent to stand trial. Ambrose argued that her bipolar disorder, unless treated with therapy and medication, would continue to make her so uncooperative that she would be unable to assist in her defense. Ambrose's request triggered the trial-within-a-trial in Diehl's already complicated case. The defense and prosecution put the actual trial on hold for years and years as they countered each other on whether Diehl was competent to stand trial in the first place. Ambrose and Michelle Hawk, his cocounsel, challenged whether Diehl had the mental wherewithal to help the defense. The District Attorney's Office questioned the degree of Diehl's mental instability while also maintaining that the prosecutors, like Diehl's defense team, wanted nothing to do with bringing a mentally unfit defendant to trial.

Ambrose had lots of information to help Fischer understand Diehl's mental state. He got access to all her previous mental health records, including those for her first treatments, at Hamot Hospital, in 1972, plus all the psychiatric reports she filed in her request to receive disability benefits. He also had the condition of Diehl's house as evidence. Ambrose's goal was to show that Diehl's bipolar disorder had made her so uncooperative that she was unable to go to trial without getting medicated for some period of time. Ambrose hinged much of his argument on the finding of the administrative law judge who in January 1984 approved Diehl for disability benefits after finding that she indeed suffered from bipolar disorder. The prosecution contended that Diehl faked or overstated her mental illness so she could get the benefits—an argument that, on its face, was not unreasonable, given Diehl's willingness to hoard government surplus food and her possessing more than $18,000 in cash despite having supposedly no verifiable income except for the disability benefits. Ambrose wrote to Judge Fischer in June 1985 contending that Diehl's lengthy mental-health history, plus the administrative law judge's ruling, should put to rest the prosecution's "concern that Marjorie's mental problems developed at or about the time she made application for Social Security Disability benefits sometime in 1982."[44]

"The bottom line is Marjorie needs medication," Ambrose continued in his letter. "Without medication it is the considered opinion of the medical physicians who have examined her that she is simply not competent to communicate in a rational manner with counsel. In reality all we are requesting is that she be afforded her basic fundamental right to medication prescribed by her physicians."[45]

Diehl, who had been prescribed Tofranil since 1977, was placed on lithium carbonate, designed to moderate her moods and control her bipolar disorder, on July 3, 1985. The recommendation for lithium came from one of the outside psychiatrists whom Ambrose hired to evaluate Diehl—Robert L. Sadoff, who would also examine Diehl in the Pizza Bomber case. She needed lithium, Sadoff wrote Ambrose in June 1985, because the bipolar disorder "has rendered Marjorie Diehl incompetent to stand trial at the present time because of her inability to communicate effectively with her counsel and her inability, because of the rapid thoughts that bombard her at once during the manic phase, to appreciate her position within this legal situation."[46]

While she was on lithium at the Erie County Prison, Diehl continued to undergo more psychiatric evaluations. Her examiners included Sadoff; Gerald Cooke, a psychologist from the Philadelphia area whom Sadoff recommended; and David B. Paul, the Erie County Prison's staff psychiatrist, who met with Diehl sixty-four times between their first visit, on August 1, 1984, and September 3, 1987, when Paul wrote to Fischer that, based on his continued analysis of Diehl's mental state, she was still incompetent to stand trial. The reports of the psychologists and psychiatrists mentioned Diehl's childhood anorexia and the blame she placed on her parents for what she considered a pressured and mostly unhappy youth. The professionals based their findings on interviews with her, but also on more objective sources, like psychological tests.

Cooke administered five tests: the Minnesota Multiphasic Personality Inventory, a personality test "indicating test-taking attitude and the nature and degree of psychopathy"; the Rotter Incomplete Sentences Blank, which provides "information on needs, attitudes, values and the quality of interpersonal relationships"; Draw-a-Person, which provides "information on the individual's self-image and the perception of interpersonal relationships"; Rorschach Inkblot Technique, meant to reveal "unconscious fears, wishes, conflicts, and the degree to which reality is accurately perceived"; and the Weschler Adult Intelligence Scale-Revised/Verbal Subscale, "to estimate intellectual functioning."[47] Based on the test results and his observations, Cooke found that Diehl's bipolar disorder, particularly her mania, and her underlying paranoia made her incompetent to stand trial at that time, in 1985. Cooke, as the social worker had done in 1972, also focused on Diehl's troubled relationships with men. He found that Diehl, despite her narcissism, had a poor self-image and needed constant attention, particularly from men, to achieve a sense of self-worth. "Because of her personality features," Cooke wrote, "she has highly conflictual relationships with others. While she experiences the kinds of angry and negative feelings toward others described, she also has strong needs for attention and nurturance, particularly from men. The result is an approach-avoidance sort of relationship leading to almost continual conflict."[48]

Cooke's evaluation was one of four that professionals performed on Diehl between 1984 and 1987; all four visits yielded the same results—the psychologist and psychiatrists determined that her mental state made Diehl unable to meaningfully and rationally participate in her trial. Faced with such findings, Judge Fischer continually ruled Diehl incompetent to stand trial. The rulings came in 1985, 1986, June 1987, and on September 9, 1987—a significant date in the homicide case against Diehl. Fischer, deciding that Diehl needed more intensive psychiatric treatment than the Erie County Prison could offer, ordered her to the Pennsylvania state prison system's Mayview State Hospital, outside Pittsburgh, about two hours south of Erie.

He ordered the staff at Mayview to perform a psychiatric exam on Diehl at least every ninety days, and to submit the reports to him.

Diehl did not want to go to Mayview; she had written Fischer in June 1987 that she feared she would lose credit for time served in prison if she were transferred to Mayview, which she called a "mental hospital."[49] Diehl in the letter blamed her lawyers for her problems; said she knew what she was doing; and, in what could be considered her understanding of the justice system, mentioned an earlier plea offer that was no longer available—a prison sentence capped at eight to sixteen years in exchange for a guilty plea to third-degree murder, or an unpremeditated killing with malice, in Bob Thomas's death.[50] The District Attorney's Office in October 1986 withdrew the offer and said it would pursue a conviction for first-degree murder, or a premeditated killing.[51] "Some mentally ill people do not recognize that they are ill," Diehl, commenting on the plea deal and other topics, wrote to Fischer in her trademark scrawl. "This isn't the case with me. I know that I am manic-depressive and at times have bad pressure of speech and flight of ideas (loose associations). Going to court will not cause me to break. I also know my strengths."[52]

Fischer had much support to send Diehl to Mayview. He had two new evaluations from medical professionals that Diehl was incompetent, including a finding from David Paul, who had seen Diehl more than any psychiatrist and perhaps more than anyone other than her lawyers. To help him in his work, Paul requested the other evaluation, by Ted S. Urban, an Erie clinical psychologist. Both were adamant that Diehl, unless rehabilitated through treatment and medication, was mentally unfit to stand trial.

As Cooke did, Urban used a battery of written tests, such as the Minnesota Multiphasic Personality Inventory, to help gauge Diehl's mental state. He never disputed the she was bipolar but found that she only exhibited mania, and no depression, when he met with her. Urban characterized Diehl as a paranoid and unusually self-aggrandizing and manipulative person, a person whose intense self-importance and anger at the world made her susceptible, at any moment, to entering into a kind of emotional fugue state that would foil her ability to cooperate with her lawyers. "Although there was no formal evidence of overt psychotic process," Urban wrote in his report, in August 1987, "it is my impression that because of the extreme degree of internal conflicts a psychotic loss of control in her perception can be easily triggered."[53]

Urban emphasized that Diehl blamed everyone except herself for her problems, including her inability to hold down a job: She was the brilliant intellect with the straight-A's in high school and the exceptional musical talent, while everyone else was an incompetent who was out to get her. She said the police entrapped her in the case that led to the filing of criminal charges when she worked at the abortion clinic; the police, she said, were working with *Hustler* magazine and the Mafia on that case. She presented her work history as "essentially successful," Urban wrote, "and she made no mention of her disability benefits."[54] Urban reported that Diehl told him she left all her jobs voluntarily or was the victim of unfair treatment. "'Rev. Wards' wife became jealous' of her and she was forced to leave," Urban wrote, quoting his conversations with Diehl. "'Mr. Locher made passes at me and I left after his wife accused me of having an affair with her husband.' 'I was fired after 4 months [from] the Welfare Office because of a personality clash—I dressed much better than her.'"[55] Diehl denied using drugs and alcohol, Urban also wrote, but "she subsequently described a relatively protracted relationship with a man with whom she got 'drunk every night.'"[56] But never did Diehl consider herself at fault, Urban wrote. She believed that her needs and comfort and well-being were more important that anyone else's, and that "if circumstances do not meet with her momentary, fleeting emotional need, her responses work to produce constant distortion."[57] Diehl, in other words, could be nasty and selfish and unbearable, but she was also mentally ill.

David Paul said he also witnessed what he characterized as Diehl's potentially self-destructive behavior. He wrote Fischer that on July 28, 1987, he sat in on a meeting between Diehl and her lawyers, and listened to her berate them, call them liars, and insist that they were no smarter than a clerk at the prison. He said she called Sadoff, who had previously examined her, a "quack," and said that some documents she was asked to complete were "foolish."[58] Paul cited Diehl's bipolar disorder, which he said manifested itself in her hostility toward her lawyers and her inability to control her behavior—traits, Paul wrote to Fischer, that would make Diehl her own worst enemy in front of a jury. Paul wrote:

> She has the typical manic's capacity for terribly poor judgment, particularly in social situations. She will insult and offend people simply because she happens to be feeling that way at the moment and, shortly thereafter, when her mood has changed, feel free to ask favors of them as though the offense she gave had never taken place. Her literality further hinders her in defending herself in a court of law by causing her to feel free to say to jurors that she believes in something like voodoo and astrology . . . , being quite without any understanding of the impression of her that she creates by so doing.
>
> If her attorneys are correct that the way she presents herself in court is of vital importance, in view of her illness and problem with self control and

judgment, I feel that she is quite incompetent to stand trial at this time and I do not feel that there is a substantial ability of attainment of competence in the foreseeable future.[59]

Paul recommended that Diehl receive hospital care to help her recover. And he said her taking lithium carbonate offered a greater likelihood that she would achieve competency.[60]

Diehl remained combative, but only to a point. She criticized her lawyers at a competency hearing before Fischer on September 4, 1987, at which she also derided the qualifications of another key defense witness—Paul, who she claimed was not board certified. She said nothing was wrong with her, based on her analysis.

> I have problems. I've tried to live with my problems. I do not try to extenuate my negatives. I try to extenuate the positive. If I was the type of person looking to my lawyers for condolences, I'd probably be like the guy that hung himself in prison because he was so, you know, obviously depressed.
> But I don't let myself get this way and I have some control. I may not have total control over my mood swings and things, I am not going to say I have that, but I have enough control over myself. I've proved it with my life. I have proved it. I don't care what Dr. Paul says. . . . I have proved it with my own life.[61]

Diehl showed no signs that she understood the absurdity of her argument—that a thirty-eight-year-old woman with a history of mental illness whose house was packed with rotting food and who was awaiting prosecution for murder had full control over her emotions and behavior. Yet Diehl, in an example of her understanding of the justice system, also pleaded with Fischer to make sure that her case would be handled quickly if he were to find her incompetent once more. "Whatever happens," she said, "I just hope it doesn't take forever to be resolved, that if I have to go to a hospital, that they give me a chance to be re-evaluated, not leaving me there for three years or something while I am waiting to be evaluated. . . . The reason I want to go to trial is to get the thing over with because it's hanging over my head. . . . I'm going on my fourth year now in prison."

"I understand," Fischer said.[62]

Diehl went to Mayview. The understanding, based on Paul's recommendations, was that she would receive medication there. But the kind of medication remained uncertain. Lithium carbonate, which Diehl had started to take on July 3, 1985, had become problematic. The development was unfortunate. Though Diehl initially took the lithium erratically, Paul wrote that she gradually "accepted the idea that medication taking was necessary if she were to have any hope of going to trial and defending herself adequately."[63] To try for further improvement, Paul supplemented the lithium with an antipsychotic drug, Mellaril (thioridazine). He aimed to have the Mellaril control Diehl's psychosis, and the lithium regulate her mood swings and maintain and stabilize her personality.[64] But the lithium-Mellaril experiment failed, Paul said, so he paired the lithium with another antipsychotic drug, Haldol (haloperidol).[65] That combination was more effective, Paul said, but then he had to discontinue the lithium and prescribe only Haldol.

The change came on April 7, 1987. A medical emergency forced it. Diehl had a reaction to the lithium carbonate—she developed severe edema, in which her ankles and feet swelled so much that Erie County Prison's medical staff grew alarmed. The prison physician prescribed a diuretic to cause Diehl to urinate more frequently and free her body of the excess water. But the diuretic also flushed massive amounts of sodium chloride, or salt, from Diehl's system, creating a chemical imbalance that posed a hazard. Due to the lack of sodium, the amount of lithium in her bloodstream risked rising to a poisonous level. Paul ordered the lithium stopped. Diehl agreed that lithium carbonate could help control her mania, but she also agreed with the decision to discontinue it. "It was a toxic level with me," she said.[66]

Diehl was taking Haldol and the antidepressant Norpramin (desipramine) shortly after she arrived at Mayview State Hospital in September 1987.[67] Diehl had been there for thirteen days when her parents drove from Erie to see her. Diehl and her mother and father got into verbal arguments that left Harold and Agnes Diehl—who were paying for their daughter's legal defense—highly upset.

"[We] won't be back," Harold Diehl said.[68]

Diehl's anger and obstinacy had become frequent by then, signaling a setback. Though anxious and apprehensive, she had been generally pleasant, even-tempered, and lucid when she arrived at Mayview, whose staff's immediate reaction was that she was competent.[69] Diehl, according to a psychologist, was "working very diligently to maintain a façade of adequacy and control. Because she is eager to get on with her trial and fears that she may be kept in the hospital for a lengthy period she is tending to minimize her problems and weaknesses. She is attempting to present herself in the best possible light and therefore seems to be denying unacceptable feelings and impulses."[70]

The façade of self-control started to collapse by the time of her parents' visit. She continued to speak to her mother constantly on the telephone, but swore at her and used obscene language. Diehl complained of the side effects of her medication, and it was discontinued in late September. "A few days later," according to a staff psychiatric report, "the patient became agitated and irritable. She then became argumentative, demanding and markedly obsessive-compulsive. . . . At times her behavior became clearly bizarre."[71] As an example, the Mayview staff placed Diehl under close observation after she was found to have caused herself to vomit in the bathroom. Diehl also became extremely preoccupied with her personal appearance, and spent long periods of time in the bathroom putting on makeup. She was increasingly rude, belligerent, and demanding with the staff, and had to be reminded repeatedly to follow the rules.[72]

Her compulsive and excessive behavior increased in October and November, particularly about her cleanliness and personal hygiene. This was the period when the staff at Mayview found that she had to brush her teeth as many as thirty-two times as part of a cycle.[73] "At the beginning of November," according to the psychiatric report, "she became increasingly grandiose and paranoid and there was rambling and pressured speech as well as loosened associations. Reasoning and judgemental capacity became markedly impaired. At that point it appeared she did indeed have Bipolar Affective disorder, mixed type."[74] The stress of her case clearly was affecting Diehl's mental stability. On November 9, 1987, the Mayview staff found her incompetent. Fischer accepted the report, and ordered Mayview to evaluate Diehl again within ninety days.

The staff in early November also placed Diehl on a new drug for her—Tegretol (carbamazepine), an anticonvulsant used to treat bipolar disorder. David Paul had told Judge Fischer at the competency hearing, in September 1987, that Tegretol someday could be used to help control Diehl's moods,[75] and the staff at Mayview found Tegretol effective. While she was on the drug in mid-November 1987, the staff started Diehl "on a highly structured and rigid behavior program to help her overcome her obsessive-compulsive behavior and aid her in compliance with ward regulations and routines."[76] She also participated in regular individual and group psychotherapy, which added to her improved behavior while she was on Tegretol.[77] As with the other drugs, however, Tegretol proved problematic for Diehl. It created severe side effects, including a rash and edema—the same condition that led Paul to order her off the lithium carbonate while Diehl was at the Erie County Prison. The staff at Mayview discontinued the Tegretol for Diehl in mid- to late December 1987. In January 1988, Diehl refused to take any medication. She cited the "unbearable side effects" the other drugs had caused her.[78] Mayview, under the law, could not involuntarily drug Diehl.[79]

About six week later, a period during which she took no drugs, the authorities at Mayview found Diehl competent to stand trial. They made their finding on January 29, 1988. It came in a report from a psychiatrist at Mayview, Duncan Campbell, and a psychologist, Howard P. Friday, the hospital's acting director of its regional psychiatric forensic center. They determined that Diehl's physical disorders were few—an apparent jaw injury, which she said was from an accident from years before; and allergies to antipsychotic medication. In terms of Diehl's mental state, Duncan and Friday determined that Diehl's bipolar disorder was "in remission," though she was no longer on medication.[80] "For the several weeks that have followed discontinuation of medication," they wrote, "she exercised good controls and was essentially cooperative and appropriate in her interactions. She has remained involved in her individual and group therapy as well as a variety of other activities here. She has had an opportunity to discuss her conflicts with the family, her attorneys and other important individuals in her life and she appears to have developed some degree of insight into the part she has played in these difficulties. It is felt that at this juncture . . . the patient is now competent to be tried and should be returned to [the] Erie County Prison."[81]

The third edition of the *Diagnostic and Statistical Manual of Mental Disorders*, or *DSM-III*, published in 1980, came into play, as Campbell and Friday used its multiaxial classification system to summarize their diagnosis of Diehl. They referred to three axes: Axis I, for clinical syndromes; Axis II, for personality disorders and specific developmental disorders; and Axis III, for physical disorders. Duncan and Friday wrote of Diehl:

Axis I: Bipolar affective disorder, mixed type, in remission.
Axis II: Mixed personality disorder with paranoid and narcissistic features.
Axis III: Multiple allergies, including allergies to Tegretol and lithium and temporomandibular joint disease.[82]

The report noted that drugs had helped. Campbell and Friday acknowledged that lithium carbonate and Tegretol had "some calming effect" on Diehl, and they called her severe reactions to the drugs regrettable. They did not eliminate the possibility that Diehl would need drugs again. They all but predicted Diehl's remission would end and her bipolar disorder would dominate her behavior once more. "It is certain," Campbell and Friday wrote, "that this individual will under stress have increasing problems with control and mood and in spite of her concerns about side effects from other psychotropic agents, she may require these at times to control symptoms of her Bipolar Disorder. Undoubtedly, she may require them periodically under the normal course of this illness." Campbell and Friday concluded: "The prognosis certainly must be guarded. This illness will manifest itself again."[83]

Diehl's lead lawyer, Leonard Ambrose, offered a more blunt analysis in his review of Campbell and Friday's report. He faulted them for failing to consider whether Diehl's present mental condition allowed her to cooperate with him (Ambrose said it did not). And even by the report's admission, Ambrose maintained, Diehl's behavior was unpredictable: "The catalyst is stress," Ambrose wrote to Judge Fischer. "In essence," he wrote, "the report paints the picture of a person who is a literal time bomb waiting to go off."[84]

Fischer accepted the Mayview report on February 17, 1988. After two years of reviewing psychiatric reports on Marjorie Diehl, he found her competent to stand trial.

At eighteen years old in 1967, Marjorie Diehl graduated 12th out of 413 students in her senior class at Academy High School in Erie, Pennsylvania. This is her yearbook photo from her senior year. Courtesy of *Erie Times-News*. Photo from the Academy High School yearbook, the *Academe*, stored at the public Blasco Library in Erie, Pennsylvania.

Marjorie Diehl at twenty or twenty-one years old, in the yearbook for the class of 1970 at Mercyhurst College in Erie, Pennsylvania. She graduated in 1970, a year early, with bachelor's degrees in sociology and social work. Two years later, at age twenty-three, she would receive her first psychiatric evaluation, with a diagnosis of a bipolar disorder. Courtesy of *Erie Times-News*. Photo from the Mercyhurst College yearbook, the *Praeterita*, stored at the public Blasco Library in Erie, Pennsylvania.

Marjorie Diehl, thirty-nine years old, walks to her trial in 1988 at the Erie County Courthouse, where she argued self-defense and was acquitted of murdering her boyfriend Bob Thomas in 1984 in Erie, Pennsylvania. Courtesy of *Erie Times-News*.

Junk filled Marjorie Diehl-Armstrong's house in Erie, Pennsylvania, when she was charged in September 2003 with killing her boyfriend Jim Roden at her house and stuffing his body in a freezer elsewhere. Authorities declared the house inhabitable. Massive hoarding was a problem for Diehl-Armstrong at the other houses where she lived. Photos entered as evidence on September 24, 2003, in *Commonwealth v. Marjorie Diehl-Armstrong*, Court of Common Pleas, Erie County, Pennsylvania, CR-374-03. Courtesy of *Erie Times-News*.

The condition of Marjorie Diehl-Armstrong's house in Erie, Pennsylvania, was so poor in September 2003 that Erie police had to dress in protective "moon suits" to remove piles of food and other trash from it during the investigation of the killing of her boyfriend Jim Roden in September 2003. Diehl-Armstrong hoarded food and other items throughout much of her adult life. Photos by Rich Forsgren. Courtesy of *Erie Times-News*.

Marjorie Diehl-Armstrong's hoarded loads of food in her house in Erie, Pennsylvania, in September 2003, when she was charged with killing her boyfriend Jim Roden, just as she hoarded food in another house in July 1984, when she was charged with killing her boyfriend Bob Thomas. Photo by Rich Forsgren. Courtesy of *Erie Times-News*.

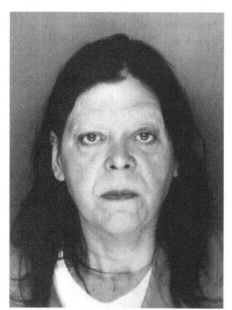

The police in Erie, Pennsylvania, released this mug shot of Marjorie Diehl-Armstrong, fifty-four years old, on September 23, 2003, after she was arrested in the killing of her boyfriend Jim Roden. She was being held at the Erie County Prison. Erie Bureau of Police via *Erie Times-News*.

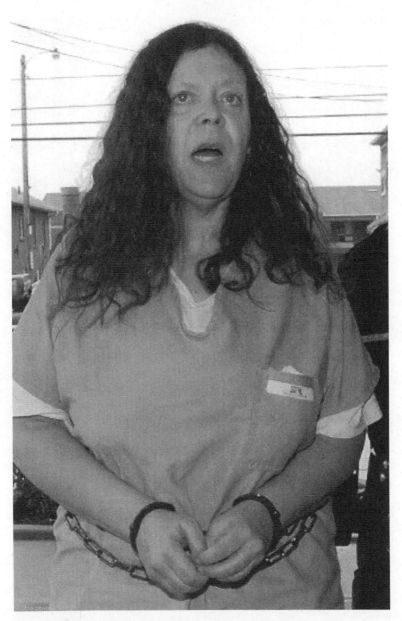

Marjorie Diehl-Armstrong, fifty-five years old, is led into the Erie County Courthouse, in Erie, Pennsylvania, for a mental competency hearing on September 8, 2004. A judge the next day ruled that she was mentally fit to stand trial in the killing of her boyfriend Jim Roden in September 2003. Diehl-Armstrong ended up pleading guilty but mentally ill to third-degree murder and was sentenced to seven to twenty years in prison in January 2005. Photo by Greg Wohlford. Courtesy of *Erie Times-News*.

Marjorie Diehl-Armstrong said her former fiancé, Bill Rothstein, framed her in the Pizza Bomber case. Rothstein helped police search her junk-strewn house in Erie, Pennsylvania, on September 23, 2003, following her arrest in the killing of her boyfriend Jim Roden. Rothstein died of cancer at sixty years old in July 2004, before he could be prosecuted in the Pizza Bomber case. Photo by Rich Forsgren. Courtesy of *Erie Times-News*.

Brian Wells, a pizza deliveryman, robs a bank outside Erie, Pennsylvania, with a bomb locked to his neck on August 28, 2003. The bomb exploded and killed Wells after he left the bank, launching the investigation into the Pizza Bomber case. Marjorie Diehl-Armstrong in November 2010 was convicted in U.S. District Court in Erie to being part of the plot, and was later sentenced to life plus thirty years in prison. Federal Bureau of Investigation via *Erie Times-News*.

Ken Barnes, center, was the main witness against Marjorie Diehl-Armstrong in the Pizza Bomber case. He pleaded guilty to his role in the plot and was sentenced to forty-five years in prison, but his sentence was cut in half because of his cooperation. Following his indictment, Barnes, fifty-four years old, is led into the United States District Courthouse in Erie, Pennsylvania, on July 12, 2007, by the lead investigator in the Pizza Bomber case, FBI Special Agent Jerry Clark, at right. At left is Clark's partner in the investigation, Jason Wick, a special agent with the Bureau of Alcohol, Tobacco, Firearms, and Explosives. Photo by Jack Hanrahan. Courtesy of *Erie Times-News.*

Brian Wells, moments after the collar bomb locked to his neck exploded after he robbed a bank near Erie, Pennsylvania, on August 28, 2003, in the Pizza Bomber case. Photo by Janet B. Kummerer. Courtesy of *Erie Times-News*.

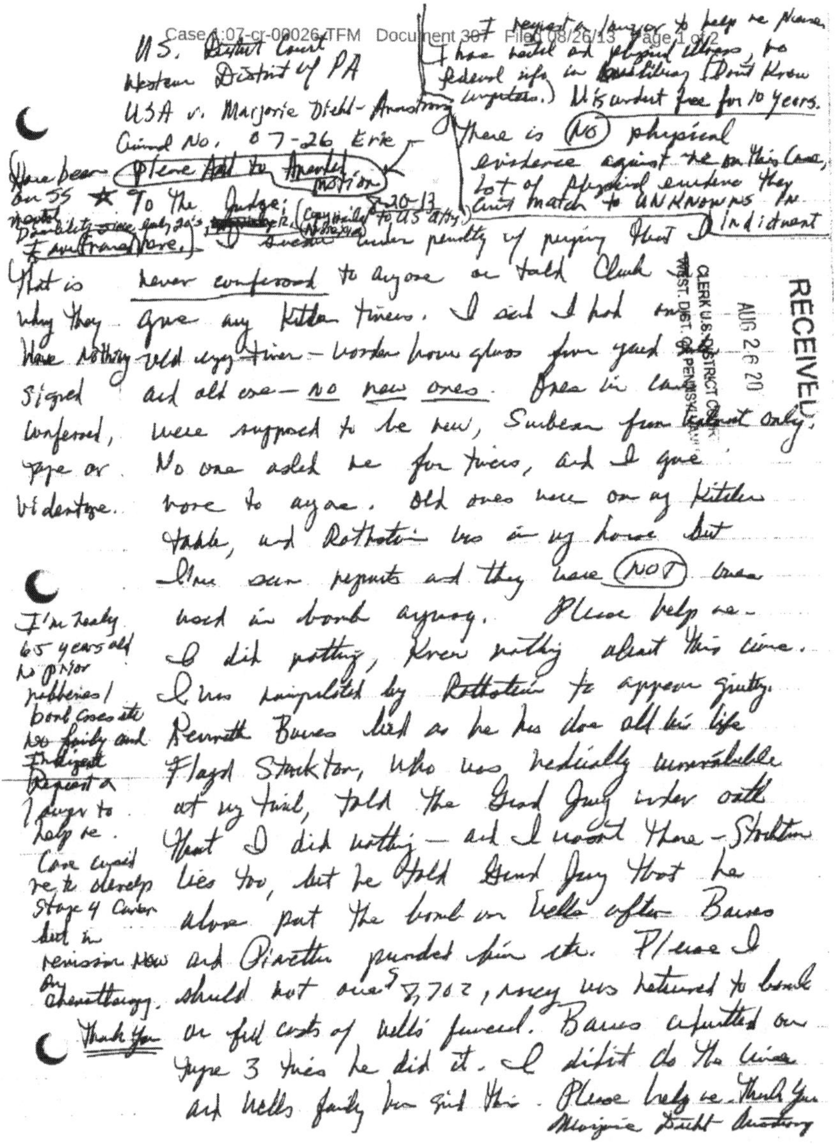

U.S. District Court
Western District of PA
USA v. Marjorie Diehl-Armstrong
Crim. No. 07-26 Erie

[handwritten letter, largely illegible]

RECEIVED
AUG 26 20[...]
CLERK U.S. DISTRICT COURT
WEST. DIST. OF PENNSYLVANIA

Throughout her legal troubles, Marjorie Diehl-Armstrong wrote judges, lawyers, and journalists, telling them she was innocent or had been wronged. She often scribbled all over the page, which psychiatrists and psychologists said was symptomatic of her mania and bipolar disorder. She wrote this letter in August 2013 to a federal judge who was reviewing one of her appeal requests in the Pizza Bomber case. The letter failed to sway the judge. Diehl-Armstrong lost all her appeals in the Pizza Bomber case. Letter entered into evidence as document 307 in *United States of America v. Marjorie Diehl-Armstrong*, United States District Court for the Western District of Pennsylvania, Crim. 07-26 Erie.

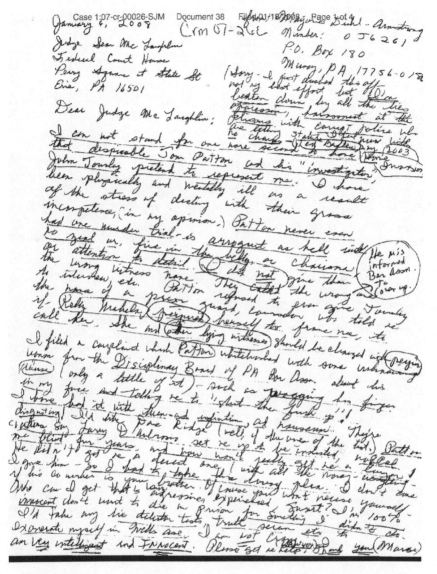

In this letter, dated January 6, 2008, Marjorie Diehl-Armstrong complains about her lawyer to United States District Judge Sean J. McLaughlin, who presided over the Pizza Bomber case. Letter entered into evidence as document 38 in *United States of America v. Marjorie Diehl-Armstrong*, United States District Court for the Western District of Pennsylvania, Crim. 07-26 Erie.

Marjorie Diehl-Armstrong fatally shot her boyfriend Jim Roden in September 2003 in what the FBI said was a murder to silence him from going to the police to report the Pizza Bomber plot. Undated mug shot from the Erie Bureau of Police via *Erie Times News*.

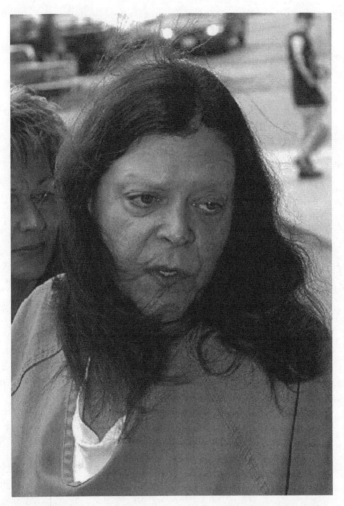

Marjorie Diehl-Armstrong, fifty-four years old, is led into the Erie County Courthouse, in Erie, Pennsylvania, on September 29, 2003, following her arrest about a week earlier in the death of her boyfriend Jim Roden. Photo by Jack Hanrahan. Courtesy of *Erie Times-News*.

Marjorie Diehl-Armstrong, fifty-four years old, shouts at reporters after her preliminary hearing on January 19, 2004, on charges that she killed her boyfriend Jim Roden in September 2003. She told the reporters that her former fiancé, Bill Rothstein, should be charged in the Pizza Bomber case. Photo by Janet B. Kummerer. Courtesy of *Erie Times-News*.

· 7 ·

"A Madman or a Natural Fool"

Determining Mental Competency

*M*arjorie Diehl clearly was mentally ill, but the degree of her imbalance represented the critical issue before and during her trial for killing Bob Thomas. Though undeniably troubled, Diehl ultimately was found not to be insane or so mentally unfit as to be unable to understand the court proceedings and assist in her defense. The Thomas case, like those that would follow for Diehl-Armstrong, including the Pizza Bomber prosecution, illustrated the interplay between insanity and mental incompetency—two categories central to the American legal system's handling of the mentally ill.

The *Diagnostic and Statistical Manual of Mental Disorders*, for all its heft, has no entry for insanity as a disorder. Insanity, as understood today, is not a psychiatric illness but a construct, "a legal term."[1] No longer is "insane" the category that applies to all the mentally ill; Emil Kraepelin ended that sweeping generalization in 1899 when he divided most mental illness into the two main categories: schizophrenia and manic-depression, or bipolar disorder. Rather than being a form of mental illness, insanity today represents mental illness with a legal and moral component; insanity, according to its most basic legal definition, means that a defendant is so mentally ill as to be unable to understand right from wrong at the time he or she committed a crime. The concepts of insanity and mental competency reside close to the core of English common law and American jurisprudence, with their emphasis on good and evil and free will. Through the insanity defense and mental incompetency, the law recognizes that a criminal defendant can be so mentally disturbed as to lack the ability to choose his or her actions. The continued existence of insanity and mental competency as legal constructs, despite their critics, indicates how the social sciences and empiricism have come to modify the justice system and its belief that choice, to varying degrees, is behind human criminal behavior.[2]

Criminal cases involving insanity and mental incompetency can be among the most highly publicized, particularly when they include murder. One study has found that 7.5 percent of crimes committed by those with serious mental disorders "were directly related to symptoms of mental illness."[3] The same study also found that "14%–16% of the 7.3 million people under correctional supervision [as of 2009] suffer from serious disorders such as schizophrenia, bipolar disorder, or major depression. This translates to approximately one million people with a major mental disorder currently involved in the criminal justice system."[4]

A temporal element differentiates the concepts of mental incompetence and insanity. The insanity defense applies to the defendant's state of mind when he or she committed a crime. Determining whether a defendant is mentally competent to stand trial focuses on his or her mental state at the time of prosecution: whether the defendant understands the legal process, and whether—as was the critical issue in Diehl's case—the defendant is able to assist the defense at trial. The concepts of legal insanity and mental incompetence recognize that a civilized society must take special precautions in criminal cases involving mentally ill defendants, though the concepts also recognize that mental illness alone does not automatically exempt a defendant from prosecution. The severity of the mental illness is the prime consideration in applying both concepts.

The concept of mental competency is the younger of the two. It is believed to have originated in the fourteenth century, when, as scholars Patricia E. Erickson and Steven E. Erickson have written, the English courts proceeded with a criminal trial only after a defendant pleaded "guilty" or "not guilty." A defendant who "stood mute" and entered no plea prompted an investigation into whether that person was faking mental illness, and thus was "mute of malice"; or was "mute by visitation of God"—truly suffering from muteness, deafness, or mental illness severe enough to be excused from trial.[5] By the eighteenth century, the preeminent English legal authority Sir William Blackstone explained how the courts must deal with a defendant who is incompetent to stand trial:

> If a man in his sound memory commits a capital offense, and before his arraignment for it, he becomes mad, he ought not be arraigned for it; because he is not able to plead to it with that advice and caution that he ought. And, after he has pleaded, the prisoner becomes mad, he shall not be tried; for how can he make is defence?[6]

The basics of Blackstone's common law definition of competency eventually became incorporated in criminal law in the United States. The Supreme Court, in the 1960 decision *Dusky v. United States*, ruled that a mentally ill defendant, to be found competent to stand trial, must have "sufficient present ability to consult with a lawyer with a reasonable degree of rational understanding" and must have a "rational as well as factual understanding of the proceedings against him."[7] The *Dusky* decision emphasized that whether a defendant could reasonably assist in his or her defense was the benchmark for legal competency, rather than whether the defendant simply had a clear understanding and recollection of the facts of the case.[8]

Later rulings refined the definition of mental competency, and set the standard for how a defendant could be restored to competency, after years of psychiatric treatment, as Marjorie Diehl was in the Thomas case. The rulings also established how often a judge must evaluate whether an incompetent defendant has been restored to competency. Once deemed competent, a mentally unstable defendant is not precluded from arguing that he or she was insane at the time of the crime, and thus not responsible for it.

As with madness, the idea that mental illness and insanity could excuse or explain criminal behavior was known to the ancient Greeks and Romans; as one historian has noted, the origins of the concept of legal insanity are "hidden in the mists of the Bosphorus," referring to the Byzantine Empire's landmark waterway, in modern Turkey, that separates Europe and Asia.[9] Ancient Jewish and Islamic law defined insanity and declared that an insane person could not be held responsible for his or her crimes.[10] Plato, reflecting thinking that continues today, proclaimed that protecting the community was more important than punishing the wrongdoer in cases of insanity:

> Someone may commit an act when mad or afflicted with disease . . . [and if so,] let him pay simply for the damage; and let him be exempt from other punishment. Except that if he has killed someone and his hands are polluted by murder, he must depart to a place in another country and live there in exile for a year.[11]

As authors Rita J. Simon and Helen Ahn-Redding have noted, Plato's thoughts on insanity included the equivalent of the civil commitment mechanism of the present, in which the law allows society to institutionalize the insane against a person's will. For Plato, the family, rather than the state, had the power: "If anyone is insane, let them not be seen openly in the city, but let relatives of such a person watch over him in the best manner they know of; and if they are negligent, let them pay a fine."[12]

Aristotle, who linked mental illness and genius, summarized the theory of criminal responsibility and its implicit holding that only someone who knowingly commits a crime could be held liable for it. In the words of two scholars who have studied criminal responsibility, "To Aristotle, knowledge, rather than forethought, was the real test of responsibility: A person is morally responsible if, with knowledge of the circumstances, and the absence of external compulsion, he deliberately chooses to commit a forbidden act."[13] And in his own words, in *The Nicomachean Ethics*, Aristotle said of responsibility for committing acts, "The agent also must be in a certain condition when he does them; in the first place he must have knowledge, secondly he must choose the acts, and choose them for their own sakes, and thirdly his action must proceed from a firm and unchangeable character."[14] Roman law, like Aristotle's ethical formulation, recognized that an insane person, like a child, lacked the requisite understanding to act as a responsible adult and could not execute an estate or take on debts: "The legal incapacity of the insane was absolute. Such persons were regarded as having no will of their own and so incapable of incurring any obligations involving consent, whether in the character of creditor or of debtor, because they entirely lack the understanding (*intellectus*) and judgment (*judicium*), or the capacity to comprehend the effects of their actions."[15]

Roman law provided the foundation that led to the development, by the end of the twelfth century, of one of the basic articles of criminal procedure: for a person to be guilty of a crime, he or she must have a *mens rea*, or a guilty mind—a trait that neither the insane nor children were said to possess.[16] Codification of Roman statutes on crime, insanity, and scores of other legal matters came during the reign of Byzantine emperor Justinian I (527–565 CE), who replaced the canon law of the Catholic Church with civil law and moved the Roman legal system away from Bible-based punishments. The Justinian Code's sophisticated analysis of insanity recognized, as today's forensics psychiatrists do, that some forms of mental illness, such as bipolar disorder, can feature cycles of bizarre and irrational behavior. The cyclical nature of some forms of mental illness would become a major part of Marjorie Diehl-Armstrong's case. So would the question of whether she was feigning mental illness, another possibility that the ancient Romans acknowledged in cases of insanity and the mentally troubled. According to Justinian's formulation:

> If you have clearly ascertained that Aelius Priscus is in such a state of insanity that he is permanently out of his mind and so entirely incapable of reasoning, and no suspicion is left that he was simulating insanity when he killed his mother, you need not concern yourself with the question how

he should be punished, as his insanity itself is punishment enough. At the same time, he must be closely confined, and, if you think it advisable, even kept in chains; this need not be done by way of punishment so much so as for his own protection and security of his neighbors. If however, as is very often the case, he has intervals of sounder mind, you must carefully investigate the question whether he may not have committed the crime on one of these occasions, and so have no claim to mercy on the ground of mental infirmity; and, if you should find that anything of this kind is the fact you must refer the case to us, so that we may consider, supposing he committed the act at a moment when he could be held to know what he was doing, whether he ought not to be visited with punishment corresponding to the enormity of the crime.[17]

Early English law adopted many of the Roman definitions of insanity and mental illness. Among its most significant features was the recognition that insanity, mental infirmity, and mental illness came in many forms and gradations. The early English defined "idiocy" as the equivalent of a permanent mental disability that existed from birth; the various forms of "idiot" included "fool," "foole natural," and "sot."[18] What society today defines as mental illness or insanity came under two categories: "lunacy" and "madness." "Madness" denoted more of "a temporary, sometimes reversible condition"[19] that was attributed to the "violently insane."[20] "Lunacy," also known as "*insanus*," described mental illness with a cyclical nature, with bouts of insanity coming in episodes, as if influenced by *luna*, or the moon: "'Lunatic' is almost always used to describe those of the insane who have lucid intervals."[21]

These definitions explain one of the more famous legal treatises on insanity in early English law, by William Lambarde, a lawyer and justice of the peace. Like the formulation of Justinian I, Lambarde's theory accounted for different kinds of mental infirmity, and it warned against malingering, or when a sane person fakes mental illness. Like the Romans, Lambarde also equated the mentally infirm and the insane with children—none are capable of using free will to knowingly choose right from wrong. In his *Archeion; or, A Discourse upon the High Courts of Justice in England*, which he finished by 1591, Lambarde wrote:

If a madman or a natural fool, or a lunatic in the time of his lunacy, or a child that apparently hath no knowledge of good or evil do kill a man, this is no felonious act, nor anything forfeited by it . . . for they cannot be said to have any understanding will. But upon examination it fall out, that they knew what they did, and this it was ill, then seemeth it otherwise.[22]

Though the early English courts recognized insanity as a defense, persuading a judge or jury to accept that defense was difficult. Another well-known definition of insanity came in 1723, at the trial in the case of *Rex v. Arnold*. The defendant, Edward "Mad Ned" Arnold, was found guilty of shooting and wounding his neighbor Lord Onslow despite testimony that Arnold was out of his mind at the time. The prosecution prevailed with its insistence that Arnold, his mental problems aside, knowingly bought the powder and the shot, and fired at Lord Onslow "in a lucid interval."[23]

Perhaps the jurors' rejection of the insanity defense was related to the instructions they received from the trial judge, Mr. Justice Tracy. He pronounced insanity a worthy and proper defense in general, but set a high standard for its successful application in the courtroom. Justice Tracy said that a truly insane person must have no more self-awareness than an undomesticated animal: "[I]t is not every kind of frantic humour, or something unaccountable in a man's actions, that points him out to be much a madman as is to be exempted from punishment: it must be a man that is totally deprived of his understanding and memory, and doth not know what he is doing, no more than an infant, than a brute or a wild beast, such a one is never the object of punishment."[24] Thus was born the "wild beast test" of insanity in English jurisprudence. Arnold, the first to fail the test, was also sentenced to die, but had the penalty set aside at the request of Lord Onslow, who "respited" him. Arnold still remained incarcerated for thirty years.[25]

Justice Tracy's instruction acknowledged that the truly insane were unable to "distinguish between good and evil."[26] English jurisprudence gradually developed an insanity formulation that progressed beyond the wild beast test. The change was complete—and the effects on Anglo-American law profound—in 1843, with "the most significant case in the history of the insanity defense in England"[27]: the case of a deranged Scottish woodcutter and assassin named Daniel M'Naghten. His prosecution has echoed through court cases ever since, including the cases of Marjorie Diehl-Armstrong. Out of his trial emerged the "M'Naghten Rules," which established the definition of legal insanity that was the standard in England and then the United States until the 1950s.

Whether M'Naghten committed his crime was never in question. He admitted that, on January 20, 1843, in London, he fatally shot Edward Drummond, secretary to Prime Minister Robert Peel; M'Naghten said he thought Drummond was Peel.[28] M'Naghten, described as "an extreme paranoiac," also blamed Peel for his financial and personal problems, and alleged that he himself was the focus of a conspiracy that involved the pope and Peel.[29] At trial, nine medical experts—including the chief medical officer at Bethlem Royal Hospital—testified that M'Naghten was insane; and even the prosecutor, Solicitor General William Follett, acknowledged that M'Naghten was mentally ill. But Follet hoped that, by relying on the wild beast test, he could also prove that M'Naghten was only partially insane when he killed Drummond and that, unlike the wild beasts, he understood right from wrong.[30]

The jury found M'Naghten not guilty on the grounds of insanity. The verdict was in line with the thoughts of the trial judge, Lord Chief Justice Tindal. He told the jurors that "the whole of medical evidence is on one side," and that they had to determine whether M'Naghten was "capable of distinguishing between right and wrong."[31] M'Naghten was sent to the mental institution at Broadmoor, where he died twenty years later.

The influence of his criminal case outlasted him. His acquittal by reason of insanity enraged the public and Queen Victoria, who countered that the evidence showed M'Naghten had his wits about him when he killed Drummond. The House of Lords summoned all fifteen members of the Supreme Court of the Judicature to define the insanity law in light of the verdict. Three months later, the justices responded with answers that became known as the M'Naghten Rules, which included the most basic rule for determining legal insanity, the rule known as the M'Naghten Test. The justices wrote:

> To establish a defense on the ground of insanity it must be clearly proved that, at the time of committing the act, the party accused was laboring under such a defect of reason, from disease of the mind, as not to know the nature and quality of the act he was doing, or he did know it, that he did not know he was doing what was wrong.[32]

The M'Naghten Test clarified the definition of legal insanity by emphasizing a right-wrong test and holding that the defendant had to be insane at the time of committing the act, which some critics said created a standard that was too rigid and failed to consider the scope of mental illness. Critics over time also said the M'Naghten Test focused too much on whether the defendant knew right from wrong, rather than on whether he or she suffered from a mental illness that would make him or her legally insane in any circumstance. The M'Naghten Test nonetheless endured, and it reflected the views on mental illness and insanity at the time—views grounded in the cognitive "right-wrong approach" that had prevailed, in various iterations, from Justinian I and the other ancients. The M'Naghten Test, like the formulations that preceded it, saw insanity as manifested in an inability to make moral decisions, rather than an inability to function because of an underlying mental illness.[33] By the mid-1800s, the M'Naghten Test had become widely accepted in most courts throughout the United States.[34]

A would-be assassin changed the scope of the insanity defense in the United States, just as Daniel M'Naghten transformed the idea of legal insanity in England. The would-be assassin in the United States was John Hinckley Jr. His acquittal by reason of insanity in the attempted murder of President Ronald Reagan, in 1981, outside a hotel in Washington, D.C., touched off a national debate whose lasting effect was the widespread acceptance of a term in the nation's legal lexicon: guilty but mentally ill.

Years before Hinckley shot Reagan, the legal definition of insanity had evolved beyond the M'Naghten Rules. The federal courts in the United States modified the rules in 1929 to include the "irresistible impulse exception," which allows for an acquittal by reason of insanity if the defendant's mental disorder prevented him or her from controlling his or her actions.[35] But the insanity defense still was largely based on a right-wrong test that emphasized moral thinking over an organic approach to mental illness—that severe mental illness in and of itself was justification enough for legal insanity.

The organic approach became enshrined in American jurisprudence, for a time, starting in 1954, when the United States Court of Appeals for the District of Columbia ruled in the case of *Durham v. United States*, in which the accused was a mentally ill housebreaker named Monte Durham. Judge David L. Bazelon, speaking on behalf of the majority, established a standard that discarded the M'Naghten Rules for a formula that was akin to what the state of New Hampshire had been following in the cases of the legally insane since 1870.[36] The new rule established in Durham, Bazelon found, "is simply that an accused is not criminally responsible if his unlawful act was the product of mental disease or mental defect."[37] In the Durham case, the Court of Appeals for the District of Columbia created a standard that was more liberal than the M'Naghten Test but was grounded in psychiatry. "This test," as one commentator has written, "would provide for the broadest range of psychiatric expert testimony."[38] It was known as the "Durham test" or the "product test."

The Durham test was law only in the District of Columbia, and it was "ultimately dismantled by the D.C. Circuit."[39] Its replacement came about through the 1972 decision in *United States v. Brawner*, which the Court of Appeals for the District of Columbia also decided. The court used the case of Archie W. Brawner Jr., convicted of second-degree murder for a 1967 slaying, to adopt the test for legal insanity that was already in the Model Penal

Code of the American Law Institute (ALI), which formulated its definition in 1962. The ALI rule, like the Durham test, was less restrictive than the M'Naghten Test, and it added an element of volition that the Durham test lacked. The ALI standard, after the Brawner ruling, became law throughout the United States. Even Judge Bazelon, who wrote the opinion in the Durham case, concurred with the findings in the Brawner case. Judge Harold Leventhal wrote in the majority opinion:

> The court adopts as the criterion of insanity, for all trials beginning after today, the rule stated . . . in the Model Penal Code of the American Law Institute. That rule, which has been adopted in essence by other Federal circuit courts of appeals, states: "A person is not responsible for criminal conduct if at the time of such conduct as a result of mental disease or defect he lacks substantial capacity to appreciate the wrongfulness of his conduct or to conform his conduct to the requirements of the law." The rule of *Durham v. United States* . . . which excused an unlawful act if it was the product of a mental disease or defect, will no longer be in effect.[40]

The ALI standard was in effect on March 30, 1981, when John Hinckley, in an attempt to impress the actress Jodie Foster, shot Ronald Reagan and wounded a police officer, a Secret Service agent, and Reagan's press secretary, James Brady, who was shot above his left eye. The twenty-five-year-old Hinckley, a failed songwriter from Oklahoma with a history of depression, pleaded not guilty by reason of insanity at his trial in United States District Court in Washington, D.C. His lead lawyer, Vincent J. Fuller, proved Hinckley's severe mental illness by focusing on, among other things, Hinckley's writings before the assassination attempt, including a letter he wrote to Foster the morning of the shooting. The writings, according to Fuller, "standing alone, strongly suggested that John Hinckley was utterly detached from reality and had no emotional or cognitive appreciation of it."[41]

The jury acquitted Hinckley by reason of insanity on June 21, 1982. He was institutionalized at St. Elizabeth's Hospital in Washington, D.C., where he remained until a federal judge in July 2016 found him no longer a danger to society and ordered him released to the custody of his ninety-year-old mother, near Williamsburg, Virginia.[42] (Monte Durham, whose case created the Durham rule, also was institutionalized at St. Elizabeth's). The public reaction to Hinckley's acquittal was swift and angry, and dismayed lawmakers nationwide immediately pushed to tighten the definition of legal insanity: "Hinckley's insanity acquittal sparked a flurry of legislative rhetoric and public inquiry about how to stop such 'abuses' in the future."[43]

For many Americans, Hinckley knew what he was doing when he shot the president of the United States, and Hinckley should have been found guilty. They were unconvinced of Hinckley's insanity despite even a bizarre four-page handwritten letter he sent to the *New York Times* two weeks after his acquittal. "The shooting outside the Washington Hilton hotel was the greatest love offering in the history of the world," he wrote. "I sacrificed myself and committed the ultimate crime in hopes of winning the heart of a girl. It was an unprecedented demonstration of love. But does the American public appreciate what I've done? Does Jodie Foster appreciate what I've done?"[44] Hinckley also wrote: "At one time Miss Foster was a star and I was the insignificant fan. Now everything is changed. I am Napoleon and she is Josephine. I am Romeo and she is Juliet. I am John Hinckley Jr. and she is Jodie Foster. The world can't touch us. Society can't bring us down. Jodie can't ignore history."[45]

The consternation over the Hinckley verdict produced the federal Insanity Defense Reform Act of 1984. The law did not abolish the insanity defense, as many wanted, but it eliminated the ALI test and established a stricter standard for the insanity defense in the federal courts. The act also shifted the burden of proof in federal insanity cases from the government to the defendant. No longer did the government have to prove beyond a reasonable doubt that the defendant was sane. The defense now had to prove by clear and convincing evidence—a lesser standard than beyond a reasonable doubt—that the defendant was legally insane at the time of the crime.

The Insanity Defense Reform Act made the standard for the insanity defense closer to the M'Naghten Test.[46] Under the act, insanity is "an affirmative defense to a prosecution under any Federal statute that, at the time of the commission of the acts constituting the offense, the defendant, as a result of a severe mental disease or defect, was unable to appreciate the nature and quality or the wrongfulness of his acts. Mental disease or defect does not otherwise constitute a defense."[47]

Three states—Montana, Idaho, and Utah—eliminated the insanity defense following the Hinckley verdict. Others adopted standards that adhered to the M'Naghten Test (as in Pennsylvania) or the Durham test, in their original or modified formats. Among the most popular of the reforms was the introduction, at the state level, of the verdict of guilty but mentally ill. The Pennsylvania General Assembly passed the law that established the verdict in that state on December 15, 1982, six months after Hinckley's acquittal. The law in Pennsylvania, as in other states, did not replace the insanity defense with the defense of guilty but mentally ill. The new defense gave juries "an alternative verdict for mentally ill offenders. Those raising the insanity defense can be found guilty, not guilty, not guilty by reason of insanity, or guilty but mentally ill."[48] A verdict of guilty but mentally ill also became an option for defendants who did not plead insanity but who still suffered from mental illness.

A defendant found guilty but mentally ill, or who pleads guilty but mentally ill, is treated the same as a guilty defendant at sentencing. But, perhaps most important for lawmakers and the public, a defendant found guilty but mentally ill is sentenced to prison, where he or she is required to get mental health treatment, rather than confined to a mental institution, where a specific length of institutionalization was never guaranteed. In Pennsylvania and elsewhere, the adoption of the alternative verdict of guilty but mentally ill signified the latest effort to deal with a legal tension that had existed since the ancients: how to recognize mental illness and protect the community: "The wave of reform following John Hinckley's acquittal in 1982 represented legislative efforts to restore a balance in the operation of the insanity defense between individual rights and public protection, a balance that the public would deem acceptable."[49]

The definition of guilty but mentally ill in Pennsylvania reads: "A person who timely offers a defense of insanity . . . may be found 'guilty but mentally ill' at trial if the trier of facts finds, beyond a reasonable doubt, that the person is guilty of an offense, was mentally ill at the time of the commission of the offense and was not legally insane at the time."[50] The definition eventually would become familiar to Marjorie Diehl-Armstrong.

• 8 •

"Scared to Death"

Marjorie Diehl's First Homicide Trial

A jury from Erie County did not decide whether Marjorie Diehl was guilty of first-degree murder in the death of Bob Thomas. The case had received so much publicity in Erie, the only place that Diehl had ever lived, that Erie County Judge Roger M. Fischer granted the defense's request for change of venire. Instead of moving the entire trial to another county—a change of venue—Fischer got permission from the Pennsylvania Supreme Court to pick a jury from Butler County, about one hour and forty-five minutes south of Erie. The jurors traveled to the Erie County Courthouse for the trial, which started with testimony on May 19, 1988, and ended with a verdict on June 1. The Butler County jurors, according to the defense's rationale, would judge Diehl only on the evidence in her case as the jury heard it, rather than rely, consciously or not, on some stray fact or misconception that they had picked up by reading Erie's newspapers or by watching local newscasts about the many facets of Diehl's case—the homicide, the food-filled house, the bond revocation, the claims of mental illness. All of those strange events had made Diehl's case more newsworthy than most. Adding to the interest was one of the case's most compelling details—that Marjorie Diehl was unique because not only was she a woman accused of killing a man but also a woman accused of killing a man because she said the man beat her.

Diehl went to trial just as the American public was becoming more aware of the prevalence of domestic violence. Battered woman syndrome had emerged as a legal foundation for self-defense around the time of Thomas's death, and the fourth edition, text revision of the *Diagnostic and Statistical Manual of Mental Disorders* (2000) would go on to identify battered woman syndrome as a subcategory of posttraumatic stress disorder.[1] Diehl's lawyers intended to present evidence that she suffered from the syndrome and acted in self-defense because of it. The Erie County District Attorney's Office blocked that strategy, arguing that the Pennsylvania Supreme Court had ruled in a 1986 case that battered woman syndrome "has not been recognized in this Commonwealth as a viable defense in the case of homicide."[2] Three years later, the Pennsylvania Supreme Court ruled, in another case, that battered woman syndrome was a viable defense in homicide cases. The justices, citing the latest scholarship on domestic violence, also said the defense had a duty to argue battered woman syndrome if the evidence supported that theory: "Because of the unique psychological condition of the battered woman and because of the myths commonly held about battered women, it is clear that where a pattern of battering has been shown, the battered woman syndrome must be presented to the jury through the introduction of relevant evidence."[3]

Diehl's lawyers had no such precedent on their side in 1988. But they were able to present plenty of evidence of what Diehl claimed was her abuse at the hands of Thomas, who was unstable with posttraumatic stress disorder and schizophrenia with paranoia. The lawyers were legally restricted from arguing a specific defense of battered woman syndrome, but Diehl in her testimony all but said she acted in a way that would have been consistent with an abused woman defending herself. She said she acted out of fear and was in a state of mind knocked out of balance by years of abuse and mental illness. Just as Diehl's lawyers never argued that she was not guilty by reason of insanity, they also never argued she was not guilty because she suffered from battered woman's syndrome. Yet the lawyers still presented evidence that, in colloquial terms, suggested that Diehl killed Thomas because she was crazy, a condition linked both to her own mental illness and the abuse she said she suffered, again and again, from Thomas. The prosecution countered with credible evidence that Diehl was indeed crazy, but crazy with a purpose and a plan, and that she plotted to kill Thomas and tried to cover up his death.

For the prosecution, Diehl was a manipulative, cold-blooded killer. For the defense she was, as her lead lawyer, Leonard G. Ambrose III, told the jury, an abused woman whose bipolar disorder only intensified her fear of Thomas, who was also mentally ill, and made her act irrationally in killing him. Perhaps the most telling detail of the defense's strategy was that Ambrose put two star witnesses on the stand: Diehl and Robert L. Sadoff, the forensic psychiatrist, who testified after Diehl to explain why she acted as she did. "My opinion," Sadoff said, concluding his direct testimony, "is within a reasonable medical certainty that at the time that Marjorie shot she was in a state of fear for her life."[4] The prosecutor objected, arguing that Ambrose had asked Sadoff to weigh in on the ultimate question in the case—whether

Marjorie Diehl was guilty or not guilty by reason of self-defense—and that Sadoff was usurping the role of the jury. Judge Fischer overruled the objection. Sadoff stated his opinion. And several days later, after deliberating eleven hours, the jury from Butler County delivered its verdict.

Diehl's outbursts had become familiar to the judge and the lawyers in the days and months leading up to the trial—how she would criticize her lawyers during the pretrial hearings and express all kinds of other opinions. Before the jury, she was controlled and even-tempered, despite David B. Paul's fear that her bipolar disorder would cause her to spout nonsense about voodoo and astrology on the witness stand, and that she would come off as a kind of dangerous freak that deserved no sympathy. That was not the Marjorie Diehl the jurors encountered. They saw more of regular Diehl, dressed in a skirt and blouse, her hair trimmed short and curled, a thirty-nine-year-old woman who, on the day testimony started, had a crown replaced on one of her beloved teeth.[5] This was the Marjorie Diehl who told the jury, point by point, and with a calm demeanor, why she opened fire on Thomas as he was on the couch the morning of July 30, 1984.

"I was scared to death at that point," she testified.[6]

That was Diehl's version. Bob Thomas was not alive to tell the jury what happened. To try to prove Diehl's premeditation, the critical element of first-degree murder, the prosecutors focused not only on the shooting, but also on the events that preceded and followed it—events where other people witnessed Diehl's behavior and heard her talk. As the defense lawyers and medical professionals had long known, Diehl liked to talk and talk.

She spoke freely when she bought the gun she used to kill Thomas, the .38-caliber snub-nosed Smith & Wesson revolver, a weapon larger than the .25-caliber Browning automatic handgun she had bought about nine years earlier and still had at the house on Sunset Boulevard. Diehl purchased the .38-caliber revolver, a box of bullets, a gun case, and a gun-cleaning mitt at an Erie sports store on July 25, 1984, five days before she shot Thomas.

"Would this gun kill someone?" Diehl, by her own admission, asked the clerk, according to testimony.[7]

Diehl also did not dispute what she told the clerk about why she wanted the gun.

"I told her it was for prowlers," Diehl testified.[8]

She also raised no challenge to another piece of indisputable evidence—that, when she filled out the form for buying the .38-caliber revolver, she stated that she had no mental illness, though she had been on Social Security disability benefits for bipolar disorder—a designation she had fought to obtain—since January 31, 1984, about five months before she purchased the gun. Diehl at the time was also on Tofranil, the antidepressant first prescribed to her in the mid-1970s. Had Diehl stated she had a mental illness on the forms at the sports store, she would have been prohibited from buying the gun.

John Bozza, one of the prosecutors, asked Diehl if she had answered the question on the form about whether she had a mental illness.

"Yes, sir," Diehl testified.

"And did you say no?" Bozza said.

"Yes, sir."

"You lied, didn't you?" Bozza said.

"No, sir," Diehl said. "As far as that question is concerned, I don't consider it a lie because I was never adjudicated to be mentally incompetent," Diehl said. "As far as I am concerned, that kind of question means do you go before a judge for a mental competency hearing, are you appointed a guardian, like you go to a state mental hospital. I had never been to a mental hospital [in 1984]. I had been to an outpatient mental hospital, but to my knowledge I was declared by the Social Security for work purposes only. I have never been told by the doctor that I am unfit mentally in other ways as far as needing a guardian to that point."

"I understand," Bozza said. "So you remember the question, then, that was asked in the questionnaire?"

"I answered you now," Diehl said.

"And you answered 'no' to that question?" Bozza said.

"Yes, I did."[9]

Whatever her reason for filling out the questionnaire the way she did, Diehl was clear at trial as to why she bought the revolver. She said it was a belated birthday present for Thomas, who had turned forty-three years old on July 14, 1984. Diehl purchased the gun eleven days later. She testified that Thomas could not own a gun of his own because he was on probation for carrying a loaded .38-caliber handgun without a license in May 1983.[10] Diehl said Thomas had also told her, in 1971, when they first met, that his then wife had filed an assault charge against him, claiming he beat her.[11] About a month before his forty-third birthday, Diehl said, Thomas started hinting that he wanted a gun: "My birthday's coming up, you know," Diehl testified about what Thomas told her, "you can get me something."[12] She said Thomas insisted that she get him only one kind of gun—a snub-nosed .38—because "that was like the one they took from him" when he was charged with carrying a handgun without a license.[13] Diehl said Thomas identified the kind of gun he wanted by showing her a picture in *The Shooter's Bible*, one of the books police found inside the house on Sunset Boulevard.[14]

"It got to be daily he got to talk to me about it," Diehl testified about Thomas's request for the unusual birthday present. "For a while there it really got to be daily right down there before I did it . . . went and bought it."[15]

In the hours after the shooting, when she talked to the Erie police, Diehl never mentioned that she had bought the gun as a birthday present for Thomas. Her remarks, as the police wrote them down, suggested that she had bought the gun as a safeguard against Thomas, who she said had been beating her. "I told him last week that I was getting a gun and I got it," Diehl said in her statement. "I told him I had the gun when he came after me, and I freaked out."[16]

At trial, the defense built its case using Diehl's explanation that the revolver was in the house only because it had been a gift for Thomas. Diehl testified she told the store clerk that the gun was for prowlers, and not a birthday present for someone else, "because you are not allowed to buy a gun for any other person, especially if the person is already on parole [it was actually probation, and it had expired] for a charge, carrying a loaded gun. You are not allowed to do that. I didn't want to get into trouble."[17]

Diehl also explained why, if the gun was supposed to have been a birthday present, she bought it eleven days after Thomas's birthday. She spoke about how Thomas had been abusing her around that time, how he beat her when they stood on line waiting for government butter and cheese. She testified she wondered whether Thomas would be dangerous with the gun, but she said she was also worried that Thomas might lash out at her if she failed to get him the gun. Buying Thomas the gun, she hoped, would "appease him."[18]

"The reason I didn't get it for him on his birthday was because I had reservations," Diehl testified. "I didn't know if it was the right thing to do. I had something telling me, you know, it's not smart. But, on the other hand, he kept on pounding to me about it. I kept thinking, Well, maybe I could handle it. It will be all right."[19]

Her lead lawyer, Ambrose, followed up.

"Did you think that buying the handgun for Bob would help the relationship?" Ambrose said.

"Yes," Diehl said.

"When you went there that Wednesday to the sports store, did you ever go to that store with the intention of buying this weapon for the purpose of killing Bob?"

"Never."[20]

Diehl said she put the gun and the bullets in a spare bedroom when she got home that day, a Wednesday. She said she intended to give Thomas the gun that Sunday night, July 29, 1984, because he was to go to the hospital for treatment of his many ailments on Monday, July 30, the day she shot him. Diehl said she had a party planned for her and Thomas on Sunday night. She said she made Thomas his favorite meal—chicken, biscuits, mashed potatoes, salad, chocolate cake, coffee, milk—and gave him the .38-caliber snub-nosed revolver as well as the box of bullets and the gun-cleaning mitt. She said Thomas was thrilled to finally have a .38 again.

"He looked happier than I had seen him in a long time," Diehl testified. "It was almost to him like . . . losing that gun had been like an extension of himself and finally, finally, he was happy again."[21]

She said Thomas promised to train her on how to use the gun, and he gave her advice right away: Never shoot a gun with no ammunition because it ruins the firing pin. Thomas, she said, opened the box of bullets, called them "well-oiled," and loaded the revolver.[22] She said he placed the gun on the coffee table, in front of the couch. It would stay there, Diehl said, until she grabbed it the next morning.

Diehl said she had no idea that watching a movie would have made Thomas so upset. After giving Thomas his birthday present, Diehl said, she suggested they watch a movie on cable television, *An Officer and a Gentleman*, the 1982 hit in which Richard Gere plays a young man training to be an officer in Navy flight school. Diehl said Thomas watched the movie begrudgingly and, as a disgruntled Navy veteran of the Vietnam War, engaged in a running commentary about how much the Navy had mistreated him and caused his mental problems.[23] Diehl said Thomas became enraged at the women in the movie and started hitting Diehl. She said Thomas got upset with her because he thought she was interested in the movie's star.

"You really go for that Richard Gere guy," Diehl testified Thomas told her.[24]

Diehl had hoped, she said, that the night would not end with a fight. Her beatings were obvious proof that she and Thomas had a violent relationship, though Diehl said Thomas could cool off as quickly as he could lose his temper. The night before, on Saturday, Diehl and Thomas had quarreled, she said, when she made him spaghetti, another of his favorite meals. Diehl said she had become exasperated when Thomas said he wanted Parmesan cheese. Diehl did not have that kind of cheese at home. But she had American cheese—thousands of pounds of which were stockpiled inside the place.

"We had tons of food in our house and God knows how many pounds of cheese, right?" Diehl testified. "And he said to me, 'I want you to go out and get Parmesan cheese. I don't want American cheese.'"[25]

Diehl said Thomas had beaten her before when his food was not quite right, so she said she went to the supermarket and bought him Parmesan cheese. She said Thomas was no longer upset.

"He was well pleased with me," she testified.[26]

On Sunday night, Diehl said, Thomas was unhappy. *An Officer and a Gentleman* ended about eleven o'clock. Diehl said Thomas wanted to have sex. She said he pulled off her silk nightgown in the bedroom and forced her to perform oral sex on him. She said he pulled her hair, slapped her, and punched her, and called her a bitch and a whore who was unable to satisfy him after more than two hours of performing fellatio against her will.

"If it was Richard Gere," Diehl said Thomas told her, "you could get him off, couldn't you?"[27]

Thomas went into the kitchen. Diehl stayed in the bedroom. Diehl said he called for her. Now wearing the silk nightgown, she walked into the kitchen, she said, where Thomas, wearing pants but no shirt, again berated her about the oral sex. She said he picked up a knife and cut her on the arm, and that they struggled and she cut him on the chest. She said the knife broke, and Thomas backed off after she pleaded with him: "Oh, God, please, please. I'm bleeding."[28]

Diehl said she went back to bed. Thomas, she said, was elsewhere in the house. She said she never called the police. She was concerned, she said, that Thomas would get angrier if she reported him, and she said she worried about the impression she would make on the police.

"I had never called the police when he beat me because . . . I was scared of him," she testified, "but also if I was to call the police in the middle of the night like that, I can't know what they would think of me. They might think I was some kind of nut or something."[29]

That morning, Diehl said, she found Thomas sitting on the couch in the living room. The loaded .38 was still on the coffee table. Diehl was wearing her nightgown. Thomas, Diehl said, told her to come and sit down. Diehl sat in a chair. She said she listened to Thomas complain about the oral sex and Richard Gere and how she did not love Thomas. Diehl said Thomas raised his hands.

"These hands are lethal weapons, do you know that?" Diehl testified he said. "They can kill you."

"You are no good," she said Thomas told her. "I should kill you."[30]

Diehl said Thomas reached for the .38 on the coffee table. Diehl said she jumped up and grabbed it first.

"Bob," she said, "I have the gun."

She said he laughed and threatened to take the gun from her.

"I believed if he got the gun from me right then and there, he was either going to kill me or beat me within an inch of my life," Diehl testified.[31]

She said Thomas again reached for the gun.

Diehl pulled the trigger again and again.

She was scared to death, she testified.

"I had no other choice," she said. "It was him or it was me, and I couldn't think. I didn't have time to think. I just fired the gun."[32]

Diehl said she felt numb. She had no idea what she was doing. She changed out of her nightgown, grabbed the cash, filled the two shopping bags with the gun, the telephone, and all the other items, and got into her Gremlin. She drove away.

About six hours later, Diehl arrived at Donna Mikolajczyk's house with a question: Would she take $25,000 to help get rid of her boyfriend's body?

The defense also presented what it considered more objective evidence. The defense called two witnesses who said they saw Thomas beat Diehl on food lines four separate times.[33] Another defense witness, a paralegal in the county public defender's office, said she took photographs of Diehl on August 2, 1984, that showed Diehl had bruises or cuts on her body.[34] The defense said the autopsy report of Thomas and other forensic evidence proved that Thomas was the aggressor and that he was not asleep or even lying down when Diehl shot him.

Making that argument was a challenge. A firearms specialist had testified for the prosecution that Diehl was standing between seven and two feet away from Thomas when she shot him. The coroner's report said police had found Thomas lying on the right side of the couch with his feet on the floor, his head lying on an armrest, and a plaid throw blanket covering the lower part of his body. The scene suggested that Thomas, before he was shot, was lying down with the blanket on him, and that he had sat up or otherwise been roused before Diehl opened fire. A pathologist testified for the prosecution that, based on the autopsy, all six bullets entered Thomas in a downward trajectory, including the bullet that severed Thomas's aorta and killed him.[35] The testimony indicated that Diehl had fired at Thomas as she stood above him, and maybe over him.

The defense said the evidence suggested otherwise. In what some spectators considered a turning point in the trial, Ambrose and his cocounsel,

Michelle Hawk, presented forensic evidence that they said showed Thomas could not have been lying on the couch when he was shot, and that he was most likely lunging at Diehl when she killed him.[36] Ambrose and Hawk had the couch, designed in a flower print, brought into the courtroom. They had a college student play the part of Thomas. A criminologist for the defense placed black stickers on the student's body to show where Thomas had been shot, and the criminologist placed dowels in the bullet holes in the couch. The criminologist said that, based on the location of the bullet holes, Thomas, when he was shot, was not in the position that the police found him—lying down, with his head on the armrest. The defense said the evidence proved that Thomas was going after Diehl.[37] The jurors got a close look at the evidence. Judge Fischer allowed them to walk around the couch and inspect the criminologist's work.[38]

The college student gave life, in a way, to Bob Thomas, by standing in for him, and portraying to the jury how the defense believed he was positioned when he was shot. The jury also got to know Thomas more intimately. Sadoff, who had never met Thomas, used Thomas's psychiatric records to tell the jury about his mental state. Thomas did not come off well. Sadoff detailed how he suffered from the "triple threat" of schizophrenia, paranoia, and posttraumatic stress disorder, and he read from documents that presented Thomas as unpredictable, angry, sarcastic, and manipulative. "Patient presented to be a very withdrawn, apathetic-looking individual who was poorly dressed and groomed," Sadoff read from a report from March 1983. "He was wearing dirty jeans, dirty shirt and red-colored leather coat which was equally dirty. His hair was disheveled. He was wearing a beard and mustache. He had a blank look in his face."[39]

In February 1984, five months before Diehl shot him, Thomas showed up at a hospital emergency room with cuts to his right wrist. As the medical records stated, Thomas had put his hand through a window "in a fit of anger."[40] Thomas complained of flashbacks and nightmares of Vietnam, and he asked for a mental health evaluation. The diagnosis: "Axis I: straight traumatic stress syndrome."[41] A ringing alarm clock would startle Thomas into believing he was in Vietnam, according to medical records, and so would certain kinds of music.[42] Once, Diehl testified, she and Thomas were watching fireworks on July 4, and Thomas became unhinged. She said he started talking about the Vietcong and the Vietnamese, and said: "Get down. Get down. We are being fired on."[43]

Yet Diehl stayed with Thomas, despite the beatings, despite his posttraumatic stress disorder, despite jealousy and suspicion so extreme that, she said, he once accused her of cheating on him when she was only at a Burger King.[44] She stayed with him despite his demand that she get him a gun that the law prohibited him from having. Diehl said she stayed with Thomas for a simple reason: "I loved him."[45] Diehl said Thomas, after the beatings and sexual abuse, was nice to her and promised to stop the beatings. She said he would pick flowers for her, and telephone her, and write letters to her, which she said she particularly liked. "I'm crazy," she said one letter read. "I know I don't love you in the normal way, but I love you in my own way."[46] Diehl thrived on the attention.

"I am a romantic person," she told the jury. "I liked it. I loved it."[47]

"We had our good times," she said. "I cared about Bob and I wanted to believe that he cared about me. We talked about getting married. He wanted a daughter. I wanted to believe the relationship would work out."[48]

Diehl's lawyers had made many points without arguing a battered woman defense. Through Diehl's testimony, the defense had all but presented her as a victim of that syndrome—a woman who, against her better judgment, kept returning to the man who abused her because she believed his promises to change, to get better, to stop the abuse. At her height (five feet, eight inches) and weight (the police listed it as 145 pounds when she was arrested), Diehl appeared as a sturdy and solid woman, and anyone around her long enough likely felt the force of her incessant talking and her endless verbal demands. But on the witness stand, on center stage in the biggest court case in Erie County in years, Diehl continued to present herself as demure, gullible, and so dependent on men for her sense of well-being that she stayed with a man she said she thought would kill her.

Diehl, under cross-examination, offered another reason she stayed with Thomas and sought no help from the police or a women's shelter. She blamed what she described as her mental disability. She said her mental illness, combined with the beatings from Thomas, removed sense from her thinking and plunged her into a cycle of abuse that she ended herself with six bullets to Thomas's chest. "You really get to the point where you are burned out," Diehl said. "You didn't stop and think. If you stopped and thought, you wouldn't be getting beatings and you wouldn't have four thousand pounds of rotten food in your house and standing in the food line if you had your mind together."[49]

For Diehl to make such statements was one matter. For an esteemed forensic psychiatrist to support Diehl's position was another. Robert Sadoff gave the defense's theory the imprimatur of medical science. Sadoff, who said he had worked on a thousand homicide cases, testified that Diehl's mental illness and abuse had made her irrational and impaired her judgment. And when Diehl's mental state was considered with Thomas's, Sadoff said, the propensity for irrational behavior multiplied, as two paranoid people tried to live with each other. How else to explain a house filled with rancid food? How else to explain the reluctance to escape an abusive relationship? How else to explain why a highly educated woman would buy a gun and bullets as a birthday present for a man she said she feared?

"It's the very weapon that could be used against her when he became violent," Sadoff testified. "So her judgment there in my opinion was also impaired."[50]

Ambrose directed Sadoff to answer what the prosecution said was the ultimate question in the case—whether Diehl acted out of fear and in self-defense. "Considering the illness as you have described, the triple threat, her illnesses, all the circumstances, dynamics of the relationship," Ambrose said, "do you have an opinion, doctor, within a reasonable degree of medical certainty as to what her state of mind was at the time she shot Robert Thomas?" Sadoff gave his response. He said Diehl was afraid Thomas would kill her.[51]

Ambrose spent ninety minutes on his closing argument. He focused—as United States District Judge Sean J. McLaughlin would more than two decades later, in the Pizza Bomber case—on what had happened to Marjorie Diehl, how her life had derailed. Ambrose held up photographs of her in college, a svelte, smiling young woman who appeared to have a sunny attitude toward life. "What causes a person to go from a person who looks like this to someone who lives like she did?" Ambrose said. "I'll tell you what does. Mental illness."[52] Given her mental illness, and her impaired judgment, Diehl had no choice but to kill Bob Thomas, Ambrose said. His argument suggested that Thomas was such a threat that Diehl would have been justified in killing him even if she were not bipolar.

"If she hadn't shot him," Ambrose told the jury, "this would not be the Commonwealth vs. Marjorie Diehl. It would be the Commonwealth vs. Robert Thomas."[53]

John Bozza, the lead prosecutor, spoke for two hours in his closing argument. His remarks echoed his cross-examination of Sadoff, in which Bozza had questioned whether psychiatry was objective or could be considered scientifically reliable: Bozza had suggested then, with Sadoff's agreement, that psychiatry "is somewhat less scientific than some of the other branches of medicine." Bozza's closing argument also touched on his cross-examination of Diehl, in which he had zeroed in on her failure to state that she was mentally ill on the forms for buying the gun. Bozza in those instances implied that Diehl was faking mental illness and that, because of the limits of psychiatry, the diagnoses of mental illness might have been misguided anyway, influenced by Diehl's constant pressure on the doctors and the social-services system to be declared mentally disabled so she could get Social Security benefits. Diehl, for the prosecution, would have readily committed such a fraud—after all, she had thousands of dollars in cash that, as far as anyone knew, she had never reported to the Social Security Administration.

Diehl, Bozza told the jury, is "a manipulative, calculating woman . . . who is more than willing to lie when it suits her purpose."[54]

Bozza all but asked the jurors not to let Diehl dupe them. He said her claim of self-defense failed to match the facts, which he said showed that she bought the .38-caliber revolver and bullets well after Thomas's birthday; that she asked the clerk whether the gun would kill someone; and that she then used the gun on the morning of July 30, 1984, to "pump six bullets" into Thomas's body as he was on the living-room couch.[55] Thomas, he said, was far from the aggressor. He said the coffee table on which Diehl said the gun had rested was undisturbed when police arrived, and that the police saw the bottom of Thomas's body covered with the plaid blanket. Bozza said the scene of the crime revealed no evidence of a struggle.[56] This was a victim who, before he was shot, was most likely, in the view of the prosecution, in a state of repose.

Diehl's actions after the shooting drew Bozza's attention, particularly the $25,000 offer to Donna Mikolajczyk. Diehl was rational when she shot Thomas, and she was rational when she tried to get rid of his body, Bozza said.

"She methodically tried to cover up her deed," he said.[57]

The jury of seven women and five men deliberated about five hours on May 31, 1984, and another six on June 1, 1984. Diehl burst into tears in Judge Fischer's courtroom when she heard the verdict at about 4:45 p.m. June 1: not guilty of homicide and possessing an instrument of crime and guilty of only carrying a firearm without a license. Several spectators in the courtroom gasped.[58] Even the defense was surprised. Ambrose told reporters he had anticipated "a compromise verdict," such as third-degree murder, which is an unpremeditated killing with malice; or manslaughter, but not an acquittal on the homicide count. "A tremendous win," he said.[59] He later said the trial, and Diehl's endless talking, exhausted him.

"It was literally, in my mind, the case from hell," Ambrose recalled. "With medication, it would kind of cut off these talks, so you could kind of have some window so you could communicate with her. It would take off the high, what I would call the nonstop verbiage."[60]

After her tears stopped following the verdict, Diehl became composed. She spoke briefly to reporters.

"I thank God and I thank the jury and everybody that's always believed in helping me get through this," she said. She was asked what she planned to do now. "Talk to God," she said.[61]

Diehl had not made such provocative statements on the witness stand, and her calm demeanor might have been her greatest asset. At a trial in which her lawyers sought to portray her as irrational at every turn, Diehl appeared rational in court. The jury foreman said Diehl's testimony, and how she presented it, "swayed us that she was trying to defend herself."[62] He said the jurors believed Diehl fired six times out of panic, and that Diehl would have only wounded Thomas (by shooting him in the kneecap, for example) had she been able to better handle a weapon and was not in fear for her life.[63] The foreman said Diehl showed remorse, and "must have been under an awful strain," which he said might have contributed to Diehl shooting Thomas six times rather than once.[64]

"If you're scared," the foreman said, "so many things can go through your mind."[65]

A little more than a month later, Diehl was back in court for her sentencing on the firearms charge. She was upset. Judge Fischer had let her out of prison following a verdict that stunned even her own lawyers, but here she was, on July 7, 1988, complaining to Fischer that she should have never been held in prison for nearly four years while she had been awaiting trial. She told reporters that she had learned her lesson and was no longer going to get into trouble. In court, where Fischer sentenced Diehl to fifteen months of probation, she said she was not dangerous but had psychological problems and knew herself best, including realizing when she needed medication. Diehl spoke with contempt—at the legal process, at the judge, at anyone who questioned whether she would be a danger now that she was no longer locked up.

"I do believe the only person who can control myself, is myself," she said. "I know when I need medication or I need a psychiatrist. I am not a dangerous person and I know myself. I am familiar with monitoring my own situation."[66]

Fischer told Diehl that he would not order her to take medication while she was on probation; he said only medical professionals could make the determination. Diehl started to sob. She had misunderstood, and thought Fischer was going to order her to take medication.

"It makes me sick," she said. "I almost died from it."[67]

She then declared, "Everybody's picking on me."[68]

Diehl would repeat that sentiment—that she was misunderstood, and persecuted, and the victim of others' manipulations—in the years ahead. She would make the comments when, still suffering from a bipolar disorder, she would plead guilty but mentally ill to murdering one man and be convicted of conspiring in the murder of another.

· 9 ·

Flight of Ideas

The Burdens of Bipolar Disorder

They were linked from the beginning, from Hippocrates on: black bile and yellow bile, depression and mania. An overabundance of black bile led to melancholy or depression—the mental imbalance that, starting in antiquity, dominated all others. But too much yellow bile created a mental imbalance that Hippocrates, Galen, and their contemporaries considered serious and debilitating in its own right—*mania*, another form of madness. The two humors, though separate, often seemed to combine. Astute observers noted how depression often followed mania—derived from the Greek *menos*, for spirit—and how mania often followed depression, in varying degrees of intensity. "Medical conceptions of mania and depression are as old as secular medicine itself," according to one comprehensive history of the condition. "From ancient times to the present, an extraordinary consistency characterizes descriptions of these conditions. Few maladies in medical history have been represented with such unvarying language."[1] The two complex maladies— depression and mania—could remain separate but also become fused in a distinct disease: manic-depressive illness, now commonly known as bipolar disorder, which, along with schizophrenia, represents one of the earliest known mental illnesses.

About 1.9 million Americans are known to suffer a form of manic-depressive illness, or about 2.6 percent of the adult population in the United States; the average age of onset is twenty-five years old.[2] The prevalence is higher among those in prison, or those who have engaged in criminal behavior—such as Marjorie Diehl-Armstrong.[3] Though she often displayed behavior that trended much more toward the manic than the depressive, the cyclical nature of her illness was apparent, especially to her. She diagnosed herself as manic depressive.

"I am a functioning bipolar," Diehl-Armstrong once said. "If you can get along in a state prison with the type of deviates they have here—if you can get along, you are maintaining your mood pretty well."[4] Several months later, also from prison, she said: "I am also a unique bipolar person. I am a rapid cycler with mixed states. They wanted to put me in a textbook. You can be manic and depressive at the same time. I don't like any of these labels. I am a unique person."[5]

Diehl-Armstrong, as frequently is the case, is correct in her analysis. She was a unique person, in the sense that manic-depressive illness affects each person differently. It is a disease that melds with each person's personality traits and magnifies them. Manic-depressive illness exhibits general symptoms that are consistent from person to person. But, on an individual level:

> Manic-depression is an equal opportunity disease: It may affect those whose underlying personality is shy or outgoing, altruistic or narcissistic, responsible or spoiled, kind or cruel. The symptoms of mania and depression interdigitate with the person's underlying personality to create a unique medley that differs not only from person to person but even from day to day within a single person as the disease process evolves. It is this interaction of disease symptoms with underlying personality that makes manic-depressive illness so difficult to comprehend for most people.[6]

Hippocrates and Aristotle made the connection between depression and mania, and so did the Greek physician Soranus of Ephesus, who practiced around 100 CE. His works included a biography of Hippocrates as well as treatises that were ahead of their time on childbirth and mental disorders. Soranus did not consider depression and mania the extreme poles of the same disease—a concept that would take more than a thousand years to develop—though he related how "melancholia and mania were two distinct diseases but with similar . . . symptoms and requiring similar treatments."[7] Soranus found that those with melancholy, though often depressed, also often displayed mania, particularly as the depression waned. Among the symptoms he observed were: "mental anguish and distress, dejection, silence and animosity towards members of the household, sometimes a desire to live and at other times a longing for death, suspicion when a plot is being hatched against them, weeping without reason, meaningless muttering and again occasional joviality."[8] The use of *again* suggests that mania frequently alternated with depression.

Aretaeus of Cappadocia, who practiced in the second century CE, is another ancient Greek physician who recognized the relationship between depression and mania. He traced the origin of mania to the heart, and considered mania and depression as corresponding ailments, with the one the inversion of the other. In yet another example of the farsightedness of the ancient physicians, Aretaeus, writing around 150 CE, explained the connection between mania and depression:

> In my opinion melancholia is without any doubt the beginning and even part of the disorder called mania. The melancholic cases tend towards depression and anxiety only . . . if, however, respite from this condition of anxiety occurs, gaiety and hilarity in the majority of cases follows, and this finally ends in mania. Summer and fall are the periods of the year most favorable for the production of this disorder, but it may occur in spring.[9]

The history of manic-depressive illness and bipolar disorder follows the pattern of the history of mental illness in general. Their insightful commentaries aside, ancient physicians like Aretaeus subscribed to humoral theory to explain manic-depression, and such thinking persisted through the Middle Ages until the Renaissance. As mental illness then became the province of asylums rather than medical hospitals, understanding of manic-depressive illness and other disorders deepened. The French psychiatrist Philippe Pinel, in his groundbreaking *Treatise on Insanity*, translated into English in 1806, described a person who suffers from manic-depressive illness as one who "gives himself up to all the extravagances of maniacal fury, or sinks inexpressibly miserable into the lowest depths of despondence and melancholy."[10]

Other French psychiatrists contributed heavily to the understanding of the disease that featured depression and mania. In 1854, Jean-Pierre Falret described manic-depressive illness as a circular disorder, or *la folie circulaire*; that same year, Jules Baillarger called the disorder *la folie á double forme*, which echoed Falret's findings and emphasized how two mental states made up a singular disease.[11] A German psychiatrist, Emanuel Ernst Mendel, in 1881 found that mania had varying levels, including hypomania, or a milder stage of mania. And another German psychiatrist, Karl Kahlbaum, described, in 1882, *cyclothemia*, or a cycling of "episodes of both depression and excitement."[12] The observations and descriptions gradually brought psychiatrists to a fuller understanding of a disorder that, though not yet named manic-depressive illness, was by now very much a hyphenated mental illness, a disease with two main elements.

The father of modern psychiatry, Emil Kraepelin, finally joined the two—depression and mania—and named the newly diagnosed disease manic-depressive insanity in the 1896 edition, the fifth, of his *Compendium der Psychiatrie*, first published in 1883. Kraepelin defined the disorder as encompassing a wide range of behavior, but with mania on one pole and depression on the other, with mixtures of each in between, which gave manic-depressive disease its cyclical nature. "Manic-depressive insanity," Kraepelin wrote, "includes on the one hand the whole domain of the so-called periodic and circular insanity, on the other hand simple mania, [and] the greater part of the morbid states called melancholia."[13]

Kraepelin's diagnosis of manic-depressive illness, a disease of doubles, is intertwined with his other major achievement: his diagnosis of dementia praecox, or schizophrenia. In one analysis, Kraepelin—as described in the 1899 edition of his textbook—defined manic-depressive illness, which he did not believe to be permanently debilitating, as a counter to schizophrenia, which he believed was permanently debilitating. The one could not exist without the other, just as manic-depressive illness could not exist without episodes of mania and depression: "Manic-depressive insanity had its place in the 1899 edition of the textbook as a foil to dementia praecox rather than a condition developed in its own right."[14] Whatever his reason for deciding upon manic-depressive insanity as a separate and distinct illness, Kraepelin's description of the disease still largely holds true today.

The characteristics of manic-depressive illness have remained consistent as well: emotional highs coupled with emotional lows, with so many variants, or mixed states, bridging the two. Mania is best described as an extreme sense of euphoria; as Kraepelin wrote, "mood is mostly exalted in mania, and in lively excitement it has the peculiar coloring of unrestrained merriment."[15] Such a feeling—a sense of heightened merriment—best fits the category of hypomania, while full-blown mania is more severe in conveying a sense of extreme awareness. In most cases of mania, no matter what the degree, the symptoms are an overly happy mood; distracted thoughts; grandiosity and an overblown sense of self-esteem; and increased activity, including increased sexual activity, excessive writing, excessive talking—the phenomenon known as "pressured speech"—and risky and bizarre behavior.[16] All these symptoms point to a mind that is all but out of control in its exuberance, a mind in which all thoughts are accelerated, no matter their importance.

As his or her mind races at full tilt, a person who suffers from manic-depressive illness or bipolar disorder often displays one of its signature traits: a flight of ideas, a rapid-fire recitation of all sorts of thoughts and beliefs, often delivered in a tone and manner that convey the speaker's belief that he or she is more brilliant than anyone. As Kraepelin wrote of a manic-depressive person caught in a flight of ideas: "In states of excitement they are not able to follow systematically a definite train of thought, but they continually jump from one series of ideas to a wholly different one and then let this one drop again immediately."[17] When a manic-depressive relates his or her flight of ideas through pressured speech, the effect on the listener can be punishing, as if caught in a barrage of words and phrases, especially when delivered in a menacing tone. The excessive writings of a manic-depressive person can produce a similar effect on the recipient: words after handwritten words fill both sides of the page, crowd into the margins, and more often than not, spread onto the envelope. No open space is left free of the writer's ideas, just as no molecule of air is left free of a manic-depressive person's pressured speech. As two psychiatrists have written in a contemporary guide to understanding manic-depressive disorder, "listening to the speech of a person in extreme mania is an unforgettable experience."[18] In terms of excessive writing, the psychiatrists have found, referring to the trademark designs and scripts on a manic-depressive person's envelopes, "Mania is the only psychiatric diagnosis that can be determined with 99 percent certainty without even opening one's correspondence."[19]

The depressive states in bipolar disorder or manic-depressive illness mirror the manic states, in reverse. The person's thoughts and activities slow; mood plummets; and self-esteem decays into self-hating behavior. "The bipolar depressive states, in sharp contrast to the manias, are usually characterized by a slowing or decrease in almost all aspects of emotion and behavior: rate of thought and speech, energy, sexuality, and the ability to experience pleasure."[20] The characteristics of bipolar depressive states emulate the characteristics of clinical depression. In either case, the person is virtually inconsolable, though the depression of the person suffering from manic-depressive disease can seem even more severe because it is coupled with mania: The depression can seem deeper because extreme highs so often precede it. Wrote Kraepelin of depression: "Mood is sometimes dominated by a profound inward dejection and gloomy hopelessness, sometimes more by indefinite anxiety and restlessness. The patient's heart is heavy, nothing can permanently rouse his interest, nothing gives him pleasure."[21] In the darkest cases, a manic-depressive person caught in a depressive state descends into a kind of emotional stupor.

A person who suffers from bipolar disorder can reside in another troubled emotional zone, one between mania and depression: the zone of mixed states, in which a person exhibits traits consistent with mania and depression at once. Some studies have suggested some 13 percent of those with bipolar disorder suffer from mixed states, while others believe mixed states are present in virtually all cases of bipolar disorder.[22] Kraepelin, again, captured the essence of two components of mixed states, describing them as "excited depression" and "anxious mania," which correspond, respectively, with states of agitated depression and dysphoric mania.[23] In mixed states, a person is neither happy nor sad, neither euphoric nor gloomy, but a combination of both. The presence of mixed states can also signal severe bipolar disorder, and, "as a rule, individuals with mixed states take longer to recover, relapse more quickly, are more resistant to medications, and are more likely to commit suicide."[24]

Marjorie Diehl-Armstrong understood all the gradations of bipolar disorder, including its mood swings and it cyclical nature. She experienced the illness time and time again, and described how she felt to numerous psychiatrists and psychologists. David B. Paul, who met with her sixty-four times, related how she described her experience with bipolar disorder to him. Paul wrote in a report in August 1985:

> She claims her pattern is one of rapidly alternating moods and claims that she does have manic episodes also. Mania is a state which she described as being like Christmas, a wonderful feeling in which she was euphoric and feared nothing. She felt like she had been given a special chemistry, which is as good a way to characterize the illness as any. However, it was accompanied at times by anxiety and, when she is manic, she neither sleeps nor eats.
>
> Sometimes, she will engage in high level productivity. Sometimes, she is too disorganized for this, with thoughts coming at her from all directions, to which she responds by crying continuously. However, she indicated that, most of the time, she has severe depressions in which she was totally dysfunctional, had a variable appetite and had a hypersomnic sleep pattern in which she could sleep all day and night.
>
> She indicated knowledge that her judgment was impaired when manic and related this to delusions of omnipotence and impulsivity. When she is depressed, she is totally occupied with her internal feelings.
>
> Depression pulls her in one direction, and mania in another, and she has times in which she yearns for a sort of a middle road of emotional stability.[25]

The *Diagnostic and Statistical Manual of Mental Disorders*—the American Psychiatric Association's handbook for psychiatrists and psychologists—changed the name of manic-depressive order to bipolar disorder in 1980, with the publication of the *DSM III*. Though less descriptive than *manic-depressive disorder*, the term *bipolar disorder* still conveys the sense of a disease of extremes, and the *DSM-5* continues to recognize that bipolar disorder is far from a singular disease. The *DSM-5* breaks down the malady into sections and subsections, each describing symptoms that swing between mania and depression and mix the two. Critical to the *DSM-5*'s analysis is the frequency and intensity of the mania as well as the prevalence of the periods of depression. Also critical for the writers of the *DSM-5* is where bipolar disorder is covered in the book: "between the chapters on schizophrenia spectrum and other psychotic disorders and depressive disorders."[26] Bipolar disorder, according to the *DSM-5*, represents a bridge between schizophrenia on the one end and other psychotic disorders on the other. It is a pivotal disease.

The *DSM-5* offers a number of diagnoses for what had been known as manic-depressive illness: bipolar I disorder, bipolar II disorder, cyclothymic disorder, bipolar disorder related to substance abuse and medications, and unspecified bipolar and related disorder. Bipolar I disorder, according to the *DSM-5*, most resembles the "classic" description of manic-depressive disorder from the nineteenth century, though a diagnosis of bipolar I requires neither psychosis nor a lifetime experience of a "major depressive episode."[27] But the *DSM-5* acknowledges that major depression is a symptom in most cases of bipolar I disorder. Bipolar II disorder, according to the *DSM-5*, requires "the lifetime experience of at least one episode of major depression and at least one hypomanic episode"; the *DSM-5* emphasizes that bipolar II disorder is not necessarily a milder form of bipolar I disorder, particularly because those who suffer from bipolar II disorder also typically experience "serious impairment in work and social functioning."[28] The National Institute of Mental Health defines bipolar I disorder as featuring "manic episodes" that last at least a week, with subsequent depressive episodes of at least two weeks. Bipolar II disorder is less severe, "defined by a pattern of depressive episodes and hypomanic episodes, but not the full-blown manic episodes" as with bipolar I disorder.[29]

Cyclothymic disorder, the third specific form of bipolar disorder, is a broad category, meant for those who experience mania and depression, but to a lesser degree than those who suffer from bipolar I disorder or bipolar II disorder. According to the *DSM-5*, "The diagnosis of cyclothymic disorder is given to adults who experience at least 2 years . . . of both hypomanic and depressive periods without ever fulfilling the criteria for an episode of mania, hypomania, or major depression."[30] Also broad is the final, and least specific, category for bipolar disorder, according to the *DSM-5*: other specified and unspecified bipolar and related disorders, which feature symptoms of bipolar disorder that differ from those of bipolar I and bipolar II disorders and cyclothymic disorder.[31]

Cyclothymic disorder and the other classifications for bipolar disorder, including bipolar I and bipolar II, allow for a broad and inclusive definition for the disease—an inclusion that the *DSM* has fostered in another way. The APA criteria for a mixed-states diagnosis broadened from the *DSM IV*, published in 1994, to the *DSM-5*, published in 2013. The *DSM-IV* required "that the individual simultaneously meet full criteria for both mania and major depressive episode."[32] The DSM-5 redefined "mixed episodes" as "mixed features."[33] While the full-blown episodes of both mania and depression are rare, "mixed states with varying degrees of mania and depression are comparatively common."[34]

For someone like Marjorie Diehl-Armstrong, the expanded definition of mixed states—a critical component of bipolar disorder—pointed to more of her behaviors as proof that she suffered from some form of bipolar disorder or manic-depression. One particularly astute definition of manic-depression accounts for the disease's reach and evolving nature:

> Manic-depression describes a mood disorder that includes at least one episode of mania or at least one period of severe depression plus one period of mild mania (hypomania, or bipolar II) or severe mania (bipolar I). The periods of severe depression or mania may or may not be accompanied by symptoms of psychosis, such as delusions and hallucinations, in addition to the mood symptoms. Cyclothymic disorder is characterized by periods of mild mania (hypomania) and mild depression.[35]

The number of symptoms for bipolar disorder and manic-depressive illness might seem limitless. So do the number of possible causes. Brain injuries and neural deformations, genetic problems, neurochemical irregularities, immune dysfunction, and endocrine dysfunction represent only several theories of causation.[36] Those searching for a definite cause for bipolar disorder will be disappointed, just as the *DSM-5* and its predecessors will disappoint those who look to those volumes for cures for all kinds of mental illness. The causes of bipolar disorder and manic-depressive illness remain as mysterious today as they were for the Greek and Roman acolytes of humoral theory. Bipolar disorder—in the case of Marjorie Diehl-Armstrong and so many others—remains a disease that psychiatrists can seek to manage and treat through medication and therapy, but a disease still without a cure. Bipolar disorder and mania and depression are in many respects lifetime illnesses, as familiar to so many Americans as the names of the medications developed to address them: mood stabilizers such as lithium and Tegretol; antipsychotic drugs such as Risperdal and Abilify; antianxiety medications such as Xanax, Klonopin, and Valium.

Also familiar is the cultural belief that links bipolar disorder to artistic creativity and intellectual brilliance. Diehl-Armstrong is one of so many people to cite the popular theory, which holds out as examples a parade of artists and writers diagnosed with "mania, severe depression, or both": Van Gogh, Michelangelo, Robert Lowell, Virginia Woolf, Walt Whitman.[37] Many creative minds, however, have thrived absent mania and depression; just as many people who suffer from bipolar disorder and manic-depressive illness lack creativity or the keen insight that artists possess. The link between creativity and bipolar disorder rests somewhere between myth and reality; the relationship acts, perhaps, as a comfort to those who suffer from what can be such a socially paralyzing disorder. Wrote one medical author in response to the question of how to gauge whether a great leader or artist was bipolar: "Try looking through history for charismatic, magnetic leaders with boundless energy, little need for sleep, wordiness, and an unquenchable sexual desire, who deteriorated as they aged. Were they bipolar? You can make up your own mind."[38]

For Marjorie Diehl-Armstrong the answer was always clear. She had most definitely made up her mind about her diagnosis: She was bipolar, and she was in good company—with Churchill and Lincoln and Van Gogh and the other famous manic-depressives—and she was blessed.

"It's the only mental illness that can also be considered a gift," Diehl-Armstrong, in one of her lengthiest reflections on her mental illness, testified at the Pizza Bomber trial. "In fact, I've had some psychiatrists that said they wished they had it. Because it's all in a continuum, the depression and the mania. My mania is hypomania. It's not a raving maniac type mania. There's some people—if you are the type of person that has that kind of hypomania, the doctors tell you that you are not going to be the raving psycho person that jumps out of the window that thinks they're a bird that can fly."[39]

Diehl-Armstrong said her mental illness helped keep her focused. She defined "hypomania" as having "a lot of energy, not requiring too much sleep. Like a photographic memory, it helps you a lot in school. It helps you be a good student. It gives you a lot of energy. And it also gives you resilience. . . . Hypomania gives you hope."[40]

"I have bipolar disorder," Diehl-Armstrong continued, talking at a rapid pace. "I get depressed and manic at the same time. And I'm rapid cycler, which means it can change really from one minute to the next. Now, the only problem it gives me with this, is sometimes perceiving situations and people, it makes me more vulnerable and easily victimized by people. It does not make me sociopathic, which I've never been."[41]

During a pause in Diehl-Armstrong's reverie about her mental illness, Sean J. McLaughlin, the judge in the Pizza Bomber case, asked her to speak more slowly. He said the stenographer, a courtroom veteran named Ron

Bench, had to be able to get all her words down. Diehl-Armstrong responded with an explanation that, with a sense of humor, again centered on her mental illness.

"Ms. Armstrong," McLaughlin said, "we want to get the whole story in, but we're going to be here a long time if you don't listen to and respond to questions, OK?"

"OK," Diehl-Armstrong said.

"Ron, are you doing all right?" McLaughlin said to the stenographer.

"Yes," he said.

"He's very good. I used to do that job for a doctor," Diehl-Armstrong said. "He's very good."

"Ms. Armstrong, you're right: he's very good, he's doing a good job," McLaughlin said.

"I'm sorry for giving you such a hard time," Diehl-Armstrong said.

Her defense lawyer, perhaps remembering Diehl-Armstrong's sense of grandiosity, asked her about the time she said she worked as a medical stenographer.

"Were you the best at it or the worst at it?" he said.

"At what, my job?" Diehl-Armstrong said. "I typed over a 100 words a minute. Being a little manic helps for that."[42]

"Freezer Queen"

Marjorie Diehl-Armstrong Kills Again

He was Marjorie Diehl's one true love. She met him in the summer of 1989, when she was about two-thirds done with her probation for the gun conviction in the slaying of Bob Thomas. Diehl had turned forty years old several months earlier, in February, and, after spending nearly four years in prison, she was thinking of trying to settle down: "Time for commitment," she recalled.[1] One day, she said, she was walking across Perry Square, the park in the center of downtown Erie, when the man first spoke to her—Richard Armstrong, who would later become her husband for twenty months, before he died of a stroke, including brain hemorrhaging, in August 1992 in the couple's house at East Seventh and Bacon streets in Erie. Eleven years later, in August 2003, in the same house, Diehl-Armstrong would fatally shoot her boyfriend Jim Roden, whose body she would help stuff in a freezer as part of the plot in the Pizza Bomber case. That murder earned Diehl-Armstrong a sinister sobriquet in prison: "Freezer Queen,"[2] which went along with her un-forgiving attitude toward Roden's demise. Diehl-Armstrong came to despise Roden, who she said could never match Armstrong. Her husband's death, she always said, saddened her the most.

"If he had not died, this wouldn't have happened to me," Diehl-Armstrong said of her conviction in the Pizza Bomber case, "because I would have never met that Jim Roden."[3] Of Roden, she also said, "He wouldn't rate a pimple on Richard's butt."[4]

Armstrong, who was black, was an Erie resident who grew up in Cleveland, Ohio. He had a criminal past and suffered from paranoid schizo-phrenia and had tried to kill himself twenty years earlier, when he was in Cleveland; the suicide attempt led to four months of hospitalization.[5] He and Diehl were both musicians; he studied and taught the trumpet while in Cleveland, and later gave trumpet lessons out of his house.[6] He attended Juniata College, in central Pennsylvania, in 1972 and 1973, but never graduated. He was an apprentice to a cobbler in Cleveland, then an apprentice to his brother, who owned an auto shop in Cleveland, and he worked at a cafeteria in Cleveland. In Erie, he moved furniture for the Erie City Mission, where he also worked as a clerk, and he worked at the Salvation Army thrift shop.[7] His mental problems, according to one account, were among the reasons he had held no job since 1984.[8]

None of this mattered to Diehl. She was smitten with Armstrong from the start, when he first talked to her in Perry Square. As Diehl-Armstrong remembered the conversation, he charmed her by immediately commenting on an aspect of her life that was so vital to her—how she looked to others, particularly men.

"Are you for real?" Diehl-Armstrong said Armstrong told her. "You look so beautiful. I can't believe that is all natural beauty."[9]

From then on, she and Armstrong were "soul mates."[10] She was dedicated to him. He was devoted to her. She said he doted on her so much that "it was crazy,"[11] and that they loved each another. She held him in high regard intellectually; he concentrated on psychology courses in college, and Diehl maintained that he had a degree in psychology, despite his only two years in higher education.[12] She saw him, in so many ways, as a once-in-a-lifetime find for her, a man who idolized her and who possessed what she considered the highest moral standards. "That is why I carry his name," Diehl-Armstrong said in 2016, twenty four years after Armstrong's death. When he died, she said, "We were getting along famously."[13]

But the relationship, like most of Diehl-Armstrong's relationships with men, was violent and volatile. Armstrong was diagnosed as psychotic.[14] He was constantly irritable, angry, and suspicious, and often punched walls. He was so delusional about the presence of germs and so fearful that his food was tainted that for a time he drank bleach with meals.[15] He assaulted Diehl early in their relationship, on the night of July, 17, 1989, around the time she said they met. Erie police accused Armstrong, who was then homeless, of throwing bricks at Diehl in the street, hurting her legs, and threatening to kill her, burn her car, and inflict permanent injury. He was also accused of denting and scratching her car by throwing bricks at it.[16] Victims in domestic violence cases often back out of pressing charges, but not in this case. Diehl told police that she feared Armstrong. Her statements led to his arrest.

Armstrong's behavior indicated he was unhinged. He wrote in court documents that he was on welfare and needed a public defender; he wrote on the application that he was suing what looked to be, according to his scrawl, a hospital for "2 trillion dollars."[17] A jury convicted Armstrong of simple assault, and he was sentenced on May 8, 1990, to six months to a year in the Erie County Prison. About two weeks before he received that sentence, Armstrong was again charged with assaulting Diehl. At Diehl's insistence, police on April 27, 1990, arrested Armstrong on charges that he hit Diehl in the face and arm and threatened to mutilate her, kill her, and burn down her house.[18] She and Armstrong were living apart when he assaulted her in that case; police listed his residence as a drop-in center for homeless men. Armstrong pleaded no contest to the misdemeanor of making terroristic threats and guilty to a summary charge of harassment. He was sentenced on January 8, 1991, to thirty days in the Erie County Prison and two years of probation, though the judge paroled him immediately because of the amount of time Armstrong had been in prison since his arrest for the second assault.[19] The parole applied to both cases.

Less than three weeks later, on January 21, 1991, Marjorie Diehl, according to her, married Richard Armstrong. How they wed remains uncertain. Diehl-Armstrong maintained that they were married in a church service, and probate records show that Diehl-Armstrong was listed as Armstrong's wife and administrator of his estate. But other court records show that Diehl-Armstrong and Armstrong were common-law spouses who were never legally married.[20] Either way, Diehl-Armstrong considered her and Armstrong husband and wife. The newlyweds moved into her house on East Seventh Street, which had been a gift to her from her father. Harold Diehl bought the house for $18,000 in March 1988, possibly so his daughter would have a place to live once she got out of prison.

The home was often unhappy. Armstrong was forty-four years old and still subject to rage; Diehl-Armstrong was forty-one years old and at a point in her life when she was able to keep her mental illness largely under control, though a psychotic break was always a possibility. A week after the marriage, Diehl-Armstrong walked into Erie's Saint Vincent Health Center for her first visit with a psychiatrist in some time. She had apparently been seeing other physicians, because she had been prescribed the antidepressant Prozac and the antianxiety drug BuSpar (buspirone). She reported that she was taking both medications on a regular basis, which had regulated her bipolar disorder.[21] "At this time she appears to be in fair remission although still exhibits, as she always has, a certain degree of pressure of speech and also an expansiveness in her mood," the psychiatrist wrote in the office report. "From what she tells me, it appears that there are times when she experiences on and off some depression as well. At this time I don't see any need for any change.

Even if I did, she would not as she has always done what she has chosen to rather than what she has been advised to do."[22] The psychiatrist kept her on Prozac and BuSpar and arranged to see her about every three months.

Richard Armstrong was receiving psychiatric treatment at around the same time. Though clearly troubled, as shown by his suicide attempt when he was in his twenties and his habit of drinking bleach with meals, Armstrong had never received formal psychiatric treatment until he was incarcerated at the Erie County Prison after assaulting Diehl in April 1990. The prison medical staff described his behavior as bizarre, withdrawn, and delusional, and he was diagnosed with schizophrenia and paranoia.[23] His behavior improved after he was prescribed the antipsychotic drug Haldol, which Diehl had taken when she was undergoing treatment at Mayview State Hospital while awaiting trial in the Bob Thomas case. Once Armstrong was paroled on January 8, 1991, he was referred to the behavioral health unit at Erie's Hamot Medical Center. His first visit was on April 25, 1991. Diehl-Armstrong accompanied him and described his strange behavior. She said he had been delusional about being the father of children by other women. She said he believed he was a famous person. The hospital staff kept Armstrong on Haldol, and ordered him to return for psychiatric evaluations every four to eight weeks.[24]

Armstrong and Diehl-Armstrong often visited their psychiatrists within days of each other. On July 31, 1991, a psychiatrist at Hamot noted that Armstrong seemed more suspicious;[25] a day earlier, a psychiatrist at Saint Vincent had listened to Diehl-Armstrong explain that she was becoming more stressed and anxious, partly because of arthritis and other physical ailments.[26] Diehl-Armstrong stayed on Prozac and BuSpar. Armstrong stayed on Haldol.

Diehl-Armstrong vented about men during her sessions; though for a long time, she never revealed she was married. On November 7, 1991, she told her psychiatrist that she felt "persecuted" by an unnamed mentally unstable man who she said wanted to become romantically involved with her against her wishes. She said she believed this same man had slashed the tires of her car in the middle of the night, though she had no proof he had committed the crime.[27] Also at the meeting on November 7, 1991, Diehl-Armstrong said she had other worries. Facing what she said were medical bills and debts related to her criminal defense in the Bob Thomas case, she said she had filed for bankruptcy protection; the petition was docketed in United States Bankruptcy Court in Erie on October 7, 1991. Bankruptcy, her lawyer in that case wrote, "has become necessary so that the Debtor may put the various financial problems related to the criminal charges behind her and have a completely fresh start in life."[28]

Diehl-Armstrong stayed on her medication. She continued to resist taking stronger antipsychotic drugs, such as lithium, because of the painful side effects, including the swelling of her legs. The psychiatrist did not argue with her, and agreed that her current hypomanic state had become stable under Prozac and BuSpar. "I am not going to make a big deal about using antipsychotic or anti-manic drugs as long as she can manage to stay out of any significant trouble," the psychiatrist wrote following a visit with Diehl-Armstrong on January 21, 1992. "It was briefly discussed that I hoped that this [hypo]manic state did not get out of hand and she [would become] outright manic and dysfunctional. She states that she realizes that and she never has [become dysfunctional] and has managed herself in the present state."[29]

In a session seven months later, on July 22, 1992, Diehl-Armstrong finally told the psychiatrist that she was married. Diehl-Armstrong was overly talkative, but her pressured speech was no more severe than usual, and she said she was starting to come out of her depression. Her psychiatrist wrote: "Today for the first time she tells me that these days she is living with her husband. She states that she has been married for two years but chose not to tell me because she feared I may not approve of the relationship."[30] The psychiatrist listened to Diehl-Armstrong describe the relationship. The office report continued:

> I am not sure how realistic of a relationship it is. However, as long as it works and she feels content that has to be fine with us. I hope that she will prepare for the next round of disappointment that may occur in the realm of interpersonal experiences and functioning. A comment about her choice for interpersonal relationships. They are either all good or all bad, nothing in between. . . . This was briefly discussed with her today.[31]

A month later, on August 24, 1992, Richard Armstrong was dead.

Armstrong's mental and physical health had been declining for months. In a visit to his psychiatrist on May 15, 1992, he was noted to be speaking in a more guarded fashion, and he displayed an appearance that was "poor at best"[32] and showed continued guarded behavior during a visit on July 10, 1992—observations that another psychiatrist said were "consistent with chronic residual symptoms of his paranoid schizophrenia."[33] Without explanation, Armstrong withdrew from psychiatric treatment. His last visit to his psychiatrist was on July 10, 1992. A short time later, Diehl-Armstrong said, her husband came down with flu-like symptoms that persisted for two weeks before his death.[34] Throughout that time, she said, he was vomiting and had diarrhea, and had stopped taking his medication for schizophrenia and for hypertension, including high blood pressure.[35] She said her husband was on medication for high blood pressure to prevent strokes. One day, she recalled, "We were going out to lunch at home, we were going to go out and buy a car, we were going out to lunch and all of a sudden he just said 'Oh,' and he had this horrible headache. He said that it felt like something busted in his head or a sledge hammer hit him."[36]

Armstrong's collapse occurred at home on August 22, 1992, two days before his death. He complained of weakness. He or Diehl-Armstrong called an ambulance,[37] which drove him to the hospital from his and Diehl-Armstrong's house on East Seventh Street; the same crew of paramedics had been to the house previously to treat him.[38] He ended up in the emergency room at Saint Vincent Health Center at around 3:20 p.m. He was conscious at first. That day, according to medical notes, Armstrong had become so weak that he fell in his living room and struck his head on a table, cutting his head and his right shoulder.[39] Armstrong, who was of medium height and weighed two hundred pounds, had not gotten up from the fall. Paramedics found him sitting on the floor, propped against a couch. He said he had been dizzy that afternoon. He said he had suffered a headache for the past two days.[40]

The attending physician saw Armstrong at the emergency room at 3:50 p.m. Armstrong was still conscious; the doctor suspected no neurological problems. He believed that Armstrong, whom he had treated before, was suffering from a viral illness.[41] Armstrong became unconscious and unresponsive at 7:30 p.m., which led the attending physician to order a CAT scan of Armstrong's head. It revealed that Armstrong was suffering from a "cerebellar bleed"—a hemorrhage to the right side of his cerebellum in the back of his brain.[42] Armstrong fell into a deep coma; he was declared brain dead. Diehl-Armstrong, when told the diagnosis, said she wanted to keep Armstrong alive because "she had serious plans of having the patient frozen in case there were medical breakthroughs in the future."[43] The hospital placed Armstrong on a ventilator. A day later, 11:05 a.m., on August 24, 1992, his heart stopped, and Richard Armstrong died.[44]

The Erie County Coroner's Office was not required to do an autopsy; Armstrong died in a hospital setting rather than at home or in another place that was not a medical facility. The Erie police were never involved; no one reported that Armstrong was suspected to have died from unnatural causes. Diehl-Armstrong, troubled about her husband's medical care, asked Saint Vincent to perform an autopsy.[45] The hospital pathologist determined the cause of death was "right cerebellar infarct with marked cerebral edema"[46]— a stroke with marked swelling of the brain. The stroke, the autopsy found, featured a hematoma and "extensive hemorrhagic necrosis"—extensive death of brain tissue due to bleeding.[47]

The autopsy findings are included in a medical malpractice and wrongful death lawsuit that Diehl-Armstrong filed against Saint Vincent Health Center and several physicians in 1994. The suit claims that the defendants were negligent in failing to diagnose Armstrong's brain hemorrhage immediately, which Diehl-Armstrong claimed would have spurred the treatment in the emergency room that would have saved her husband's life. The defendants argued they acted properly. The full circumstances surrounding Armstrong's death were never developed fully, and in public, at a trial. The case settled for $250,000 in November 1998, four years after Diehl-Armstrong filed the suit. Her lawyers got $75,000. She got the rest: $175,000, most likely the most money she ever had up until that time in her life. Though the case ended in a settlement, Diehl-Armstrong was the clear victor. The defendants initially offered her only $15,000 to end the suit.[48] Diehl-Armstrong still was upset with her award.

"I got a quarter million dollars," she recalled. "But I didn't think that was that good because it should have been more. By the time I paid my lawyers, I only got $175,000. That really wasn't much for a man's life, at only forty-four years of age, college-educated, intelligent man."[49] She also recalled of Armstrong: "My husband was a psychologist. He was a good husband. I would be still married to him had he not had his stroke. When I met him, he had a drinking problem. Then I helped him with it and he got over it. In the beginning of our relationship we had a few problems, he was still a little abusive and stuff. I told him, 'You know, I'm not going to put up with that.' And he stopped the drinking; he stopped all that and we had a happy marriage. But, unfortunately . . . he had a familial tendency to strokes."[50]

Diehl-Armstrong was distraught. She spoke about her loss to her psychiatrist on January 28, 1993, her first visit since Armstrong's death. She said his death plunged her into a period of grief and left her suicidal.[51] Diehl-Armstrong also spoke of Armstrong in glowing terms, which caught the attention of the psychiatrist. According to the notes: "I am aware that while they were married or immediately prior . . . they did have fairly significant interpersonal difficulties, however in today's interview, this patient describes her deceased husband as a 'perfect saint.'"[52] The psychiatrist explained why Diehl-Armstrong thought of Armstrong in that way: "Nothing unusual for a manic depressive, who does tend to either overvalue in a very exaggerated manner or to completely undervalue, particularly the qualities in people who they are in a relationship with, and who at one point they like and at other times they don't."[53]

Diehl-Armstrong said she would love her husband until the end. She had his body cremated. That way, she told the psychiatrist, she "could live with the ashes for the rest of her life."[54]

Diehl-Armstrong stayed in mourning for a while longer. She considered herself old-fashioned in her belief that a widowed woman should not date another man for at least a year after her spouse's death, especially if the woman had been "really in love with [her] mate."[55] She said her friends wanted her to go out, but she refused. Based on her recollection, she most likely would have remained unattached for years had she not received mystical guidance from a psychic. Astrology and numerology and the occult had enthralled Diehl-Armstrong for most of her adult life, so her visiting a psychic in 1993 was unsurprising. She met the psychic at Lily Dale, a spiritualist enclave just east of Erie, over the Pennsylvania line in Chautauqua County, New York. She said she made the trip to connect with the spirit of her husband, because she missed him so much. She said she had no plans to ask about her prospects with living men. But then the psychic predicted another man would soon steal her heart.

"You're going to meet this other man. He's going to come from around Cleveland," the psychic said, according to Diehl-Armstrong. The psychic told her the man would be tall, and "he's going to be ten years younger and he's going to have thick red hair and a beard. He's going to be a major love in your life."

"I don't really want to hear that," Diehl-Armstrong said.

"Well, it won't happen for nine months, but it's going to happen," the psychic said.[56]

About nine months later, Diehl-Armstrong said, she met Jim Roden. The encounter led her to declare, "I kind of believed in fate."[57]

Diehl-Armstrong said she met Jim Roden in 1993 at a tavern when she was on a date with another man. Roden, a divorced alcoholic, had recently moved to Erie from Cleveland, and he sat at the end of the bar looking at Diehl-Armstrong. She thought he looked nice. He came over to her table and asked if she and her date were married. He offered to buy them drinks. He matched the psychic's description: he was thirty-five years old, or a decade younger than Diehl-Armstrong; he was from Cleveland; he was tall, at six feet and 140 pounds with a waist size no larger than twenty-seven inches; and he had thick hair and a red beard. He was in Erie looking for work laying carpet. "I was intrigued with him. I was flattered by him, of course," Diehl-Armstrong recalled.[58]

She and her date and Roden stayed at the bar until two in the morning and then went to breakfast. She liked his intensity.[59] She and her date
dropped off Roden at his motel, but that was not the last she saw of him. He
kept calling her and showing up at her house. Diehl-Armstrong introduced
him to her mother, who thought he was handsome, and Diehl-Armstrong
learned more about him: how he suffered brain damage in a tractor-trailer
accident years ago, and that the injury left him prone to rage. He kept pursu-
ing her.

Eventually, a taxicab dropped off Roden at her house on East Seventh
Street with all his belongings. He put everything on the front porch. He
moved in. She welcomed him, and their relationship blossomed—at first.

"He was kind of like a dog that followed me home," Diehl-Armstrong
recalled. "I don't like to put it that way; I'm not calling him a dog at that
point. I called him a dog later when I got to know him."[60]

Their relationship quickly turned violent. In July 1994, Erie police accused Roden of cutting Diehl-Armstrong's thigh by pushing her into the
broken glass panel of a stove door at the house on East Seventh Street. She
needed six stitches. Harold Diehl posted a $250 bond for Roden. He pleaded
guilty and was sentenced in November 1994 to three months to a year in
the Erie County Prison and a year of probation.[61] Roden was already in
prison at the time. In August 1994, Erie police charged him with violating
a restraining order Diehl-Armstrong took out against him when he cut her
thigh. She said Roden, who was then homeless, showed up at her house and
threatened to kill her and burn down her house. Roden was found guilty and
in September 1994 was sentenced to six months in the Erie County Prison.
The case drew attention from officials at the Erie County Courthouse. On
the form that accompanied Diehl-Armstrong's claim that Roden had violated
the restraining order, a court official wrote that the county probation department was familiar with her. "Marjorie Armstrong is Marjorie Diehl," the note
read. "They consider her dangerous."[62]

About ten months later, Roden was in trouble again. Diehl-Armstrong
in July 1995 accused him of violating another restraining order by bruising
and scratching her leg and threatening "to burn down the house with her
in it" and ruin the pool that was at the East Seventh Street house.[63] Roden
was convicted of violating that restraining order and sentenced to six months
in prison. Court officials again noted the probation department's concerns
about Diehl-Armstrong, the petitioner in the case. "Probation . . . said they
consider petitioner dangerous," according to a notation in court records.
"Dealings with her have been far from pleasant."[64] Once Roden got out of
prison, he and Diehl-Armstrong reunited.

Their living arrangements were a ruse. Though she and Roden lived together for years in the house on East Seventh Street, Diehl-Armstrong eventually converted the attic into an apartment where Roden could live. Roden and Diehl-Armstrong built the apartment so they could tell the welfare officials that Roden was her tenant, rather than her live-in companion, so that she and Roden could both continue to get government subsidies for heating bills and other expenses. The two would have received only one subsidy if they had been living together. They wanted "to build an upstairs apartment in her house so that it would look like they had an apartment rather than it just being a one-family home,"[65] one of their friends said.

Diehl-Armstrong and Roden lived in squalor. The house on East Seventh Street was a duplicate of the house on Sunset Boulevard, in terms of the junk, though the East Seventh Street also had a pool. Diehl-Armstrong's hoarding had gone unchecked. Her obsession just moved to a new location. Calling the 1,010-square-foot residence a home might have been an exaggeration. With all the debris and garbage inside, the place was more like an indoor dump. Like she had done when she lived on Sunset Boulevard, Diehl-Armstrong navigated the inside of the house on East Seventh Street by squeezing through "goat paths." The rooms were lined from floor to ceiling with toys, furniture, food, clothing, and junk such as an artificial Christmas tree and shopping carts. Cockroaches and other insects overran the kitchen and other rooms; feces covered the floor from Diehl-Armstrong's seven cats, some of them feral, and two dogs—a pug named Peanut and a chow named Bandit. Bags of garbage, stuffed animals, broken furniture, and a set of box springs crowded one room. Bags of trash covered the kitchen counters and pushed against the stove; at the top of one heap teetered an upside-down baby carriage whose wheel nearly touched the ceiling.[66] Water and sewage had backed up into the basement. When Erie police officers searched the house after Roden's death, in 2003, they wore masks and white hazardous-material suits that made them look like they were prepared to blast off into outer space. The stench was overwhelming at the East Seventh Street house, just as it had been on Sunset Boulevard.

"I've dealt with a lot of things," a longtime Erie police officer said after going through the East Seventh Street House. "I've dealt with corpses with the flesh falling off. This is worse."[67]

The moon-suited police officers and detectives filled several garbage trucks with bags of rubbish hauled from the house. The police fumigated the place. The fleas still covered the junk inside.

"I guess it didn't get through all the layers of fleas," a detective said of the initial fumigation. "I think the fleas ate the cockroaches."[68]

Diehl-Armstrong said the items in her house were not junk. She said they were new objects, especially Beanie Babies and other stuffed animals, which she said she adored. Some people smoke, she said, and other people drink, but she collected things. "The stuff in the garbage bags was not garbage," she said. "It was new stuff."[69] She said of what she considered her hobby of collecting: "I have my eccentricities. At least I wasn't at bars picking up guys. It was clean and honest."[70]

Diehl-Armstrong appeared stable during many of her thirty-six psychiatric visits to Saint Vincent Health Center, which occurred from one to six months apart between January 1991 and May 2003. Psychiatrists noted her behavior was calm, more or less, and that Prozac, though an antidepressant, and BuSpar, though for antianxiety, seemed to keep her mania in check. "I have not been able to understand how Prozac and Buspar [sic] control what one might consider hypomanic symptoms," one psychiatrist wrote in 1996.[71] Diehl-Armstrong still displayed pressured speech and had flights of ideas, and much of the conversations with the psychiatrists focused on her relationship with her parents and with unnamed men. She spoke with anger about some situations, but also held extended discussions about her past and what could be considered her propensity for violence. During one visit, Diehl-Armstrong explained how one man

> was trying to hound or persecute her and he stopped. Then some time was spen[t] exploring the possibility of her acting out in a violent manner, in self defense. This has happened in the past. She vehemently denies and says that she is not a person of violence, that she has learned her lessons and she would not buy a gun even if someone paid her to buy one. Says that she would deal with such situations in a legal way or with the help of the police.[72]

Diehl-Armstrong continued to blame her problems on others, even if the accusations came in a more controlled tone. She said her father never let her grow up and be an adult, and raised concerns about her current boyfriend, presumed to be Roden, and even her deceased husband. "She believes none of these people will give her any due for worth for what she is rather than use her for her own benefits and exploitation," one psychiatrist wrote. "States that it is very hard for her to trust them and wonders when she is going to be free of such neurotic bondage."[73] Steep depression struck more than mania, which continued to puzzle the psychiatrists, who knew how Diehl-Armstrong could be frantic. "When she feels depressed," one psychiatrist wrote, "she feels down in the dumps and she does not [know] what is the reason, then she thinks about all of her life she wasted, but now, she is not going to cry over that. She is going to see that she will do well with whatever she has. She stated that she is not suicidal."[74]

A psychiatrist changed Diehl-Armstrong's drug treatment for the first time in years in October 1999. She continued to take Prozac (forty milligrams in the morning) and BuSpar (ten milligrams twice a day), but was also prescribed 0.5 milligrams of the sedative Klonopin (clonazepam), because of insomnia. Her prescriptions continued to change more, along with her behavior; she was diagnosed with "bipolar disorder mixed with intact cognition" (October 1999),[75] and schizoaffective disorder (November 1999).[76] Her thinking had become more disoriented in the spring of 2000; during one visit, she went on about how she was "fed up with this world," including her parents and disrespectful "young kids."[77] A psychiatrist in April 2000 kept her on the Prozac, BuSpar, and Klonopin, and added Risperdal (risperidone), an antipsychotic used to treat bipolar disorder. The addition of Risperdal appeared to make Diehl-Armstrong think in a more organized manner, even if she was delusional. She told a psychiatrist in May 2000 that she was cleaning her house, without describing the house's condition. Diehl-Armstrong said she was "putting stuff back together and everything in order so her friend can come and visit."[78] A psychiatrist kept her on all the same medications, but added Synthroid (levothyroxine sodium), a hormone replacement used to treat hypothyroidism and mood swings, both of which she had.

The cocktail of prescriptions seemed to work, for a time. Her mood swings, according to the psychiatrist's report, had become less frequent in the summer of 2000—until an event that sent Diehl-Armstrong into mental disarray. Her mother, one of the biggest influences on her life and, in Diehl-Armstrong's view, her psychosis, died on July 16, 2000. Diehl-Armstrong grieved. Then she raged. Agnes Diehl's death triggered a fight over her estate that, according to the FBI, would shape Diehl-Armstrong's behavior in the Pizza Bomber case. "My mother was a clean-living woman," Diehl-Amstrong said. "I loved my mother. I might have had differences with her, but she was all I had."[79]

Agnes Diehl was eighty-three years old when she collapsed in the bedroom of her and Harold Diehl's house, where their only child had grown up. Agnes Diehl suffered from hypertension; the coroner ruled she died of coronary occlusion, or a blocked artery, and acute coronary thrombosis, or a blood clot in the heart.[80] Death by natural causes made no sense to Diehl-Armstrong. She considered her mother's death suspicious. She claimed her father failed to make sure her mother was taking her medication. She claimed her father was nonchalant about the death. "Harold A. Diehl told Marjorie

Armstrong that he knew her mother was dying for a long time," Diehl-Armstrong's lawyer, Larry D'Ambrosio, declared in court papers. "During the week following her death, Harold A. Diehl asked Marjorie Armstrong on four different occasions if she was going to try to put him in jail for her mother's death."[81]

The allegations about Harold Diehl were false, based on the coroner's report. But D'Ambrosio, at Diehl-Armstrong's request, cited the claims in an effort to get Harold Diehl removed as the administrator of Agnes Diehl's estate and replaced with a neutral party. Diehl-Armstrong wanted more control over the assets, which included a brokerage account valued at $150,867, which were distributed according to her mother's will. Agnes Diehl wrote the will on the back of an envelope, and she had firm directions regarding her daughter's share: "Remember," it said, "make a trust fund for Marjorie with a bank person in charge."[82] Jim Roden signed on as potential witness for Diehl-Armstrong in the estate challenge, though the challenge to the administration of her mother's estate went nowhere. The settlement of the estate initially left Harold Diehl with $84,200 and his daughter with $54,200.[83]

Diehl-Armstrong remained concerned about the money she did not get: When Agnes Diehl died, she and her husband held municipal bonds whose face value was $1.8 million.[84] Harold Diehl was in control of those funds, and Diehl-Armstrong was worried about the fate of that money—money, as D'Ambrosio wrote in the court filing, that Diehl-Armstrong believed was hers alone. The filing referred to the Wolfendens, Diehl-Armstrong's beloved maternal grandparents, and alluded to how they had shown her the safe in their house when she was a child. The Wolfendens, D'Ambrosio wrote, "said all the money was from her side of the family, and that they and Agnes E. Diehl all agreed it was to go to Marjorie Diehl at her mother's death."[85] Diehl-Armstrong expressed her fears about the money to her psychiatrist at an appointment on November 15, 2000, the first after her mother's death. She "started talking about her mother who recently died," the psychiatrist noted, "and she thinks her father is getting quite irrational, showing very poor judgment that he is giving away money to everybody else, but not to her and she thinks her father should have [a] guardian."[86] The fear of missing out on her inheritance would haunt Diehl-Armstrong for the rest of her life.

Diehl-Armstrong's unsuccessful challenge to remove her father as administrator upset her. So did an incident related to the estate fight, in which she tangled with a bank. Though many of Diehl-Armstrong's over-the-top claims were untrue or distorted, her grievances often had rational underpinnings. Despite her mental illness and her medication, she remained intellectually sharp and well-read and, when competent, had a clear under-standing of the law. She used her knowledge of Pennsylvania estate and inher-itance regulations to argue with a branch of PNC Bank, in Erie, about access to her mother's safe-deposit box. She claimed the bank violated state law by letting her father get into the box the day after her mother's death without the bank making a required official inventory. Diehl-Armstrong said the access allowed her father to take what was in the box on his own. Diehl-Armstrong cited the incident in her failed attempt to get her father removed as admin-istrator of the estate, and she wrote a letter to the Pennsylvania Department of Revenue asking for an investigation of the PNC Bank branch, which had indeed allowed her father access to the safe-deposit box without an inventory of its contents. The letter detailed how Diehl-Armstrong and D'Ambrosio had a confrontation with the bank branch manager. Diehl-Armstrong wrote that she wanted action immediately, though nothing is known to have come of her demand. She included with the letter photocopies of the pertinent Pennsylvania estate and inheritance laws. "Please see attached laws and penal-ties which I <u>thank you</u> for enforcing," Diehl-Armstrong wrote.[87]

The fight over the safe-deposit box stoked Diehl-Armstrong's obsession with money, particularly her father's money, and it embittered her against PNC Bank, the institution that she believed was holding that money. Diehl-Armstrong's paranoia, a symptom of her bipolar disorder, deepened.

Jim Roden stayed by her side. She looked past the abuse she said he inflicted on her and fashioned a role for herself as Roden's protector, the one person who could make him better by keeping him away from alcohol. Diehl-Armstrong found the best way to keep Roden sober was to do things with him outdoors. One of their favorite hobbies was fishing. They made for an interesting couple, Diehl-Armstrong and Roden, as they cast their lines. She had wild hair and a large frame and talked nonstop, mostly with exple-tives. Roden, with his thin build, was less demonstrative but still capable of losing his temper. The two fished constantly from Erie's South Pier, on one side of the channel that connects Erie's Presque Isle Bay to Lake Erie. Diehl-Armstrong said she had enjoyed fishing since her father taught her how to fish when she was twelve years old—which she said was one of the few good things her father did for her. "He taught me to drive and he taught me to fish, that's about all I can say," she recalled.[88] She said she had liked to fish with her dad, she had liked to boat and swim with Edwin Carey, and she liked to spend hours at the South Pier with Roden, hauling in catfish and other fish to eat and give to friends. Diehl-Armstrong described herself as a gourmet cook. She was fond of making fish dinners.[89]

Fishing on the South Pier is how Diehl-Armstrong met Erie resident Kenneth E. Barnes, who would become one of her main links to the Pizza Bomber plot. Barnes, who was four years older than Diehl-Armstrong, was a television repairman, computer whiz, and drug dealer whose clutter-filled house in Erie was just as bad as Diehl-Armstrong's. Barnes and Diehl-Armstrong's friendship was strong enough that, according to him, he once accompanied her to Lily Dale, the spiritualist enclave, where Barnes said Diehl-Armstrong wanted Barnes to meet with a medium to determine "if I was psychically in tune with her realm of reality."[90] The psychic was not there. Barnes said he and Diehl-Armstrong walked around in the woods and looked at the animals.[91]

By the spring and summer of 2003, Barnes had become a regular at Diehl-Armstrong's house. He was also a handyman, and he was helping her build the upstairs apartment for Roden. The apartment and the deceptive cost-cutting rationale behind it had grown into a kind of obsession for Diehl-Armstrong by that time. Barnes listened to her talk constantly about money. Diehl-Armstrong was worried that her father was giving away her inheritance to friends and neighbors. She was correct about her father's largesse. He did indeed go on to make gifts that included $1,000 to the mail carrier, $100,000 to one friend, $50,000 to another, and $100,000 to still another.[92] "These people are vultures," Diehl-Armstrong said of the recipients. "They are all vultures."[93] But Diehl-Armstrong was wrong that the money her father was giving away could be considered hers. Her father was still very much alive, and he was free to do what he wanted with his fortune. Whether he wanted to put his only child in his will would be his decision, though he seemed inclined not to bequeath her much, if anything. He once told the Erie police that he knew his daughter was upset with him for giving money away, but that "her elevator doesn't go all the way to the top and she's not dealing with a full deck."[94]

Diehl-Armstrong by then had plenty of money and assets of her own, but seemed intent on getting more. She relied on Social Security disability payments for her main income. She also said she delivered newspapers—as many as six routes a day, given her mania—in the late 1990s.[95] Diehl-Armstrong had amassed a small fortune. It included the $175,000 she received in the malpractice case over her husband's death; the $54,200 she had inherited from her mother; and another $180,000 she eventually received after her mother's death from a joint account for which Diehl-Armstrong had the right of survivorship.[96] The cash added up to $409,200. Diehl-Armstrong had other assets. Her father in 2000 had deeded the house on East Seventh Street to her for free. In February 1999, she paid $65,000 in cash for a cottage in Harborcreek Township, east of Erie; the cottage was set back from a cliff that overlooks Lake Erie. Diehl-Armstrong also owned a Jeep Cherokee, a Chevrolet Camaro sports car, and a Chevrolet Blazer, and she claimed she had other automobiles, including a motor home, as well.[97] Though she was often known to exaggerate about her wealth, Diehl-Armstrong, at this point in her life, really did possess financial means.

But she wanted more money. Diehl-Armstrong wanted to make sure her father's money was left for her. She continued to complain about her father during her regular psychiatric appointments at Saint Vincent Health Center. "He is giving away his money to friends and everybody else but not to her," according to the notes of a meeting on June 26, 2001.[98] "She thinks she is the only child and the father should give all the money to her," according to the notes of a meeting on August 1, 2001.[99] And in the notes of a meeting on April 23, 2003, a psychiatrist wrote: "She talked nonstop about her father who is giving away money to everyone else but her and she was upset about that. . . . I did try calling her father. He thought that his daughter wants money, but otherwise she doesn't need anything. He was going to give her 20% of his income, but now he is getting to the point where he does not care about his daughter. The patient was upset over that."[100] The psychiatrist increased the dosage of Diehl-Armstrong's medications because she seemed "to be very angry, upset and delusional."[101] Diehl-Armstrong was still taking Klonopin, Synthroid, and BuSpar, but was no longer on Risperdal or Prozac. She was instead taking the antidepressant Wellbutrin (bupropion) and the antipsychotic Stelazine (trifluoperazine).[102] She had previously also been on the antipsychotic Seroquel (quetiapine), but no longer had a prescription by the spring of 2003. "I was on these drugs and I was doped up, like you would drug up a cow or a horse," she once said.[103]

Diehl-Armstrong was back taking BuSpar as well as Stelazine, Klonopin, and Synthroid when she visited the psychiatrist on May 21, 2003. "She was very circumstantial and tangential," the psychiatrist noted. "It was hard to bring her back to her original thoughts. She was talking about six years ago or talking about last week; it was hard to understand. She kept talking, not making any sense."[104] The psychiatrist prescribed her a four-month supply of drugs and told her to visit again in four months. Diehl-Armstrong never kept the appointment. The visit on May 21, 2003, was the last she would have with a psychiatrist outside a prison setting.

Ken Barnes heard Diehl-Armstrong complain more than ever about her father and his money in the spring of 2003, as Barnes worked on remodeling Diehl-Armstrong's attic into the apartment for Roden. He said she grew increasingly agitated. In the spring and summer of 2003, he would later testify, Diehl-Armstrong asked him if he wanted to help her rob a bank. Barnes said he was not interested.[105] He said she had another question: "She asked me then if I would make a bomb for her or I knew how to make a bomb."[106] Barnes said he told her he knew how to make a bomb but was not interested in helping her.[107] The questions kept coming. "She asked me if I would kill her father for her," Barnes testified. "She asked me how much I'd charge."[108] Barnes said he was joking when he set a price of $250,000. He said Diehl-Armstrong told him she wanted her father dead because "he was spending her inheritance that she had from her mother. She said he was giving his money away to the church and to the neighbors; she didn't like it because it was her money."[109] As for what bank to target in a robbery, Barnes said Diehl-Armstrong was angry at one bank in particular: PNC.

Marjorie Diehl-Armstrong went to the classified section in the *Erie Times-News* to buy the 12-gauge shotgun that she used to kill Jim Roden. The ad for the gun ran on August 2, 2003. Diehl-Armstrong showed up at the seller's house about a week later. She smelled strongly of cat urine, looked anxious and tired, and she was carrying lots of cash, mostly $20 bills.[110] She paid the asking price for the gun—$450.[111] Diehl-Armstrong told the seller that she wanted the gun for home defense because of break-ins in her neighborhood. She told him how, over that Memorial Day weekend, she had reported to the Erie police that a "coked-up biker" had broken into her house shortly before four in the morning on May 30, 2003. She said she was sleeping in her nightgown on the couch in the living room, with her purse and a plastic shopping bag filled with $2,300 in cash hidden underneath the couch cushions.[112] She said someone in a black jacket climbed through the window, held a knife to her chest, shouted, three times, "I'll kill you, bitch, if you don't give me your money," and ran off with the cash.[113] Diehl-Armstrong first told the police the thief had stolen $2,300, then the number became $2,800, and finally $133,000. Diehl-Armstrong blamed Barnes for the heist. Police never charged anyone, given Diehl-Armstrong's mental state and her inconsistency about how much money was stolen.

Diehl-Armstrong insisted that the burglary happened. She said she needed a gun for protection. In 1984, when she bought the handgun she used to kill Bob Thomas, she said she needed it for prowlers. In August 2003, she said the threat was burglars and robbers. When she bought the handgun in 1984, Diehl-Armstrong failed to disclose her mental illness, which, if known, would have disqualified her from gun ownership. In August 2003, she bought the shotgun in a private sale, through the classified ad, and did not disclose her mental problems. She asked the seller if he was a cop, an immediate indication that she was worried about someone knowing she was buying a gun. She said nothing about her bipolar disorder when she bought the shotgun, a semiautomatic Remington Model 11-87 with a shiny walnut stock and a twenty-six-inch barrel made of high-gloss metal that glowed blue. The shotgun could hold three rounds—one in the chamber and two in the magazine. She wanted to know how to break it down, and what would happen when she fired it.

"If I was to shoot the gun," she said to the seller, "if I needed to use the gun in the house, would it put a big hole in the wall?"[114]

The seller chuckled.

"Yeah," he said. "It's going to put a big hole in the wall if you miss whoever or whatever your aiming at."[115]

"I don't want to kill anybody," Diehl-Armstrong said. "I would just shoot them in the foot to scare them."[116]

Jim Roden was defenseless when Marjorie Diehl-Armstrong shot him. He was lying facedown in his single bed, in the attic apartment in the house on East Seventh Street, at about two o'clock, during a stormy morning on August 10, 2003. He might have been sleeping.[117] She carried the 12-gauge Remington shotgun as she crossed through the maze of trash downstairs and climbed the fifteen stairs to the attic. She walked into the bedroom and stood five to seven feet from Roden's bed. She fired once. The shotgun recoiled, but she was able to handle the force of the kick. She fired again. She shot Roden in the middle of the back, just below the right shoulder blade. The two wounds were nearly side by side. Roden curled in the fetal position. He died instantly as his blood covered his bed.[118]

Roden's body was left unmoved for two days. The outside temperature hit highs of seventy-eight degrees; the attic must have been sweltering. Diehl-Armstrong avoided the heat and stench by living out of her car—the red Jeep Cherokee, which she filled with papers and clothes and stuffed animals and other junk; it was like her house, but on wheels. She parked it in the lot at the Walmart south of Erie. She used the Walmart bathroom to wash. She spent most of her days trying to figure out what to do with Roden's body. She called the one person she knew who would have the expertise and the inclination to assist her in her plan, no matter how nefarious. She called her onetime fiancé, Bill Rothstein.

Though they had long ago stopped being lovers, Diehl-Armstrong and Rothstein had continued to stay in touch, even if the contact was infrequent. His life, like hers, had reached something of a dead end. The two of them were so much alike in that regard: they were both highly intelligent, even brilliant, but they were also both condescending and arrogant and unwilling to accept that someone, anyone, could be smarter than they were. So Diehl-Armstrong, beset by mental illness, had embarked on a life of instability and abusive relationships. Rothstein, who never exhibited signs of mental illness, got by as a handyman, electrician, and substitute teacher who taught robotics; he was so good with his hands that a principal and the athletic director at the Erie School District hired him to do work at their houses.[119] Rothstein was fifty-nine years old in the summer of 2003, unmarried and still living alone with his German shepherd in the house where he had grown up, at 8645 Peach Street, just south of Erie. He had lived there with his mother until she died in 2000, at age eighty-five. The house, like the residences of Diehl-Armstrong and Barnes, was a mess, filled with junk and papers and hardware products, such as scrap metal. The houses were in such disarray that an investigator searching for evidence in any of them would have no idea where to begin to look, which was maybe the point.

Rothstein liked the house; it resembled the house of a mad genius, which is what he held himself out to be. His physique had changed little over the years. He was still big in the summer of 2003—six feet, two inches tall; 319 pounds; and shoe size twelve EEE, a size so big that he complained he could rarely find shoes that fit. He wore the same type of clothes most every day, whether he was on a handyman job or teaching as a substitute: thick-rimmed glasses, a work shirt, denim bib overalls, and boots.[120] He looked like a pig farmer.

Diehl-Armstrong's views of Rothstein fluctuated. She never denied that she loved him when they were engaged to be married, but later in life she found herself exasperated with him. Once she was indicted in the Pizza Bomber case, she came to demonize her former fiancé. She called him "a devious piece of shit"[121] and a "sicko,"[122] but readily acknowledged his intellect. "Rothstein was a brilliant guy," she recalled. "You fuck with the master, you fuck with disaster."[123] Rothstein, according to the FBI, was the mastermind behind the Pizza Bomber plot.

Diehl-Armstrong had no hesitation in turning to the master for help in getting rid of Roden's body. As Rothstein recalled, she showed up at his house several days after Roden's death; thirty years earlier, when she and Rothstein were engaged, she had lived in that house with him. Now she was a visitor in a panic. Diehl-Armstrong told him about Roden's death. She said something—or so Rothstein testified—about killing Roden because he was not doing enough to help her track down the crackhead biker who broke into her house over Memorial Day weekend. She also blamed Roden for introducing her to Barnes, who she believed was responsible for the burglary.[124] Rothstein said she gave him $78,000 in cash to help get rid of Roden's body and for safekeeping; she put the number at $100,000, but said she told Rothstein she hoped to get $10,000 of it back, to go to California to get her teeth fixed.[125] She also said she gave Rothstein so much cash because she had been in shock over Roden's death.[126] Whatever the amount, Rothstein, with the money in hand, said he was more than willing to participate to make Roden's body go away.

"I wanted to help her," he testified, "because I thought maybe this will straighten her out, because she was going to give up on guys, because she kept going around with the wrong guys she claimed, so I thought maybe I could help her out with this."[127]

Rothstein also said of their relationship, "Usually I would hear from her . . . she would call up with some kind of complaint or something, and if I could help her I would, but usually I tried to avoid her as much as possible, unless I really thought I could help her."[128]

Rothstein also agreed to dispose of the Remington shotgun, the murder weapon. That part was easy. He said he used a reciprocating saw to cut it up and used an acetylene torch to melt down the fragments. He said he got rid of the scraps by throwing them out his car window as he drove around Erie County early one morning. Rothstein had experience in such tactics. In 1979, he testified in an Erie County murder trial that he had unsuccessfully tried to burn the pistol that his friend had used to fatally shoot a man in a dispute over a girlfriend. The burning failed to melt the pistol, which Rothstein, testifying for the prosecution, said he threw in the trash. He had no qualms in engaging in such behavior.[129]

With Roden's death and its aftermath, the past had also come full circle for Diehl-Armstrong. Here she was, nineteen years after she killed Bob Thomas, in the same situation. She had fatally shot another boyfriend while he was in what authorities said was a resting position—Thomas on the couch, Roden face down on the bed—and then offered a friend tens of thousands of dollars to help make the body disappear. As she had been after Thomas's death, she was frantic now, over the fate of Roden. One night, in mid-August, she and Rothstein wrapped Roden's body in a plastic tarp, hauled it out of the house on East Seventh Street, drove it in a van up to Rothstein's house, and, in the garage, stuffed it into a working chest freezer that Rothstein had purchased for that purpose. They went back to the East Seventh Street house and scrubbed the blood-stained attic with bleach and other solvents, painted the walls, and moved out almost everything that had been in the attic, including the blood-stained mattress and box springs. Rothstein dropped all the junk off at his house, and then dumped it at the landfill—a total of 1,040 pounds, or more than a half ton. He and Diehl-Armstrong, whose houses looked like junk yards, suddenly went into a cleaning frenzy. They did all they could to erase evidence of the crime, including Roden. Rothstein said he went along with the plot to provide Diehl-Armstrong a sense of peace: If all the evidence was gone, all her worries might disappear as well. "If she didn't have that hanging over her head," he said, "she might be allowed to be free."[130]

More than two weeks after Roden's death, on August 28, 2003, Brian Wells was killed in the bomb blast as he tried to rob the PNC Bank branch in Summit Township, not far from Rothstein's house. Police quickly determined that Wells, as a pizza deliveryman, had, minutes before the bank robbery, delivered two pizzas to a clearing at the end of a dirt road that ran beside Rothstein's house at 8645 Peach Street, in Summit Township. From that site, Wells, now wearing a bomb locked to his neck, drove to the bank. When Wells drove along the dirt road, past Rothstein's house, he also drove by Rothstein's cluttered garage, which held the chest freezer that, at that moment, contained Jim Roden's frozen body. Police and the FBI at the time of Wells's death had no idea that Roden was even dead. They had no idea that Diehl-Armstrong and Rothstein might be connected to the murders of both Roden and Wells. Those links would come much later.

Even Bill Rothstein had his limits. He said he started to get worried when Diehl-Armstrong became serious about cutting up Roden's body—an idea that Rothstein said he raised with her. "In theory," he said, "that's the best way to do things. It's the same way with the gun. It's best to just chop it up in as many pieces and spread it around as [much as] possible, but that doesn't mean I thought it had to happen."[131] He said he realized that Diehl-Armstrong really was serious about cutting up Roden's body when the two drove to a kitchen-supply store on September 20, 2003. They went there to buy a meat grinder or an ice crusher; Diehl-Armstrong walked out with the ice crusher, but the purchase was as baffling as it was frightful. She had purchased the type of ice crusher a party host would use to break up ice cubes for cocktails; a chunk of ice deposited in a slot in the top went through a grinder and ice cubes and shards came out the side. The ice crusher cost $94.34, including tax. Diehl-Armstrong carried it to Rothstein's van in a box.[132] Who knew how much time they would need to dismember Roden's body and run it through this ice crusher? The task seemed impossible and absurd. But the possibility that Diehl-Armstrong was committed to carrying out the task, Rothstein said, frightened him. And so, perhaps, did the possibility that the highly anxious, nervous, and, most likely, unmedicated Marjorie Diehl-Armstrong might have been preparing to gun down Bill Rothstein next, and make him her latest victim.

For whatever reason, Rothstein decided to act. He got in his van, drove away from his house, and called 911 at 8:15 p.m. on September 20.

"At 8645 Peach Street, in the garage, there is a frozen body; it's in the freezer in the garage," Rothstein told the operator. "There is a woman there you might want to pick up and question."[133]

Rothstein gave the operator the woman's name: Marjorie Diehl.

"Who is she to you?" the operator said.

"I helped her do stuff I shouldn't do," Rothstein said, "but I never killed anyone. So I just want that known."[134]

Erie police arrested Diehl-Armstrong at Rothstein's house in the early morning of September 2, 2003. Detectives charged her with homicide, aggravated assault, possession of an instrument of crime, tampering with evidence, abuse of a corpse, and criminal conspiracy to tamper with evidence and abuse a corpse. She had $4,200 in her purse and another $781 at her house on East Seventh Street.[135] Unlike in the Thomas case, she was mostly quiet. After her arrest, while sitting on a bench at the state police barracks, she muttered that Jim Roden had been shot, and she said that, over the years, she had experienced "poor luck" with men.[136] She said little after that, upon her incarceration without bond at the Erie County Prison, and during her contacts with the District Attorney's Office and the Erie police, who handled the case because Roden was killed in Erie and his body moved to Summit Township. In the Thomas case, Diehl-Armstrong immediately told investigators—and then could not stop telling investigators—that she killed Thomas because he abused her. She could have made the same argument in the murder of Roden; once again, the victim had a documented history of violence toward her and the victim was dead. No direct witnesses would have existed to counter Diehl-Armstrong's claims of self-defense if she chose to raise them. But Diehl-Armstrong, despite her inclination toward pressured speech, stayed quiet over why Roden was killed.

Diehl-Armstrong's reputation preceded her when she arrived at the Erie County Prison in late September 2003, shortly after her arrest in Roden's death, and she enjoyed the attention she received from the infamous Thomas case. While at the prison, she was diagnosed with schizoaffective disorder and prescribed familiar medications: Wellbutrin, Synthroid, BuSpar, and Klonopin.[137]

Diehl-Armstrong's mental problems and the strange nature of her current case were well known among her fellow female inmates. One inmate recalled how she was sitting at a table with her and other inmates when Diehl-Armstrong said she did not like another prisoner, that "when she saw her in the med line, she wanted to smash her head like a watermelon and watch the seeds pop out."[138] The inmate at the table joked about why the other inmates had to be wary around Diehl-Armstrong.

"I dubbed her the Freezer Queen," the inmate said. "I said it doesn't pay to piss off the Freezer Queen. You end up an entrée."

The inmate said Diehl-Armstrong pointed at her, gesturing that she found the joke funny.

"She thought it was hysterical," the inmate recalled.[139]

Diehl-Armstrong still kept quiet about the details of her case. Her preliminary hearing was on January 20, 2004; a magistrate ruled that the District Attorney's Office had presented enough evidence for the case to go to trial. The main witness was Rothstein, who showed up at the Erie County Courthouse wearing, in a rare sartorial break, a jacket and tie rather than overalls and a work shirt. He testified that he helped Diehl-Armstrong put Roden's body in the freezer, but did not kill Roden. He said Diehl-Armstrong told him that she was the one who fired the shotgun. He explained that putting the body in a freezer was one thing, but cutting it into pieces was another.

"I couldn't see myself cutting up a body like that," he testified, "and I don't think she would, and she wanted me to, she indicated she wanted me to, and I couldn't do it."[140]

The police charged Rothstein with abuse of a corpse, tampering with evidence, and conspiracy to abuse a corpse and tamper with evidence. He was not charged with homicide. He was to be the star witness at Diehl-Armstrong's trial.

Though Diehl-Armstrong did not testify during the preliminary hearing, as is usually the case for defendants at such proceedings, she made a brief comment afterward. She looked straight at the television cameras as sheriff's deputies led her out of the courtroom in handcuffs. She snarled, "Rothstein is a filthy liar. Rothstein should be charged with the death of Brian Wells and a lot of other charges."[141] She said nothing else.

Diehl-Armstrong remained at the Erie County Prison. Outside, her problems worsened. On January 9, 2004, fire destroyed her cottage on the cliff above Lake Erie. No one was home and no one was injured, but the fire burned through heaps of the treasures that Diehl-Armstrong had spread throughout the place. Garbage bags filled with debris were piled four to five feet high in the rooms and hallways. In October 2003, while looking for evidence in Roden's death, Erie police had worn white moon suits inside the cottage. The inside was covered in animal feces, and at least two dead cats were found inside as well. The stench from the house could be smelled several blocks away.[142] Now, three months later, the junk created problems for firefighters, who suspected that workers checking on the furnace might have started the blaze. The firefighters had to get out of the house rather than knock down the flames from the inside. The junk in the house put them at risk of getting trapped. The cottage was a total loss. "It's no fault of the firefighters," said the Pennsylvania State Police trooper who investigated the fire. "They made a quick response. But they were met with such a mess."[143]

Chaos struck Marjorie Diehl-Armstrong's personal affairs because of the fire. One of her recurring fears—that someone would burn down her house—had come to pass. She had no insurance on the cottage. She had hoped to sell some of her valuables in the cottage to help pay for her defense in the Roden case, but now those assets were gone. She saw the loss of the cottage as another example of the constant destruction of nice things in her life, the things she deserved. "It's one of the best and it was big," she said of her cottage as compared to the others in the neighborhood. "It had four bedrooms; it was very exclusive property."[144]

Diehl-Armstrong's mental state remained unstable, just as it had in the Bob Thomas case; her incarceration and the fire and the loss of her valuables had to unnerve her. At a bond hearing on February 12, 2004, Diehl-Armstrong rambled. She talked about her assets. She talked about her case. She talked about Rothstein, saying he was "shifty" and wanted to have "perverted sex" with her. She talked about the probate dispute with her father over her mother's estate. She talked about her lawyers, who were public defenders; she called them "public pretenders."[145] A judge ruled that Diehl-Armstrong could not pay for her own lawyer. He ruled that her assets were tied up as evidence because of the allegation she used tens of thousands of dollars to pay Rothstein to dispose of Roden's body. In between all the legal discussions about the availability of her money, Diehl-Armstrong also talked about her manic-depression.

"Severe, very severe," she said of the extent of her mental illness, "but not violent."[146]

Diehl-Armstrong's lawyers in March 2004 asked a judge to send her to Mayview State Hospital to determine her competency to stand trial—the same place she had gone in the Bob Thomas case. For proof of Diehl-Armstrong's mental issues, her lawyers cited her psychiatric history, the condition of her house on East Seventh Street—which the city of Erie had determined was unfit for human occupancy—and the psychotropic drugs police had found inside the house. They included Wellbutrin, BuSpar, Klonopin, Stelazine, and the sedative Librium (chlordiazepoxide).

The judge, Shad Connelly, issued an order on March 22, 2004, that sent Diehl-Armstrong to Mayview for a six-month evaluation. She was admitted to Mayview on April 1, 2004. She refused medication and started rambling in her first interviews. She said she owned her own firm and consulting business. She spoke of Roden's death, and identified no suspects by name, but clearly believed Rothstein had something to do with the murder. "The patient stated that prior to the alleged crime a friend who wants to be a boyfriend was hanging around a lot and insisting on a relation with her, but she does not love him and he wants only her money," the examining psychiatrist wrote. "She stated that she is an independent, high functioning person who 'has been framed' and accused of this crime because they were jealous of her that she acquired a lot of money through her consulting business."[147] She said the police were prejudiced against her because she had killed her previous boyfriend, and that police did not believe her story then, so she saw no need to report Roden's death because no one would have believed what she had to say. "I was very angry that my friend bought a freezer and kept the body in the freezer all this time," she said. "That is not what I asked him to do."[148] Because she was in a mental institution when she made the comments, the authorities could not use them against her in the Roden case.

Despite her initial flight of ideas, Diehl-Armstrong soon was ready to head to trial. She continued to refuse medication for a time, saying the drugs would make her "a zombie,"[149] but she eventually relented; as the examining psychiatrist, Laszlo Petras, MD, wrote, "without any antipsychotic medication or mood stabilizer, her signs and symptoms of mania appeared to increase."[150] The Mayview staff gradually discontinued her use of Wellbutrin and prescribed her Seroquel. That drug did not help, and Diehl-Armstrong complained of the side effects, so the staff put her on a drug that was new to her: the antipsychotic Geodon (ziprasidone), used to treat schizophrenia and bipolar disorder. Diehl-Armstrong's condition improved with the Geodon, the Mayview staff said, and a prescription for Klonopin aided her sleep. She also took Synthroid again, for her hypothyroidism.

With her mood stabilized, Diehl-Armstrong was calm enough to attend group sessions on legal issues while at Mayview. She said she did not think she needed medication, but said she would take her prescriptions if that is what the staff wanted her to do. Petras, the psychiatrist, evaluated Diehl-Armstrong using the fourth edition, text revision, of the *Diagnostic and*

Statistical Manual of Mental Disorders (*DSM IV-TR*). He found her competent for trial with this diagnosis:

Axis I: "Bipolar disorder, manic phase, in partial remission";
Axis II: None.
Axis III: Hypothyroidism, obesity, history of water retention; history of
   allergic reactions to some drugs;
Axis IV: Incarcerated, "pending serious charges, minimal social support."
Axis V: About 50.[151] This referred to the Global Assessment of Functioning scale, from 1 to 100. The higher the score, the better the coping skills.

Petras and LuAnn Cochenour, the director of Mayview's psychiatric forensic center, also wrote of Diehl-Armstrong:

She clearly understands the nature of the crime, although her view of it is somewhat distorted. She understands the seriousness of the charges. She understands the legal system and her options of trial by judge or jury, the possibility of plea bargaining and the need to cooperate and work with her lawyer to assist her case. Unfortunately, the patient still has not achieved full understanding of the seriousness of her mental illness throughout the years and its consequences. She still has a tendency to use defense mechanisms, which are self-defeating, including denial, projection, intellectualization and rationalization. This is interfering with her fully understanding the need for treatment and the seriousness of the consequences when she is not complying with mental health treatment in the community.[152]

Diehl-Armstrong was returned to Erie County, where she had a competency hearing at the county courthouse on September 8, 2004. Petras, a witness, testified about what he had written in the report: that, under the current medication, Diehl-Armstrong's mania was in remission and she was competent to stand trial. Judge Connelly listened to Petras and reviewed Diehl-Armstrong's mental health records back to the early 1970s. The next day, on September 9, 2004, Connelly ruled that Diehl-Armstrong was competent for trial.

Four months later, the case was over. Diehl-Armstrong arrived at the Erie County Courthouse on January 7, 2005, for a plea hearing and sentencing. The plea: guilty but mentally ill. It applied to third-degree murder and abuse of a corpse in Roden's death. Connelly sentenced her to seven to twenty years in a state prison; the maximum sentence for third-degree murder alone was twenty to forty years. The sentence, which the District Attorney's Office found agreeable, represented a break. Diehl-Armstrong avoided getting the maximum for third-degree murder, or an unpremeditated homicide with malice, and avoided prosecution for first-degree murder, or a premeditated homicide, a conviction for which carries a mandatory life sentence with no parole in Pennsylvania. Diehl-Armstrong got a break for a reason. Bill Rothstein, the main witness against her in the Roden case, had died in the county nursing home on July 30, 2004, at age sixty. He suffered from stage IV non-Hodgkin's lymphoma; the cancer had spread from his lymph nodes to other organs.

With Rothstein dead, the District Attorney's Office used the plea bargain to secure a conviction. By pleading guilty but mentally ill, Diehl-Armstrong guaranteed that she would initially serve her sentence at Mayview, where she would receive additional mental health treatment, and then get moved into the regular Pennsylvania state prison system. She would also be eligible for parole after seven years, though early release seemed unlikely, given her violent past. If she served her entire maximum sentence of twenty years, Diehl-Armstrong would not be free until she was in her late seventies. The lengthy sentence, Judge Connelly said, was appropriate.

"The defendant's background is familiar to the court, including her prior contacts with the law," Connelly said at the sentencing. "The court is also familiar with the fact that Ms. Diehl has an education. She is intelligent, as the psychological reports indicate, with an average to superior IQ. The court is also familiar with the fact that she has had mental health problems now for well over twenty years that have been consistent and resistant to treatment."[153] He called Diehl-Armstrong "severely mentally disabled."[154]

As United States District Judge Sean J. McLaughlin would do years later, at Diehl-Armstrong's sentencing in the Pizza Bomber case, Connelly recounted how Diehl-Armstrong's conduct had cut short the life of another—Jim Roden—and devastated the victim's family. He said Diehl-Armstrong had "recognized her need for treatment on a continuing basis at this point," and suggested that her mental deterioration represented another sad facet of the case. "As in cases of this nature," Connelly said, "it's a tragedy in several aspects, but none more so than by the fact that a life has been lost as a result of the actions of the defendant."[155]

Diehl-Armstrong sobbed as she apologized and said she was not "a bad person."[156] She explained how she understood the terms of the plea, in which she agreed to plead guilty but mentally ill to killing Roden directly or as an accomplice with Rothstein. The District Attorney's Office contended that Diehl-Armstrong shot Roden. Diehl-Armstrong, in her explanation, told the judge: "I just want to say . . . that I'm only pleading guilty to this because of the complicity clause, that I would have liked to have had the strength to stand trial and claim not guilty to these charges. And I feel badly about this, and I want to apologize to the family, his [Roden's] relatives and friends for what happened. I'm so sorry."[157]

Jim Roden's mother, Jean Roden, said she always thought Diehl-Armstrong was "really a nice person," based on her son's letters home. "I don't believe she should be on the streets," Jean Roden said of Diehl-Armstrong. "She's a danger to society. . . . I had no idea it would turn out like this."[158]

The district attorney, Brad Foulk, who had gone to Academy High School with Diehl-Armstrong, recounted Diehl-Armstrong's violent past, including the death of Bob Thomas. Foulk characterized Diehl-Armstrong as an unrelenting threat to Erie:

> I know the court cannot take into account the acquittal [of] a number of years ago, but I think it's important to note that the conduct she engaged in the late '80s was almost identical to this particular conduct. And I know she's pleading guilty but mentally ill today, and I think the psychiatric reports reflect a woman who is suffering from a mental disorder that without question, without question, if she were ever placed on the streets again she would kill another man.

Diehl-Armstrong interrupted, her voice rising in anger. "Oh, how can he say that?"[159]

$\cdot$ *11* $\cdot$

The Fractured Intellectuals

The Pizza Bomber Plot Unravels

*M*arjorie Diehl-Armstrong used her mental illness to explain why she killed two of her boyfriends. She said her bipolar disorder and paranoia had heightened her fears about an abusive Bob Thomas, so she pumped six bullets into him while he was on a living room couch, unarmed. She said she was equally unstable when she blasted Jim Roden in the back with a shotgun while he was resting or sleeping on his bed. Stuffing Roden's body into a freezer was, for her, yet another example of her untethered mind. She pleaded guilty but mentally ill, after all, in Roden's murder, and certainly no one in that case questioned that she suffered from bipolar disorder and other forms of serious mental illness.

Diehl-Armstrong and her lawyers used her mental illness in a different way in the Pizza Bomber case, her strangest and most diabolical plot. They argued that her mental illness made her participation in the case so unlikely as to be impossible. Her paranoia, they said, made her apt to stay by herself rather than associate with others, particularly those of the ilk of Bill Rothstein and Ken Barnes. Her extreme narcissism and grandiosity, she and members of her defense team said, made Diehl-Armstrong a poor candidate for working with someone else, even someone as brilliant as Rothstein. And Diehl-Armstrong's bipolar disorder, they said, made her so unstable, so impulsive, so prone to wild swings between depression and mania, that she lacked any capacity to concentrate and think through a plan as complex as the one that led to Brian Wells's bombing death on August 28, 2003.

"It just doesn't follow that someone with that type of personality would have the ability to be a planner, to deliberate. Over a long period of time," her trial lawyer told the jury in his closing argument in the Pizza Bomber case.[1] Regarding the allegation that Diehl-Armstrong was a member of a wide-ranging conspiracy, the lawyer, Douglas Sughrue, told the jury that the United States Attorney's Office had done nothing more than show Diehl-Armstrong hung around with "bad company"—an association that, in her case, in no way could be considered a crime.[2]

Those arguments failed badly. On November 1, 2010, the jury in United States District Court in Erie convicted Diehl-Armstrong of all the charges against her in the Pizza Bomber case: conspiring with Ken Barnes to commit armed robbery; aiding and abetting an armed bank robbery involving a death; and aiding and abetting the use of a destructive device—the bomb—in a crime of violence. For the jury, Diehl-Armstrong's involvement in the Pizza Bomber plot made sense, despite her mental illness and despite her claims that the evidence was deficient. Seven women and five men deliberated eleven hours and thirty minutes over two days at the end of Diehl-Armstrong's ten-day trial in the Pizza Bomber case. They found that the government's theory of the case—a theory that the evidence more than supported—showed that Diehl-Armstrong was voluntarily involved in the Pizza Bomber plot and knew what she was doing. No one disputed Diehl-Armstrong's mental illness. But that mental illness did nothing, in the end, to excuse Diehl-Armstrong's behavior in the Pizza Bomber case. The plot was bizarre and often hard to accept as being based in reality. But as the federal prosecutor in the case, Marshall Piccinini, explained to the jurors, the evidence, no matter how dark and disturbing, was undeniable: Marjorie Diehl-Armstrong was at the center of one of the most horrific crimes that the FBI had ever investigated.

"The evidence in this case proves that a twisted scheme was executed on August 28, 2003," Piccinini said in his closing argument. "The evidence shows that the conspirators who concocted this scheme were arrogant, narcissistic individuals, who the evidence shows believed they were smarter than anyone else."[3] Piccinini also reminded the jury of a hard truth: that even in Erie, Pennsylvania, a group of weird and violent misfits could exist and carry out such an odd and deadly scheme. The trial, he said, revealed how a group of people sank to the "depths of human depravity" and came up with "this maniacal plan, this stupid, overworked, overblown, ridiculous plan."[4]

Marjorie Diehl-Armstrong, Ken Barnes, Bill Rothstein, and the others involved in the Pizza Bomber plot had a name for their crew: the Fractured Intellectuals. The lead investigator, FBI Special Agent Jerry Clark, based in Erie, and his partner in the investigation, Jason Wick, a special agent with the Bureau of Alcohol, Tobacco, Firearms, and Explosives, started calling the group that name as well. Diehl-Armstrong, Rothstein, and the others were all were bright and at one time possessed much potential. But by the time they had reached late midlife—Diehl-Armstrong was fifty-four years old in August 2003, Rothstein was fifty-nine, and Barnes was fifty-one—each had become a broken criminal, because of mental illness, drug abuse, or sociopathic behavior that Piccinini, the prosecutor, said was rooted in two base elements: evil and greed. Diehl-Armstrong always claimed she distanced herself from Rothstein and Barnes. She repeatedly described Rothstein, in addition to being a "sicko," as a jilted and jealous lover who was upset that she rejected him. She had harsher words for Barnes, whom she accused of being kind of subhuman. "It is always a bad day when I cross Ken Barnes. He is like a skunk," she once said.[5] In another moment of rage, she said, "Ken Barnes is nothing but a criminal. Someone once told me all Ken Barnes cares about is sex and money. That is not me. I am higher on the food chain than Ken Barnes."[6]

The final remark captured Diehl-Armstrong's supreme arrogance. Even as she was relegated to an existence of collecting $580 in monthly Social Security disability payments, living in dilapidated and sordid houses, and holding down no jobs except delivering newspapers while in her early fifties, Diehl-Armstrong thrived as a know-it-all and manipulative narcissist. Each of the Fractured Intellectuals had no shortage of ego. Diehl-Armstrong saw herself as one of the smartest of them all. She was like self-crowned royalty in the underworld of Erie's crooked.

"I didn't hang around with those unsavory guys," she once said. "I may not be perfect, but I've got my standards too."[7]

The Pizza Bomber plot—what Piccinini called that "stupid, overworked, overblown, ridiculous plan"—seemed destined to fail from the start. Brian Wells did not fit the profile of a bank robber. At forty-six years old, he had spent most of his adult life delivering pizzas. He was a high school dropout who liked puzzles and watching movies, particularly *Jesus Christ Superstar*, with his mother. He was also a recovering alcoholic known to use cocaine and frequent prostitutes, including his favorite, a woman by the name of Jessica Hoopsick, whose pimp was Ken Barnes.[8]

On the afternoon of August 28, 2003, Wells, a driver for Mama Mia's Pizza-Ria, just south of Erie, took an order for two small pizzas with pepperoni and sausage. He got behind the wheel of his 1996 Chevrolet Geo Metro and delivered the pizzas to the clearing at the end of the dirt road that went past Bill Rothstein's house at 8645 Peach Street in Summit Township. He passed Rothstein's garage, where Jim Roden's dead body had been inside a freezer for at least a week. Wells dropped off the pizzas at the clearing. A gun went off. Then he drove back down the dirt road. Wells was wearing something different than when he left Mama Mia's. Now he was wearing the ticking time bomb locked around his neck. It looked like a giant handcuff.

Wells parked his Geo outside the PNC Bank branch at 7200 Peach Street, several minutes away from the clearing where he made his final delivery. He was carrying a shotgun shaped like a cane; sucking on a lollipop; and wearing an oversized white T-shirt with "GUESS Jeans" on the front, as if to convey a taunt: Guess what is going on? Guess who did this? The T-shirt concealed the bomb, which hung from his neck and rested against his chest. Wells waited on line and strolled up to the counter. He asked the teller for $250,000—an outrageous amount of money to demand during a bank robbery—and gave her a four-page demand note that looked like someone had written by tracing over typed print. "Act Now, Think Later Or You Will Die," part of the note read. The teller put all the money in her drawer inside a canvas bag: $8,702. Wells complained that the cash was not enough, but he left the bank anyway. He walked slowly. He continued to suck on the lollipop.

Wells drove his Geo to a McDonald's just east of the bank. He got out of the car, walked over to the drive-through sign, and picked up a rock. He removed a note that had been stuck to the bottom of the rock. He read the note, got back in his Geo and drove east. He headed toward one of the interstates that ran near Erie.

Troopers with the Pennsylvania State Police stopped Wells before he could reach his destination. Squad cars pulled over the Geo in the parking lot of an eyeglass store just east of the McDonald's. The troopers ordered Wells out of the Geo. He sat cross-legged in the parking lot and complained that the bomb around his neck was heavy and was going to go off soon. He said his name. He said he worked for Mama Mia's. He said black men had forced him to wear the bomb and rob the bank. The only bomb squad in the area, for the Erie police, was rushing to the scene, but was still six miles to the north and driving through heavy traffic. Wells continued to talk. He said at least three people were watching him to make sure he robbed the bank. He said the bomb had locks that, when turned with keys, could give him more time. The explosive device was made of two pipe bombs wired to two kitchen timers. Wells pleaded with the troopers to do something. He talked more about a black guy he said had overpowered him.

A camera operator for a local television station, WJET-TV, filmed Wells's final minutes.

"He pulled a key out and started a timer," Wells said. "I heard the thing ticking when he did it."

"It's gonna go off," Wells said. "I'm not lying."[9]

Brian Wells had taken the pizza delivery order at 1:15 that afternoon, and walked into the bank at 2:27 p.m. At 3:18 p.m. on August 28, 2003, the bomb around Wells's neck exploded. It blew a hole in his chest. He died instantly, moments before the bomb squad arrived.

Jerry Clark and the other FBI agents and police officers and ATF agents had no idea what they were dealing with. The terrorist attacks of 9/11 had happened just two years earlier, so no one disregarded the thought that Wells's death was the result of an organized assault that might be repeated soon, with other victims. But soon the investigators pursued a theory that, in many respects, was even more baffling than the prospect of a rogue state somehow targeting Erie, Pennsylvania. Clark and the other agents found notes in Wells's car similar to the notes he left at the bank. The writings, nine pages in all, including what he showed the teller, directed him on a kind of scavenger hunt through Erie County. After he robbed the bank, Wells was supposed to have driven to no less than three other locations, where he would have found more instructions on how to get keys to deactivate the bomb. The way the device was designed, it gave Wells a total of fifty-five minutes on each kitchen timer. But one timer was never activated—Wells was supposed to have used another key for that—so Wells only had fifty-five minutes to complete a complicated route made even more complex because Wells would have been anxious and in a hurry, as he tried whatever he could to stop the bomb from exploding. Clark and others later drove the route and determined that Wells would have had no chance to finish it and stay alive. He really would not have had enough time. This sick game of death was rigged against him.

More clues surfaced in the hours after the fatal explosion. Investigators searched Wells's house, a sparsely furnished bungalow in suburban Erie. They discovered no bomb-making materials, which would have immediately suggested that Wells was in on the plot. They did find a spiral notebook filled with the names and telephone numbers of just about everyone Wells knew. The names and telephone numbers of his friends and relatives were on the list. So were the names and numbers of two Erie women who worked as prostitutes. One of them was Jessica Hoopsick, who worked for Ken Barnes. Agents tracked down both women, who denied having anything to do with Wells's death.

At the same time, Clark and the other investigators had to try to develop leads based on the theory of the case that their superiors found to be, at that moment, most plausible. As evidence technicians gathered the bits of the bomb for an eventual reassembly, Clark's superiors asked him to piece together whatever he could find about the black man or men who Wells said had placed the bomb around his neck and sent him on his deadly way. The state troopers who had pulled over Wells were skeptical that searching for this unknown black man would be worthwhile. When Wells blamed a black man for his plight, one of the troopers wondered if his accusation was just another example of a white person faulting a black person for his or her problems, whether real or imagined.[10]

Clark too had his doubts about the theory centering on the mysterious black man, but he and other investigators conceded that they could not simply ignore the possibility that Wells had been telling the truth when he gave his fevered explanation of how he had ended up in such an unfathomable situation. When he was talking as the bomb was ticking, Wells was offering the equivalent of a deathbed confession: he had nothing to lose by telling the truth. Deathbed confessions are considered so reliable that they are admissible as evidence in court though they are hearsay and not subject to cross-examination. Who is so brazen as to lie on his or her deathbed? Why would Brian Wells lace his last words with deception?

The pursuit of that strand of the investigation soon slowed, however, as another death required the attention of Clark and most of the other federal agents, who at the height of the investigation numbered as many as seventy five; the FBI had jurisdiction because of the bank robbery. This was a major case, Major Case 203, which meant the FBI was prepared to use all of its resources to solve it as quickly as possible. Three days after Wells was killed, his close friend and fellow pizza delivery driver, a forty-three-year-old recovering alcoholic by the name of Robert Pinetti, was found dead of an apparent drug overdose at his mother's house outside Erie, where he had been staying. An FBI agent had tried to interview Pinetti the day after Wells was killed, but Pinetti, who had reported to work to deliver pizzas, put off the agent for another day. The interview never took place. Then Pinetti, who would have been able to provide intimate information about Wells, was dead.

Then the FBI and police in the early morning of September 21, three weeks after Wells's death, discovered the corpse of Jim Roden after Bill Rothstein, supposedly alarmed at Marjorie Diehl-Armstrong's purchase of the ice crusher, got in his van the night before, drove away from his mother's house, and called 911. He and his former fiancée soon were under arrest. The Pizza Bomber investigation appeared to have taken on yet another dimension.

The connection seemed so obvious as to be absurd. The FBI had indisputable evidence that Brian Wells's final delivery, the delivery at which he was forced to wear a bomb, occurred at the clearing at the end of the dirt road that ran next to Rothstein's house. And Rothstein had a body in a freezer in his garage. And the deceased, Jim Roden, had been shot to death at Marjorie Diehl-Armstrong's bug-infested and junk-strewn house in Erie. This was the same Bill Rothstein known to be adept an anything involving electronics, and who taught robotics as a substitute teacher. And this was the same Marjorie Diehl-Armstrong who had shot her boyfriend to death in 1984. What would have prevented her from killing Brian Wells as well as Jim Roden, maybe as part of the same plot? And what would have prevented Bill Rothstein, the stereotypical pack rat and eccentric handyman, from assembling the collar bomb?

Adding to the evidence was a suicide note that investigators found inside Rothstein's wreck of house after Roden's death. The note, which Rothstein never acted on, read:

1. This has nothing to do with the Wells case.
2. The body in the freezer in the garage is Jim Roden.
3. I did not kill him, nor participate in his death.
4. My apologies to those who cared for me or about me. I am sorry that I let them down.
5. I am sorry to leave you this mess.[11]

Rothstein was intelligent. Why did he feel the need, in what was like his own deathbed confession, to disavow himself of a crime for which he had not been charged? For Clark and Jason Wick, his counterpart with the ATF, Rothstein was protesting too much.

The investigation seemed ready to be closed, less than a month after Wells's murder. "Handyman-Wells Link?" declared the front-page headline in the *Erie Times-News* on September 27, 2003. The FBI's reaction to the possible connection was much more muted. "All I can say at this time," a supervisor with the bureau said in the story, "is we have no evidence that would suggest Rothstein was associated with this crime. I don't mean to close the door on all possibilities."[12] For the supervisor and other authorities in the FBI, Rothstein's involvement in the Pizza Bomber case was unlikely, in part, because it seemed so obvious. In their view, Bill Rothstein was too smart to have taken part in the Wells case and then drawn attention to himself by hiding a dead body in his freezer. The Pizza Bomber case remained open. Rothstein, when questioned about what he had been doing when Wells was killed, told investigators that he and Marjorie Diehl-Armstrong had been in the vineyards east of Erie, on Lake Erie, sampling wine. At first, the FBI took him at his word. The agents once again redirected most of their energy trying to find the elusive black man.

The Erie police had other uses for Rothstein. They put him up in a hotel room after Roden's death and treated him as a star witness, the one person who could finger Diehl-Armstrong as Roden's killer as the Erie County District Attorney's Office prepared to prosecute the Roden case. Rothstein took the police on a tour of Diehl-Armstrong's house, where he explained how he found Roden's body and how he and Diehl-Armstrong cleaned up the premises; and he took police on a tour of his house, where he explained how Roden's body ended up in the freezer. As he walked the police through the two houses, Rothstein enjoyed his moment on the stage. He chatted with the police, laughed with the police, and showed no signs of being worried. During the tour of his house, a state trooper asked him about the suicide note, and why Rothstein felt compelled to write that he had nothing to do with the Wells case. Rothstein gave a Gallic shrug. "So you wouldn't go hog wild, saying this has to do with the Wells shit," he said.[13]

Diehl-Armstrong wanted nothing to do with the police. She continued to keep to herself while at the Erie County Prison, awaiting prosecution in the Roden case. She attracted attention with her outburst after her preliminary hearing, in January 2004, when she declared to reporters that "Rothstein should be charged with the death of Brian Wells and a lot of other charges." But her mental illness helped her maintain her silence and keep the investigators away. Jerry Clark and Jason Wick wanted to interview her for information in the Wells case. But she was off limits starting in March 2004, when Erie County Judge Shad Connelly ordered her to receive psychiatric treatment and undergo a competency examination at Mayview State Hospital, with her return to court not scheduled until September 29, 2004. While at Mayview, Diehl-Armstrong was not mentally stable enough to even consent to being interviewed. Clark and Wick could not get near her.

By the middle of 2004, Clark and Wick had become convinced, despite the beliefs of their superiors, that Diehl-Armstrong had participated somehow in the Pizza Bomber plot. They appreciated the concerns that Rothstein was too intelligent to connect himself to a crime in so obvious a fashion, but they also knew that Rothstein and Diehl-Armstrong and the others were not normal. Rational behavior did not apply in this case. Clark and Wick also knew that questioning Diehl-Armstrong about the case would give them more leads. Their desire to interrogate Diehl-Armstrong intensified after Bill Rothstein died on July 27, 2004. Clark had interviewed Rothstein three days earlier in his bed at the county home, and Rothstein said he could not remember what he was doing the day Wells was killed; this contradicted his earlier statement that he and Diehl-Armstrong had been touring Erie County's vineyards. Several hours before Rothstein died, two reporters with the *Erie Times-News*, Ed Palattella and Tim Hahn, interviewed Rothstein in his bed. They started asking him questions about the Wells case. He lifted one arm high above his head, and sketched in the air, with his index finger, one word: NO. "No!" Rothstein groaned to the reporters. "Nooo!"[14]

With Rothstein dead, and Diehl-Armstrong found to be competent in the fall of 2004, the Erie County District Attorney's Office offered her the plea deal in Roden's death: guilty but mentally ill to third-degree murder and other charges. The mentally ill aspect of the plea created more problems for Clark and Wick. The plea required Judge Connelly to make sure Diehl-Armstrong got mental health treatment at the start of her sentence of seven to twenty years. Connelly ordered her to begin the sentence at Mayview State Hospital, where Clark and Wick could not visit.

Their fortunes changed on March 16, 2005. Diehl-Armstrong was transferred from Mayview to the Pennsylvania State Correctional Institution at Muncy, the women's prison in the middle of the state. Clark and Wick visited her there on April 27, 2005. They were not treating her as a suspect, so they did not read her Miranda rights. She was unmedicated. Shortly after her arrival at Mayview, in early January 2005, Diehl-Armstrong was prescribed the antipsychotic Abilify (aripiprazole), used to treat schizophrenia, bipolar disorder, and depression. Diehl-Armstrong had initially refused any medication at Mayview in January 2005, but eventually agreed to take Abilify, mainly because she had not tried it before and she did not perceive any side effects.[15] She soon stopped taking Abilify; she said it made her shake and rock, a phenomenon known as tardive dyskinesia. She was not known to use psychotropic drugs again.

Clark and Wick would go on to interview Diehl-Armstrong a total of eight times while she was in prison in 2005 and 2006. She was careful in each interview not to implicate herself, but she gave the investigators enough information for them to conclude that she had played a role in Brian Wells's death. She would have been unable to know such details had she been out of the plot completely. In the first interview, on April 27, 2005, for example, Diehl-Armstrong seemed to relax and open up when Clark, knowing of her obsession with her teeth, greeted her with a bit of flattery: "Marge," he said, "you have a million-dollar smile."[16] Diehl-Armstrong insisted that she had no part in Wells's death, though she said Rothstein confessed to her that he was involved. She said Rothstein was lying when he told Clark that he and Diehl-Armstrong had been on a wine-tasting tour the afternoon Wells was killed.

Clark and Wick then asked about Jim Roden's body.

"Why was Roden killed?" Clark said.

"I can't answer that," Diehl-Armstrong said.[17]

In another prison interview, on July 5, 2005, Diehl-Armstrong was more forthcoming. Her personal lawyer, Larry D'Ambrosio, who also had her power of attorney, was with her, which protected Clark and Wick against any claims that she was talking to them against her will. Diehl-Armstrong asked D'Ambrosio if she needed an immunity deal before she spoke, which was odd, given that no one had accused her of doing anything wrong. D'Ambrosio assured her that she was safe to talk, and she did. Using the passive voice, she said Roden was killed over an argument in the Pizza Bomber plot, and that Rothstein was present when he was shot. She said Roden was killed because he had threatened to reveal the bank-robbery plan to another, unnamed person. At D'Ambrosio's prodding, Diehl-Armstrong also said that she gave Rothstein, at his request, two fairly new kitchen timers in June 2003. She said she saw Rothstein cut open shotgun shells—a key admission, because Clark and Wick knew that the explosive powder in the bomb had been made out of shot from shotgun shells. Diehl-Armstrong talked more, but suddenly stopped the interview.

"If I say any more, I'm dead," she said. "I've hung myself already."[18]

Diehl-Armstrong could not keep her mouth shut all the time while she was in prison. Her compulsive talking and pressured speech—symptoms of her mental illness—led to her undoing. No fewer than six female inmates reported to the FBI that Diehl-Armstrong told them in prison, repeatedly, that she was involved in the Pizza Bomber plot. One inmate, Kelly Makela, took twenty-four pages of handwritten notes of her conversations with Diehl-Armstrong. Makela said she talked constantly, and quickly. "Slow down," Makela said she once told her, "I can't write that fast."[19] Makela and the other inmates independently told Clark and Wick what they said Diehl-Armstrong told them: that she killed Roden because he had threatened to go to the police about the Pizza Bomber plot, in which he was supposed to have been a driver; that she helped measure Brian Wells's neck for the bomb; that Rothstein called in the final pizza order for Wells from a pay phone; and that the entire plot revolved around money and Diehl-Armstrong's hatred of her father for dissipating what she considered her fortune. "She didn't like her father very much," one of the inmates reported. "She felt that he had squandered her inheritance."[20] When asked what Diehl-Armstrong said was the motive behind the plot, the inmate said: "That was money. That was all about money."[21]

Clark and Wick kept interviewing Diehl-Armstrong in prison, without letting her know that they had been talking to the other inmates. In one interview, she provided Clark and Wick with information that led them to talk to someone Diehl-Armstrong had come to know well: Ken Barnes, Diehl-Armstrong's fishing buddy. Clark and Wick spent days tracking down Barnes, whom they called "the hobo" for his penchant for walking around Erie constantly, looking for drugs and money. When he was not walking around, Barnes was selling crack at his house, which, like Diehl-Armstrong and Rothstein's, was overrun with junk. Barnes never let his two dogs— Gizmo and Peanut—out of the house, and he was so desperate for money that he heated his kitchen—the only room in the house that was warm—with a space heater hooked up to a car battery. Over a series of interviews in the summer, fall, and winter of 2005, Barnes laid out the Pizza Bomber plot. He said he knew Wells because Wells would have sex in exchange for drugs at his house with the prostitute Jessica Hoopsick. That admission connected all the major players in the case: Wells knew Barnes, who fished with Roden and Diehl-Armstrong, who was close to Rothstein. Wells, from what Barnes said, was not an unwitting pizza delivery driver, but someone the other plotters knew. Wells was part of the plan.

Barnes's interviews unraveled the conspiracy. He said Diehl-Armstrong in the spring of 2003 had asked him to kill her father so that Diehl-Armstrong could get her inheritance of $1.8 million before he gave it all away to his friends and neighbors. Barnes said he wanted $250,000 to do the hit. Though she had a lot of money, Diehl-Armstrong did not have that much on hand. Barnes said he and Rothstein and Diehl-Armstrong came up with the plan to get the $250,000 in cash by robbing a bank—a branch of PNC, which had angered Diehl-Armstrong over its handling of the safe-deposit box after her mother's death, in 2000.

Brian Wells, who at first appeared to be an innocent victim, knew what was going on, Barnes said. He said Wells was in on the planning of the bank robbery but always thought that the bomb would be fake; in a practice session the day before the heist, Barnes said, Rothstein, with Diehl-Armstrong watching and measuring Wells's neck, had him try on a device that was indeed phony. That all changed on August 28, 2003. Barnes said Wells, as planned, drove to the clearing near Rothstein's house to deliver the pizzas and put on the bomb. This device, however, was heavier, and it was real. Rothstein and Diehl-Armstrong were at the scene, Barnes said, and so was Robert Pinetti, Wells's friend and coworker, who Barnes said had helped talk Wells into participating in the scheme. Also at the scene, Barnes said, was another member of the conspiracy: Floyd A. Stockton, a fifty-six-year-old fugitive on the lam from charges that he had raped a mentally disabled nineteen-year-old woman in Washington State in 2002. Stockton had been hiding out with Rothstein, one of his closest friends.

Wells tried to escape, but could not. Barnes described the scene in what would become some of the most riveting testimony in the Pizza Bomber trial. Barnes said of Brian Wells:

> When he came, he brought the pizza out that they had ordered, and he set it on the hood of Bill's van. And then Mr. Stockton came out from behind the one building that was down there, carrying this device. And he brought it up like towards Bill, and while Brian was looking at it, he got a look on his face, it was like, you know, I think at that point he realized this thing was real. Because as far as I knew, it wasn't supposed to be. It was supposed to be just a gag to . . . get the teller to give him some money. . . . He [Brian Wells] turned to run, and when he went to run, Bill fired a pistol up in the air. At the same time, Mr. Pinetti and Mr. Stockton tackled him, Brian, and got him down on the ground and was scuffling around with him a little bit. Then they come up holding him up. By then Marjorie and Bill were over there beside, Marjorie was helping hold the device while Bill was strapping it on. And he was yelling, he didn't want to be a part of it anymore. I walked over to him and punched him in the face, not real hard, but just light. And I regret doing that because back then I was just thinking of my own greed about getting the money, I really wasn't concerned for his health and safety at that point.[22]

Barnes said his only concern was that he be able to get money and leave so he could buy crack cocaine. After Wells had the bomb locked to his neck, Barnes ate pizza with Diehl-Armstrong, and the two then drove away to act as lookouts during the bank robbery, Barnes testified.[23] He said he and Diehl-Armstrong parked in a lot of an Eat'n Park restaurant, across from the road to the PNC Bank branch, and used binoculars to watch Wells drive to and from the bank in his Geo, wearing the bomb and with the cane gun and the notes. Barnes said Diehl-Armstrong saw the state police troopers stop Wells after the robbery. He said she commented: "Looks like the bank was robbed. Ha, ha."[24]

Barnes's account was consistent with information the inmates said Diehl-Armstrong had told them about the Pizza Bomber plot. More evidence from Barnes, the inmates, and others filled in details. Roden was supposed to have driven a car in the scheme and was shot because he threatened to go to the police. Pinetti overdosed on a mixture of the sedative Xanax and methadone, a combination known on the street as a "hot shot." The dose was most likely meant to be fatal, but investigators were never able to find out who gave Pinetti the drugs.[25] Wells was to have used the cane gun to intimidate the tellers if they refused to give him money. After the bank robbery,

Wells was supposed to have handed off the money to Rothstein, who was waiting near the bank. And Rothstein was supposed to have given the money to Stockton, who was to have set it aside so everyone could, as Barnes said, "divvy it up later."[26] Rothstein was the mastermind. Based on what Barnes and others said, he concocted the Pizza Bomber plot, made the bomb, and came up with the plan to send Wells on the scavenger hunt after he held up the bank. If Wells was caught before the bomb went off, he was supposed to have told the police he was delivering pizzas until he was forced to wear a bomb and a rob a bank as "bomb hostage," according to the notes he gave to the teller.[27] As a hostage, Wells would not be charged, Rothstein and the others assured him.

No black men were involved. One of the enduring mysteries in the Pizza Bomber case would be why Wells, up until his final breath, said that a group of African Americans were responsible for locking the bomb to his neck. Wells, until the very end, was complicit in telling a story that he knew was not true. Clark and Wick theorized that Wells's decision to stick to the script was made out of fear. Wells knew that Barnes, Diehl-Armstrong, and the others would be watching him, and possibly listening to him, and he was worried that they would kill him if he departed from the plan. Wells, according to this theory, also was holding on to the slight hope that the bomb really was fake, as it had been the day before. As he was on his deathbed, Wells came to the undeniable conclusion that the device was a live bomb, and that his friends had double-crossed him into wearing it. By then, Wells had no time to divert from his script—a script that he had followed because he believed his friends would kill him if he did otherwise.

As Marshall Piccinini would later tell the jury at Diehl-Armstrong's trial, the Pizza Bomber plot was too overcomplicated to succeed. Brian Wells would have had a better chance of robbing the bank by doing what most thieves did—walk into the place, demand money, and run out. Nothing was simple in the Pizza Bomber plot. Before Rothstein became a suspect, the FBI released a behavioral profile of the person the bureau believed was behind the Pizza Bomber scheme and who wrote the notes that directed Wells on his final journey. That person, the FBI said, "is a manipulator who manipulates the actions of others. He is like a puppeteer."[28] The description fit Rothstein. Clark came to believe that Rothstein used Diehl-Armstrong's demand for money to kill her father as an impetus to launch the Pizza Bomber plot. Rothstein was the architect. He crafted the framework, and Diehl-Armstrong acted as the catalyst to put that framework into use. Rothstein did not care whether Brian Wells lived or died. Clark came to believe that, by the summer of 2003, Rothstein knew he was dying of cancer, and he wanted to execute what he considered the perfect crime before his time on earth expired. Bill Rothstein was playing God on August 28, 2003, when he and Diehl-Armstrong and Barnes and Pinetti and Stockton joined together to hitch Brian Wells to the device that would kill him. Wells never had a chance.

The last time Jerry Clark and Jason Wick met with Marjorie Diehl-Armstrong was on May 10, 2006. After listening to her Miranda rights, she took a drive with them and her lawyer, Larry D'Ambrosio, to locations that were critical to the Pizza Bomber case. She said she was at the various spots on August 28, 2003. She said she was near the clearing where Wells made his final delivery, but said she did not go all the way back to the site with Rothstein, Stockton, Barnes, and Wells. She said she parked at the Eat'n Park where Barnes said they acted as lookouts. She said she might have driven on the highway—Interstate 79, which ran to the west of Erie—after Wells was killed. This admission was crucial: Barnes had said he was driving the wrong way on I-79 with Diehl-Armstrong following the bombing, which made sense, because Wells, at the direction of the notes, was to have stopped along I-79 to gather clues to deactivate the bomb. Barnes could have been driving to or from one of those spots, to place or collect the notes. The FBI had solid evidence to back up Barnes. Another motorist was unequivocal in telling the FBI that, around the time of Wells's death, he had seen a woman who looked like Diehl-Armstrong in a car that was driving the wrong way on I-79.

Diehl-Armstrong quickly ended the interview on May 10, 2006. She and D'Ambrosio had thought her cooperation would give her leverage with the FBI. Diehl-Armstrong would later criticize D'Ambrosio's advice as misguided. At the same time, her trip with Clark and Wick put her at the center of attention and allowed her to spar with special agents from the FBI and ATF. She believed she had been holding her own with them, until she realized what her talking had done. "I've put my head in the lion's mouth," she said at the end of the interview.[29]

Diehl-Armstrong soon got an enforcer to keep her quiet. She was assigned an assistant federal public defender on September 26, 2006. Though not yet indicted, she qualified for representation because she had become the target of a criminal investigation and because she lacked the assets to hire a lawyer of her own. The assistant federal public defender, Thomas Patton, her initial lawyer, was a well-regarded attorney who was a veteran of the intricacies of federal court. He immediately shut off Diehl-Armstrong from Clark and Wick. Patton reasoned that she had spoken too much already.

The Pizza Bomber investigation proceeded. Clark and Wick gathered additional evidence. Jessica Hoopsick, the prostitute, was now cooperating and confirmed the link between her and Wells and Barnes. The FBI shortly after Wells's death had determined that the call for the pizza delivery had come from a particular pay phone in a kiosk outside a gas station not far from Rothstein's house. But the FBI had been unsure who had made the call. Clark and Wick got a statement from a UPS driver who said he saw Rothstein using the phone at the same time Wells received his final pizza delivery order on August 28, 2003. The UPS driver, whose family had lived near Rothstein, had recognized Rothstein at the phone kiosk and said a woman was standing next to him as he made the call. He said he recognized the woman as Marjorie Diehl-Armstrong.[30]

The federal grand jury indictments against Diehl-Armstrong and Ken Barnes were unsealed on July 11, 2007. The two were both accused in Wells's death. Diehl-Armstrong had become very much alone among the Fractured Intellectuals. Rothstein was dead. His friend Floyd Stockton had agreed to cooperate with the United States Attorney's Office against Diehl-Armstrong and Barnes in exchange for immunity. Barnes had been cooperating with the FBI as well. He would be expected to testify against Diehl-Armstrong at trial, in exchange for a plea deal. Diehl-Armstrong seemed to have little room to maneuver. When she said, of her life and her legal plight, "I'm the pickle in the middle with hell on all sides," she was correct.[31] She called her indictment "the worst thing that happened in American history."[32]

Patton, her lawyer, moved quickly to make sure that she continued to keep her mouth shut. On July 12, 2007, he went to court with an unusual request. He asked a federal magistrate judge to prohibit Clark and Wick from driving Diehl-Armstrong from the state prison at Muncy to Erie for her arraignment. Patton said Diehl-Armstrong's mental condition and uncontrollable urge to speak meant that she would most likely jabber on and on during the four-and-a-half-hour car ride. Who knew what she might say?

"She is mentally ill, has been diagnosed with bipolar disorder," Patton told United States Magistrate Judge Susan Paradise Baxter. "She is almost constantly in a manic state. She is on no psychotropic medications. She cannot control herself when she's in the manic state about speaking."[33]

Diehl-Armstrong ended up waiving her right to be present at her arraignment, so she did not make the trip from Muncy to Erie. Patton nonetheless had scored a minor victory in the earliest stage of the case. His petition to the court, just a day after Diehl-Armstrong's indictment was made public, also signaled how the defense was going to attack the government's evidence in the long term. Diehl-Armstrong's mental illness would be at the forefront of yet another homicide case.

Far from the courtroom, Harold Diehl put in everyday language what Patton had set forth in legal terms about his daughter's mental state.

"She'd have a tendency to do anything that's possible because I think her mind is a little goofed up," Diehl, then eighty-eight years old, said when asked about the newly unsealed indictment. "I don't think she's completely sane."[34]

The indictment alleged that the Pizza Bomber plot included Diehl-Armstrong's solicitation of Barnes to kill Harold Diehl for what Diehl-Armstrong said was her inheritance. Diehl, interviewed on the front porch swing of his house, was asked about whether he believed that his daughter had put a hit on him.

"I wouldn't doubt that," he said. "I heard that years ago and I believe it. Don't forget: Her mind is, in my estimation, not the mind of a stable person."[35]

"I've been told she's wanted to kill me before," Harold Diehl also said. "She figured if she killed me . . . she'd have this house—if I got a million dollars, she'd get it. She's got a demented mind. If she wanted a million dollars, she wouldn't ask me for it. She'd try to kill me.

"She didn't realize I could give it to the next-door neighbor and not her."[36]

Psyche on Trial

Marjorie Diehl-Armstrong's Final Verdict

$\mathscr{R}$obert L. Sadoff had returned. Twenty-three years after the forensic psychiatrist first examined Marjorie Diehl in the Bob Thomas case, a defense lawyer called upon him once more, this time to offer his professional opinion on whether Marjorie Diehl-Armstrong was mentally competent to stand trial in the Pizza Bomber case. Sadoff's involvement with Diehl-Armstrong over so many years, and in two homicide cases, underscored how deeply ingrained her patterns of dysfunction had become. Yet again, according to Sadoff's analysis, was Diehl-Armstrong displaying manic-depressive behavior. And yet again, Sadoff said, was that behavior preventing her from assisting in her defense. Her psyche had changed little. She still talked incessantly. She still considered herself smarter than anyone else, including her lawyer; she still portrayed herself as a victim; and, in Sadoff's view, she still suffered from bipolar disorder and was out of control, particularly with no medication. In the Pizza Bomber case, Sadoff found, Diehl-Armstrong's delusions had elevated to a new level. In her previous homicide cases, she at least understood that the charges were simply not going to go away. In the Pizza Bomber case, the most serious case against her, Diehl-Armstrong believed that the prosecution should just vanish.

"When I asked Marjorie what she wants, she states that she wants to go to court and wants this whole case to be discharged, because she didn't do anything wrong," Sadoff wrote to Thomas Patton, Diehl-Armstrong's initial lawyer in the Pizza Bomber case, on January 15, 2008. "She wants to get it over with and be put on parole because, she says, she has been a good prisoner and has done her time."[1]

Sadoff said Diehl-Armstrong was incompetent to stand trial. His opinion, though unsurprising, given his depth of knowledge of Diehl-Armstrong, triggered a legal fight whose intensity was unlike that of any other courtroom dispute over Diehl-Armstrong's mental health. She was now indicted in an internationally known criminal case of unprecedented complexity and horror, and she was in federal court, where the United States Attorney's Office and the FBI could rely on the government's unlimited resources to prove their points. The government put everything about Marjorie Diehl-Armstrong under review in the Pizza Bomber case as it raised the bedrock question. It was a question that psychologists and psychiatrists, using time-tested theories and modern tools of behavioral analysis, such as the *Diagnostic and Statistical Manual of Mental Disorders*, had tried to answer since Marjorie Diehl-Armstrong was in her early twenties: Was she really mentally ill? And why?

Diehl-Armstrong and her lawyers never raised the insanity defense in the Pizza Bomber case, just as they had never pursued it in her previous homicide cases. The focus, once again, was on whether Diehl-Armstrong was competent to stand trial. And, once again, the debate over competency centered on one issue: not whether Diehl-Armstrong was capable of understanding the legal process, which she was, but whether she was able to assist in her defense—specifically, by being able to cooperate with Patton, her lawyer. That question was nothing new to anyone who had followed Diehl-Armstrong's tortured journeys through the criminal justice system. In each case, she fought with the lawyers who initially handled her case, claiming that they were incompetent and unworthy of representing her. She got her way in the Bob Thomas case, when her parents paid $60,000 to lawyer Leonard G. Ambrose III and his cocounsel, Michelle Hawk, to take over the defense from two public defenders; and Diehl-Armstrong got her way in the Jim Roden case, when she was able to pay a private lawyer, John Moore, $41,000 to represent her instead of the two public defenders who initially handled that case—two lawyers that Diehl-Armstrong had called "public pretenders." Moore's fee was paid out of the approximately $75,000 that Diehl-Armstrong had given to Bill Rothstein to help get rid of Roden's body. Once that cash was recovered, a judge distributed it to a number of parties, including the Erie police, to reimburse the city for overtime and costs of cleaning up Diehl-Armstrong's house on East Seventh Street. Moore got what was left over—a substantial amount of money.[2]

Diehl-Armstrong had no stacks of cash to pay a lawyer in the Pizza Bomber case; and, unlike in the previous cases, her father was not going to come to her financial rescue. She had to make do with whatever lawyer the federal government gave her. The situation galled her and her inflated sense of self, but it also gave her Tom Patton, a fine defense attorney who was unafraid of going up against the United States Attorney's Office from the beginning of the case. He fought to have Jerry Clark and Jason Wick prohibited from driving Diehl-Armstrong from the state prison at Muncy to Erie. A shrewd move, but one that Diehl-Armstrong failed to appreciate. Almost from the time she met Patton, she said she could not stand him and would not cooperate with him.

She refused to listen to Patton, even when he told her to stop using the prison telephone to call the *Erie Times-News* to talk about the Pizza Bomber case. She had started making daily calls—sometimes two or three times a day—to reporter Ed Palattella on November 7, 2007, four months after her indictment. She called in response to a letter Palattella wrote to her. Though Diehl-Armstrong never revealed incriminating details during the telephone calls—she always insisted she was innocent—she discussed evidence and trial strategy. The FBI and United States Attorney's Office listened to recordings of the phone calls, as Diehl-Armstrong knew they would. A recorded message at the start of each call from prison told the participants they were being taped. Diehl-Armstrong also knew the FBI and United States Attorney's Office were allowed to listen, because no attorney-client privilege was involved. But Diehl-Armstrong made the calls, again and again, and she talked nonstop, often complaining about Patton.

"I want someone who has a little experience," she said to Palattella in their first telephone conversation, in which she talked without a break for thirteen minutes and nine seconds. "I am a thousand percent innocent. I am trying to get extricated from this maze. I am trying to see daylight. My time is running out here. This is a very high-profile case. I think someone should do it for the publicity. I want someone who really cares for this case."[3]

At the end of the conversation, which concluded only because of prison-imposed time limits for phone calls, Diehl-Armstrong sought to clear up what she thought was a misconception about her past.

"I am not a man hater at all," she said.[4]

In the early phone conversations, Diehl-Armstrong also clarified what would be her defense. She acknowledged that she was at incriminating places on August 28, 2003, the day Wells was killed, such as with Bill Rothstein when he called in the pizza order from the pay phone. But she said she would argue that she had no knowledge of the plot and that a jealous Rothstein manipulated her into being at the spots. She said Rothstein was angry with her because she refused his sexual advances. Diehl-Armstrong, the master manipulator, was admitting to getting played herself. Her "bad company" defense was taking shape. "I am going to get framed for life," she said.[5]

"Rothstein had me around him to make it look like I was involved in the Wells case," she said. "Rothstein was very intelligent. What Rothstein did: If he couldn't have me, no one could."[6]

At Patton's request, Sadoff interviewed Diehl-Armstrong at the state prison at Muncy for three hours on June 19, 2007, and another three hours on October 22, 2007. Patton asked Sadoff to evalaute Diehl-Armstrong's competence for trial. Sadoff, in his letter of January 15, 2008, said Diehl-Armstrong was incompetent—because of her inability to cooperate with Patton, a situation that Sadoff attributed to Diehl-Armstrong's bipolar disorder and paranoia. Sadoff wrote:

> Her paranoid ideation is focused sometimes on her attorney, whom she does not trust and cannot work with. She does not follow his instructions, and she often takes matters into her own hands, especially by contacting the newspapers against her attorney's advice.
> She is not able to focus in a rational manner when working with her attorney, a dyadic relationship that I have observed personally. She is not taking medication, and her manic symptoms are quite apparent. . . . As long as she continues to be manic and depressed, she does not think rationally and cannot work in a rational manner with her attorney in order to prepare a rational defense. Her symptoms of bipolar disorder go back many, many years, even to the time I saw her in 1985.[7]

After decades of psychiatric evaluations of Marjorie Diehl-Armstrong, the pattern diverged on April 15, 2008. The unprecedented finding came in a report from William J. Ryan, PhD, a forensic psychologist at the Metropolitan Correctional Center in New York City. In response to Sadoff's letter about Diehl-Armstrong's competency, the judge in the Pizza Bomber case, Sean J. McLaughlin, on February 11, 2008, ordered Diehl-Armstrong to undergo a mental health exam to determine her competency. Diehl-Armstrong was flown from the state prison at Muncy to the Metropolitan Correctional Center, on the southeastern tip of Manhattan, just north of the ramps to the Brooklyn Bridge. She arrived on March 5, 2008. Ryan examined her the next day, and on seven other days, through April 10, 2008. In his report, filed five days later, he found that Diehl-Armstrong suffered not from bipolar disorder, but from posttraumatic stress disorder and a personality order not otherwise specified, with borderline paranoid and narcissistic traits.[8] Marshall Piccinini, the assistant United States attorney on the case, characterized the diagnosis as "personality disorder or bipolar disorder in remission."[9] Either way, the *Diagnostic and Statistical Manual of Mental Disorders* does not consider a personality disorder a serious mental illness, and, under federal law, "a personality disorder is not a sufficient mental illness to render an individual incompetent."[10] Ryan concluded that, despite what had been the diagnosis of ten psychologists and psychiatrists since the early 1980s, Diehl-Armstrong was not bipolar. Using the taxonomy of the *DSM-IV-TR*, Ryan wrote of his diagnostic impressions of Diehl-Armstrong:

> Axis I: Post-traumatic stress disorder, due to her reported "long history of physical abuse"; ruled out history of bipolar I disorder, severe without psychotic features, most recent episode hypomanic.
>
> Axis II: Personality disorder not otherwise specified (NOS), with borderline paranoid narcissistic traits.
>
> Axis III: Medical problems: glaucoma, hypothyroidism, and hypertension.
>
> Axis IV: Current psychological stressors: recent history of arrest and incarceration.
>
> Axis V: Global Assessment of Functioning—on the scale from 1 to 100—was listed as a 60, due to unstable mood and thought process.[11]

Ryan's analysis focused on Diehl-Armstrong's history of manipulation. He found that Diehl-Armstrong had been diagnosed as bipolar not because she truly suffered from manic-depression, but because she had tricked and worn down mental health professionals into making that determination. As anyone knew who had listened to Diehl-Armstrong, the temptation was just to give her what she wanted so she would go away. "Ms. Armstrong has unscrupulous methods when dealing with others," Ryan wrote in his report, in which he detailed how she had interacted with the mental health evaluators at the Metropolitan Correctional Center. "She demonstrated single-mindedness as she made one statement repeatedly and refused to answer any other questions. She would often lie and try to bully the evaluator."[12] Ryan wrote that Diehl-Armstrong told the evaluator she had been trying to get disability benefits when her mental health came up for review before. Ryan wrote that Diehl-Armstrong often would keep talking about the same issue. "After multiple interviews," Ryan wrote, "it became clear this is Ms. Armstrong's way of dealing with someone she views as an adversary. Her manner of talking in circles appeared to be her way of 'hammering a point home.'"[13]

The contention that Diehl-Armstrong feigned mental illness to get disability benefits was a prominent theme not only in Ryan's report. Piccinini, amplifying Ryan's conclusions, made the same argument before Judge

McLaughlin at a competency hearing for Diehl-Armstrong in United States District Court in Erie in May 2008. Piccinini said Diehl-Armstrong suffered only from a personality disorder and was competent for trial. Piccinini referred to the letter that Diehl wrote to one of her psychiatrists, Paul Francis, in the early 1980s, when she had been unable to get disability benefits: "Will you help me by documenting as best you can, that I have a 'permanent disability' psychologically?" Piccinini, as Ryan did, acknowledged that Diehl did win Social Security benefits in 1984, based on the finding that she was manic depressive. Piccinini questioned whether that initial landmark diagnosis was accurate; in doing so, Piccinini sought to undermine Diehl-Armstrong's entire mental health history. Diehl-Armstrong's mental health background, Piccinini wrote, "is accordingly tainted by Ms. Diehl's early attempts to over-inflate the degree of her mental illness to support her efforts to obtain Social Security disability benefits."[14]

Piccinini and Ryan looked for supporting evidence that Diehl-Armstrong was a malingerer and was only portraying herself as mentally ill. Piccinini had an investigator interview guards and other officials at the state prison at Muncy. "She is crazy like a fox and has a reason behind everything she says," a lieutenant at the prison said.[15] A guard reported that his experiences with Diehl-Armstrong revealed that she was "not crazy, just nasty."[16]

That statement summarized the government's position regarding Diehl-Armstrong's competence for trial. Using Ryan's report as his main piece of evidence, Piccinini argued that Diehl-Armstrong was difficult to get along with because she was arrogant and unpleasant, not because she was mentally ill. No one denied that Diehl-Armstrong refused to cooperate with Tom Patton; but for Piccinini, the lack of cooperation had nothing to do with Diehl-Armstrong being bipolar and everything to do with her being a person who was obstreperous, self-centered, and mean to the extreme—a person who had a personality disorder with narcissistic traits, but who was not mentally ill.

Piccinini's theory, while raised in the context of competency, had deep ramifications; if true, the theory meant that Diehl-Armstrong's behavior was more sinister than what anyone had previously imagined. Her mental illness, while it did nothing to excuse her violent behavior, at least provided some explanation for it: Diehl-Armstrong was a serial killer partly because illness had invaded her mind. If Marjorie Diehl-Armstrong were not mentally ill, her behavior was even more frightening. With no bipolar disorder, with no manic-depression, she was a killer solely because she wanted to be. She was evil as a matter of choice. For Patton, that scenario was impossible, based on the consistent findings of the ten psychologists and psychiatrists—excluding

Ryan—who had examined Diehl-Armstrong over thirty years and found that she was severely mentally ill.

"All these prior mental health experts are wrong?" Patton said at the competency hearing. "My client is not difficult because she is just a nasty person. She is difficult because she is mentally ill."[17]

The competency hearing spanned May 21–22, 2008. The main witnesses were Ryan for the government and Sadoff for the defense. Diehl-Armstrong was flown back from New York City for the hearing and did not testify, though what she said and did at the hearing was of great importance, especially her antics during the hearing's first day of testimony, which lasted nine hours. Diehl-Armstrong maintained that she was competent, which put her in conflict with Patton, who was arguing that she was incompetent. As she had done before with so many of her lawyers, Diehl-Armstrong fought with Patton in court and spoke up frequently. "Liar, liar!" she screamed at one point, referring to testimony that she had given investigators statements that linked her to the Pizza Bomber case.[18] "They are corrupt!" she shouted at Piccinini and agents Jerry Clark and Jason Wick.[19] To no one in particular, she declared, "I am innocent. Period."[20] And, when the testimony focused on her previous homicide cases, in which the victims were Bob Thomas and Jim Roden, Diehl-Armstrong called out "self-defense."[21]

Diehl-Armstrong had planned to make a scene, if doing so would help her cause. "Who knows?" she said before the hearing. "I'll do whatever I want. If I feel it necessary, I will create a disturbance. If the judge is not acting right, I don't care. I'm not going to sit there for my hanging like a Girl Scout."[22]

During much of the hearing, however, she was also calm. Even when disruptive, she was still in control, which impressed Ryan. He said Diehl-Armstrong during the hearing displayed no signs of hypomania or bipolar disorder. "I see nothing remotely suggesting hypomania," Ryan said. "There is nothing. She looks like she has a personality disorder and is competent to stand trial."[23] He described Diehl-Armstrong's mental issues as "characterogical," or related to personality traits, rather than symptomatic of a mental illness. He called Diehl-Armstrong a "conversational bully" who stopped attacking him with words once he told her he was going to find her competent, as she insisted she was; then, Ryan testified, "she seemed to me a different person. She was perfect."[24]

Patton countered with Sadoff, who reached back thirty years to retrieve the first evidence that Diehl-Armstrong was bipolar and, without medication, incompetent. He referred to the condition of her house in the Bob Thomas case, with all the rotting surplus butter and cheese, and referred to the condition of her house in the Jim Roden case, which was not much better. Sadoff said he could not discount that evidence nor could he disregard the findings of all the others who had examined Diehl-Armstrong over her lifetime and found her to be bipolar. In some respects, Sadoff's answers in federal court in Erie in May 2008 resembled those he had given in Erie County Court in May 1988, during Diehl's competency hearing in the Thomas case. Sadoff again acknowledged that psychiatry, though not an exact science, nonetheless is grounded in scientific tenets, such as observation. In Diehl-Armstrong's case, Sadoff testified before Judge McLaughlin, if ten people "from different places observe that, and I observe similar things, then to me it is a no-brainer," referring to the diagnosis of bipolar disorder. "She is bipolar. She is extremely bright. But that doesn't take away from that fact that she is bipolar."[25] Of the condition of Diehl-Armstrong's houses, he said, "It is the breakdown of the personality that leads to the chaos we see."[26] Even Ryan agreed, as McLaughlin later noted, that Diehl-Armstrong's extreme hoarding in her houses "is not the type of behavior that one would expect from a person suffering from only a personality disorder and is more consistent with major mental illness."[27]

During the hearing's second day, Patton built on Sadoff's comments with the testimony of Leonard Ambrose, who had represented Diehl-Armstrong in the Thomas case. Mainly because of Diehl-Armstrong's endless talking and belligerent behavior, Ambrose said, the Thomas case, for him, was "the case from hell."[28] He said Diehl-Armstrong needed medication.

Diehl-Armstrong was unimpressed. At the end of the first day of testimony, she spoke of Ryan and Sadoff in yet another telephone interview with Palattella from prison. "I don't think either of them really explained me," she said. "But some of what they both said was true."[29] She also said that a psychic had recently communicated with her and told her she was innocent in the Pizza Bomber case. "She is right on the money," Diehl-Armstrong said.[30]

Several days after the hearing, Diehl-Armstrong remained defiant as she stewed over what Ambrose, Sadoff, Ryan, and others had said about her in court. "I'm not that loony," she said. "I did not have a house full of garbage. OK, it got a little confusing with Rothstein around and Roden's body upstairs."[31] Then she repeated what had become something of a mantra: "I am not crazy. I am damn not crazy."[32]

Judge McLaughlin's ruling on Diehl-Armstrong's competency, issued July 29, 2008, was foremost a legal document. Yet the fifty-nine-page decision, with its detailed and sweeping analysis of Diehl-Armstrong's past, also represented the most comprehensive report on her mental health to date. McLaughlin found Diehl-Armstrong incompetent for trial and in need of more mental health therapy before he would again evaluate her mental state. Just as importantly, McLaughlin found that Diehl-Armstrong was indeed mentally ill, suffering from bipolar disorder, and that she had responded to some medications in the past, such as Geodon. McLaughlin relied heavily on Sadoff's analysis, and he focused on Diehl-Armstrong's hoarding as evidence of her psychotic thinking and irrational behavior—behavior that McLaughlin said often prevented her from cooperating with Patton. McLaughlin said Diehl-Armstrong suffered from a personality disorder, but also bipolar disorder.

One of Diehl-Armstrong's dominant personality traits, McLaughlin wrote, was her tendency to manipulate others. Yet he said this behavior did not mean that Diehl-Armstrong was feigning mental illness, nor did it mean that her first diagnosis of manic-depression, in the course of seeking disability benefits, was fraudulent. McLaughlin wrote:

> The evidence does indeed suggest that the Defendant engaged in an overt attempt in the early 1980s to highlight her mental illness as a means of obtaining disability benefits. However, it does not follow, and this Court does not believe, that the Defendant's treating physicians thereby ceded to her demands and diagnosed bipolar disorder without any legitimate basis. Similarly, while it may have been to the Defendant's legal advantage to highlight her mental illness as part of her defense in the Robert Thomas case, that fact does not necessarily undermine the validity of her bipolar diagnosis. . . . In short, Dr. Ryan's diagnosis can only be accepted as accurate by concluding that every other clinician who has diagnosed the defendant with bipolar disorder did so in error. I do not find the record supports that conclusion."[33]

McLaughlin found that Diehl-Armstrong's bipolar disorder was behind the behavior that made her so hostile to Patton and thus incompetent to stand trial. Diehl-Armstrong responded to the ruling by saying she would demand a conference with McLaughlin and that she would eventually be declared competent, but would refuse to take medication. She insisted on her innocence in her new home: the 1,466-inmate women's Federal Medical Center-Carswell, Texas, in Fort Worth, where she was sent to undergo further examinations.

"Everybody in here is guilty," she said, "except me."[34]

Back in Erie, the case against Diehl-Armstrong was tightening. Diehl-Armstrong still maintained that Rothstein framed her, and made her be at certain incriminating places as the Pizza Bomber plot unfolded. But the United States Attorney's Office had gained a valuable witness to debunk that theory and prove Diehl-Armstrong's firsthand knowledge and participation. On September 3, 2008, Ken Barnes, now fifty-four years old and in declining health from kidney problems, pleaded guilty to two of the three charges against him—conspiracy to commit armed bank robbery and aiding and abetting the use of a destructive device in a crime of violence. As part of the plea bargain, Barnes agreed to testify against Diehl-Armstrong at trial, and Piccinini dropped the most serious charge against Barnes, aiding and abetting an armed bank robbery, which would have carried a life sentence because Brian Wells had been killed during the heist. Barnes still faced a sentence of thirty-five years to life, which meant that he was all but certain to die in federal prison.

McLaughlin sentenced Barnes on December 3, 2008. He gave him forty-five years. Barnes would be incarcerated until he was one hundred years old. Barnes apologized to members of Brian Wells's family, who were in the courtroom. "What happened to him," he said, referring to Wells, "was something that was not supposed to happen."[35] Piccinini and McLaughlin had little sympathy for Barnes. Piccinini said Barnes had participated "in one of the most bizarre criminal acts we have ever seen."[36] McLaughlin characterized Barnes as depraved. "The callousness and complete lack of regard for human life exhibited by this defendant is, in a word, chilling," he said. "This case represents the unfortunate combination of the incredibly bizarre and the sadly tragic."[37]

A few days after Barnes's plea of guilty, McLaughlin issued a ruling on a second competency hearing for Diehl-Armstrong partially based on the findings of the professionals who had examined her over four months at the Federal Medical Center-Carswell. This time, McLaughlin ruled Diehl-Armstrong competent to stand trial. He issued his sixty-four-page decision on September 8, 2009. One of the key differences in their reports, as opposed to the findings of William Ryan, was that Diehl-Armstrong indeed suffered from a bipolar disorder, which, under the law, qualified as a mental illness that could render a defendant incompetent for trial. The lead examiner at Carswell, Leslie Powers, PhD, a forensic psychologist, offered this diagnosis, following the *DSM-IV-TR*:

> Axis I: Bipolar I disorder, most recent episode hypomanic (by history).
> Axis II: Personality disorder not otherwise specified (NOS), with borderline paranoid and narcissistic traits.
> Axis III: Hypothyroidism and glaucoma.

Axis IV: Current psychological stressors: legal problems, lack of social support.

Axis V: Global Assessment of Functioning—on the scale from 1 to 100—was listed as a 60.[38]

Though Powers found Diehl-Armstrong suffered from bipolar disorder, she also concluded that Diehl-Armstrong, who remained unmedicated, "did not satisfy the criteria for a hypomanic or depressive episode during the period of the evaluation."[39] Diehl-Armstrong's bipolar disorder, according to that analysis, was in remission. And Powers, in a part of her report that McLaughlin cited, found that Diehl-Armstrong's behavioral problems, such as pressured speech and irritable mood—"which, in the past, had been reported as manifestations of [her] mania"—were better explained "as symptoms of [her] personality disorder."[40]

McLaughlin acknowledged the findings of Sadoff and others, who continued to maintain that Diehl-Armstrong was incompetent for trial. One expert for the defense in the second competency evaluation, Frank Dattilio, a forensic psychologist, called Diehl-Armstrong "one of the most complex, difficult types of personalities that I've seen in my thirty years of experience."[41] But McLaughlin also found that, since the first competency hearing in the Pizza Bomber case, Diehl-Armstrong had changed, and that her current mental state was stable enough for her to be competent and cooperate with her lawyer. While Diehl-Armstrong was at the federal prison at Carswell, McLaughlin wrote, her "bipolar disorder was in a state of quiescence . . . and that the symptoms during that time did not suggest the presence of any mania."[42]

McLaughlin wrote that he agreed with Sadoff, who said Diehl-Armstrong's "mental profile is complex and that her competency involves a degree of fluidity."[43] McLaughlin also wrote:

> I continue to credit past medical evidence suggesting that stress, when severe enough, may cause the Defendant to lose a degree of control over her mental state. For present purposes, however, I find by a preponderance of evidence that the Defendant has recovered to such an extent that she is able to understand the nature and consequences of the proceedings against her and to assist properly in her own defense.[44]

To evaluate Diehl-Armstrong's relationship with Tom Patton, her lawyer, McLaughlin noted how Diehl-Armstrong acted in court, during the second competency hearing on April 27, 2009. McLaughlin several times had to tell Diehl-Armstrong to calm down; at one point, when Powers was testifying, Diehl-Armstrong shouted from the defense table: "I am done with her. I don't care what she says."[45] Though Diehl-Armstrong's outburst was rude, McLaughlin found that it was grounded in reason: Diehl-Armstrong was upset about a genuine misstatement in Powers's testimony. McLaughlin also noticed how Diehl-Armstrong acted when he told the deputy United States marshals in the courtroom, "One more outburst, take her out in the holding cell."[46] Diehl-Armstrong was quiet after that. McLaughlin concluded that Diehl-Armstrong knew what was happening in court, as her anger at Powers showed, and could control her behavior when she had to, as she showed when she calmed down after hearing the threat that she would go to the holding cell. Her fights with Patton, McLaughlin wrote, were more about Diehl-Armstrong's single-mindedness than the result of delusional behavior. Diehl-Armstrong's desired defense strategy might make no sense, but that did not mean she was out of her mind. Diehl-Armstrong's "refusal to heed the advice of her lawyer may be unwise in the extreme," he wrote, "but it does not necessarily demonstrate an inability to consult with her lawyer with a reasonable degree of rational understanding."[47]

McLaughlin's handling of Diehl-Armstrong's competency was based on common sense as much as it was on psychiatric findings. Because Diehl-Armstrong clearly had mental problems, McLaughlin would have risked getting overturned on appeal had he ruled her competent right away, especially considering her lengthy psychiatric history. By ruling her competent after a second evaluation and hearing, McLaughlin showed that he had been particularly careful in gauging Diehl-Armstrong's mental state. The defense would have a hard time convincing an appeals court that McLaughlin had acted rashly. The judge subsequently displayed that same type of caution at a hearing on September 17, 2009, when he let Diehl-Armstrong fire Tom Patton. McLaughlin regarded Patton highly, but forcing Diehl-Armstrong to continue to use him as her lawyer, despite her hostility, would have given the defense a legitimate issue on appeal. McLaughlin cited the defendant's "deep-seated distrust and antipathy" in removing Patton, whom he called "one of the pre-eminent defense attorneys in the area."[48] He said Patton had become "a distinct psychological stressor" for Diehl-Armstrong.[49] He warned Diehl-Armstrong that she would not get another chance to pick a lawyer. He said she was entitled to a court-appointed lawyer but was not guaranteed a lawyer of her choice.

Diehl-Armstrong moved little from her chair at the defense table as Patton, now officially fired, got up to leave.

"Good luck, Marge," he said as he walked away.[50]

Diehl-Armstrong liked her new court-appointed lawyer, at first. He was Douglas Sughrue, an experienced attorney from Pittsburgh. She initially praised the choice, saying it fit her horoscope. She enjoyed the attention as Sughrue brought her catalogs in prison to help pick her dress for trial, which McLaughlin scheduled for August 2010. She liked Coldwater Creek's apparel the best. Soon, though, as had been the case with most of Diehl-Armstrong's relationships with men, she turned on Sughrue and said he was incompetent. She said she didn't like his courtroom style—not aggressive enough—the way he looked, and even his name: "Doug Screw-you," was how she repeatedly referred to him in her phone calls with Palattella. Diehl-Armstrong wanted to fire Sughrue, but McLaughlin refused. "The pattern which emerges," he said at a hearing, "is one where the defendant is never satisfied with counsel, whoever it might be, because she tends to view herself as smarter and more informed than anyone else."

The remark upset Diehl-Armstrong.

"I don't want to hear this!" she shouted.[51]

Diehl-Armstrong's relationship with Sughrue worsened, but McLaughlin refused to let her fire him.

"Leave me the fuck alone!" she once shouted at Sughrue in court.[52]

She questioned his trial strategy by showcasing her knowledge of a memorable German defeat in the Second World War.

"I'm tanking like the Bismarck," she said.[53]

And on another day, with the jurors out of the courtroom, she berated Sughrue, who kept a calm demeanor and responded to her tongue lashings with a wry smile.

"I want rid of you," she told him. "You make me sick."[54]

Hearing that remark, McLaughlin asked her if she wanted to leave the courtroom. She said she did.

"This is a kangaroo court," she shouted as the marshals led her to a holding cell. "I am being railroaded."[55]

Diehl-Armstrong had other problems. She was diagnosed with cancer. She had a malignant lump removed from her neck in mid-March 2010. The question became whether the cancer, which originated in her breast and spread to her lymph nodes, was terminal. Piccinini, the prosecutor, said he would not take the case to trial if Diehl-Armstrong's death was imminent. The government and the defense waited on a second opinion, which would clarify Diehl-Armstrong's life expectancy. The situation was not unlike what had happened with Diehl-Armstrong's competency. The United States Attorney's Office wanted her found competent so she could stand trial, and the United States Attorney's Office intended to prosecute Diehl-Armstrong if she was expected to live a substantial amount of time. Diehl-Armstrong said she was taking a practical approach to the latest development in her case.

"I have fucking cancer somewhere," she told Palattella. "We are all terminal in this world. It's not like it makes me a bad person. We are all going to die sometime; death is part of life. But I'm not ashamed. A lot of people get cancer. I just happen to be one. It's out of my control."[56]

She said she was now focused on her health, rather than the Pizza Bomber case, "which is crazy, because before I thought about it all the time."[57] She said, no matter what happened with the cancer, she would never admit to being part of the plot that ended in Brian Wells's death. In that regard, she was like Bill Rothstein and Wells, who, on their deathbeds, had refused to reveal the truth.

"I'm telling you that if I died today, I would never confess that," she said. "I'm not going to say I did something that I didn't do. This case is killing me."[58]

"Don't fear the reaper," she also said, referring to the Blue Öyster Cult hit from 1976. "That is my favorite song."[59]

The second opinion came in August 2010. Diehl-Armstrong had cancer of the glands—adenocarcinoma—that originated in a breast. Magee Women's Hospital in Pittsburgh determined that Diehl-Armstrong, sixty-one years old, had three to seven years to live. McLaughlin agreed that such a life expectancy was adequate. He set her trial for October 2010. Diehl-Armstrong said she was looking forward to testifying. She said she rejected a plea deal that would have sent her to prison for another five years, after she finished the seven to twenty years she was still serving for Jim Roden's death.

"I'll tell them not only to wipe their ass with it," she said of the plea offer, "but to shove it up their ass."[60]

At this point, Diehl-Armstrong had nothing to lose. Whether her life expectancy was three years or seven years, she was dying.

"I take one day a time," she once said. "I hope for the best and expect the worst. We are all ashes: ashes to ashes and dust to dust."[61]

Diehl-Armstrong was headed to court after more than a year of some of the most thorough mental examinations she had ever experienced. And yet, like her cancer, her mental illness was a condition without a cure, a disease with no known origin. William Ryan, like so many psychologists and psychiatrists before him, noted Diehl-Armstrong's hostility toward her parents and her claims of abuse, all of which provided him enough evidence to diagnose Diehl-Armstrong with posttraumatic stress disorder.

But pinpointing the roots of her mental dysfunction remained an elusive effort. Whether anyone could truly penetrate Diehl-Armstrong's mind was an open question, just as the scientific nature of psychiatry remained open to debate, even in the centuries following the work of Philippe Pinel, Benjamin Rush, Emil Kraepelin, and other founders of modern psychiatry. Marjorie Diehl-Armstrong remained a puzzle of conflicting thoughts and ideas. She was undeniably erudite. Not only did she compare herself to Lincoln and Churchill and other historical figures; she also spoke fluently about literature and the arts. The poet Sylvia Plath could be a subject in one conversation[62] and Elisabeth Kübler-Ross and her five stages of grief in another.[63] To boost her spirits in prison, to help her realize that everyone had a purpose in life, she said she got inspiration from the final line of John Milton's poem, "On His Blindness": "They also serve who only stand and wait."[64] When she spoke of the intricacies of her father's estate, which she comprehended better than any estate lawyer, Diehl-Armstrong used an allusion that made perfect literary sense. She said the case was like the endless probate fight in Charles Dickens's *Bleak House.*[65]

Diehl-Armstrong's mental illness, whatever its cause, had prevented her from experiencing a promising and fulfilling life of music and academics. She could be charming and sympathetic; however, she always displayed that narcissism, that grandiosity, that exaggerated sense of importance that made her come across as mostly arrogant and condescending. Her attitude made any sympathy for her hard to maintain. Her unbridled egotism, based on what she told the psychiatrists and psychologists, most likely originated with her mother, who saw her only daughter as a precious child worthy of only the best. Somehow—whether through abuse or due to some other cause—Diehl-Armstrong's sense of self-esteem became so oversized as to be dysfunctional. Her anorexia showed how her desire to become perfect eroded her mental health to the point that she was starving herself. Perhaps she would have turned out differently if she had received mental health treatment at that moment, at the fragile point when she matured from a girl to a troubled young woman. From then on, she seemed to pursue her dreams of perfection and self-entitlement in perverse ways, such as by hoarding rotting food or killing men she once considered ideal but soon found to be tiresome, moronic, and abusive. She thought herself gorgeous and witty, but gravitated mainly toward abusive men, maybe because they were the only kind of men who would live with her or maybe because she believed, despite her outward confidence, that she could do no better. When reality failed to deliver on her expectations, she turned to the occult—to astrology, horoscopes, and psychics—to reaffirm that she was bound for the greatness she deserved. She even said she had supernatural powers to put a spell on those who would thwart her and that those she had hexed had "dropped over dead."[66]

Judging from all the mental health analyses, for Marjorie Diehl-Armstrong, everything was about her. She thought herself special, but she was also insecure; she would declare that beauty was superficial, but then rail against how she looked in a mug shot. Her unbridled narcissism spawned her greed, which produced, in the view of the United States Attorney's Office, a desire for money so extreme that she would stop at nothing to satiate it, even participating in a conspiracy in which the ultimate target was her elderly father—a conspiracy in which a man was killed by a bomb locked to his neck. As Marshall Piccinini would remark at Diehl-Armstrong's sentencing, she presented the unique combination of mental illness and evil.

As for Diehl-Armstrong, she never stopped seeing herself as the victim. "I am fully aware of my flaws," she once said. "I am fully aware of my crazy parents. One of my biggest flaws is I am a little bit gullible. I was an only child, and lived an isolated life. I lived in my mind."[67] She said the men she had killed deserved their fate and that she was no serial killer. Yet, in response to her indictment in the Pizza Bomber case, she also expressed regret. "I'm glad my mother is not alive to see this day," she said.[68]

Her attempts to play the role of victim fell short in the Pizza Bomber trial, in which opening statements started at 1 p.m. on October 15, 2010. Diehl-Armstrong and Doug Sughrue, her lawyer, lost two major arguments right away. Judge McLaughlin refused to grant Diehl-Armstrong a change of venue or venire, as had happened, with a change of venire, in the Bob Thomas case. Though the Pizza Bomber case had drawn intense media coverage, McLaughlin found that much of the publicity was due to Diehl-Armstrong's constant telephone calls to Ed Palattella at the *Erie Times-News*, who would write stories about what she said. In his other major pretrial ruling, McLaughlin refused to reschedule the trial to allow Robert Sadoff to testify for the defense.

Sadoff was prepared to take the stand to reprise a version of the argument he had made in the Bob Thomas case—that Diehl-Armstrong's mental illness explained and excused how she acted—this time in the Pizza Bomber case. He was set to tell the jury that Diehl-Armstrong's paranoia and other mental problems prevented her from actively participating in the plot. Sadoff's approach was not without its risks for the defense. In a five-page letter to Sughrue on September 13, 2010, in which he detailed his position, Sadoff acknowledged the strength of the evidence that Diehl-Armstrong was with Bill Rothstein and Ken Barnes in crucial spots and at crucial times before and after Brian Wells was killed. But he said that Diehl-Armstrong did not willingly participate in the overall plot. Sadoff wrote:

> I am aware that Diehl-Armstrong's behavior is consistent with the allegations by the government against her. What is in dispute, however, is her state of mind, her ability to act willingly and voluntarily, knowingly aiding and abetting in this conspiracy. The government appears to be drawing conclusions about her state of mind from her behavior. In most cases, with reasonable individuals, that is a valid presumption. However, in the case of Marjorie Diehl-Armstrong, we are dealing with a woman who has a psychotic mental disorder called bipolar disorder, during which when she becomes manic, she is out of control, psychotic and not acting according to logic or the way non-psychotic people would react. . . . In addition, Ms. Diehl-Armstrong has a personality disorder, with borderline features and paranoid features. She is very suspicious of others, does not trust them and has great difficulty working with them. . . . In addition, she had a borderline personality disorder as part of her overall mental illness. Borderline personality disordered people see events either in black or white and very little shades of gray. They tend to focus on the extremes rather than the middle. They are also self-destructive and have difficulty with boundaries between themselves and others.[69]

Sadoff focused on the government's evidence that Diehl-Armstrong killed Jim Roden and helped put his body in the freezer to silence him in the Pizza Bomber plot. He said he believed she killed Roden not as part of a cover-up, but for reasons she gave—the claims of abuse and Roden's refusal, in her view, to find the burglars who had terrorized her over Memorial Day weekend 2003—"which are more personal."[70] Sadoff said she got entangled in the Pizza Bomber plot when she went along with putting Roden's body in the freezer. Sadoff said she cooperated with Rothstein in that regard to achieve her singular goal: to get back the $75,000 that she had given him for safekeeping. That goal was also why Diehl-Armstrong was with Rothstein and the others when Wells was killed, Sadoff said. He said Diehl-Armstrong had no reason to participate in the bank-robbery scheme to raise money for a hit on her father because "she had money to pay for what she wished to have done."[71] Sadoff wrote:

> It is my opinion that if she were told that her goals would be achieved, i.e., she would get her $75,000 and Roden's body would be disposed of without her being detected or arrested for killing him, she would participate with the others in order to achieve her goals. She would have no particular interest in their intent to rob the bank, except to go along until her goals were achieved.

Her actions are always designed to help herself, not to participate in the conspiracy to help others. What was "reasonably foreseeable" for her was that she would get her money and be safe from arrest for killing Roden. It was not "reasonably foreseeable" for her, as she perceived it, because of the nature of her mental illness, that the bank would be robbed or Wells would be killed. In essence, she would not have been able to "foresee" the consequences of their behavior which did not benefit her. All she could focus on, because of her personality disorder and her psychotic mental illness, was her own reality, i.e., her goals would be achieved.

In summary, it is my opinion that Ms. Diehl-Armstrong could participate in the behaviors outlined by the government without forming the intent that is necessary for the conspiracy. It would appear, to the average person, that her behavior was, in fact, part of the conspiracy, but because of her mental illness and her personality disorders, she could not participate with the willful intent and foreseeability of the normal, non-psychotic individual.[72]

Logistics and the law influenced McLaughlin's decision that prohibited Sughrue from calling Sadoff as a witness at trial. Sadoff was out of the country and McLaughlin would have had to delay the trial to allow Sadoff to attend. Sadoff also was apparently unable to testify via videoconference. McLaughlin on October 25, 2010, ruled that delaying the trial—the jury had already been empanelled and heard a week of evidence—would increase the risk that the jurors would be exposed to media reports about the case. He said the delay would diminish the jurors' ability to remember the evidence that Sughrue and Marshall Piccinini had already presented.

McLaughlin also agreed with Piccinini and found that Sadoff's testimony would have been irrelevant in any case because Diehl-Armstrong was not presenting an insanity defense. "It is not even clear that Dr. Sadoff's opinions could be used logically to support the defendant's stated theory," McLaughlin said in an opinion. "The mere fact that the defendant tends to distrust other people and has a difficult time working in an agreeable and cooperative manner with others is not necessarily at odds with the allegation that she was part of the conspiracy." To prove conspiracy, he said, the government "does not need to prove an express agreement spelling out all the details or understanding," but only that "two or more persons in some way or manner arrived at some type of agreement, mutual understanding or meeting of the minds to try to accomplish a common goal and unlawful objective."[73]

Despite Sadoff's absence, Sughrue and Diehl-Armstrong still presented Sadoff's basic theory of defense, but without the aura of psychiatric certainty that Sadoff's testimony would have provided. Diehl-Armstrong and Sughrue argued that any willing participation in the Pizza Bomber plot by her made no sense, psychologically and factually. Sughrue said Diehl-Armstrong's narcissistic personality made her a poor if not impossible candidate to have an active role in such a complex scheme that took so many others to carry out. Diehl-Armstrong, through her testimony, tried to point out that she had no reason to have been part of the conspiracy with Bill Rothstein, Ken Barnes, Floyd Stockton, Robert Pinetti, and Wells. She said she did not want her father killed, and that, even if she did, she had plenty of her own money to pay for the hit; she also said she once had plenty of valuable objects stored at her houses, which showed she was a woman of means. She said she was used to having money because she was raised with it. She said Barnes repulsed her, especially after, according to her, he helped burglarize her house over Memorial Day weekend 2003; she said she had no desire to be around Barnes after that. She said she was around Rothstein only because she wanted to get back her $75,000. She said Rothstein then framed her by having her be with him before and after Brian Wells was killed.

Through the entire, convoluted plot, Diehl-Armstrong said, she had no idea what was going on, even as she stood near Rothstein while he called in the pizza order from the pay phone. She admitted she was beside him as he made the call. But she said she did not know what was happening.

"Do you have any idea who he called, where he called or what the substance of the conversation was?" Sughrue asked Diehl-Armstrong.

"He didn't want me to hear it," she said. "I did hear him saying something later, though."

"That's what I was going to get to," Sughrue said. "Did the phone call take long?"

"It took a little while, wasn't a real long phone call, no," she said.

"Did you have any conversations with Bill after the phone call was over?" Sughrue said.

"Yeah, I says, I'm getting hungry, I want to have some lunch, I haven't had lunch yet," Diehl-Armstrong testified. "He says, I just called in a couple pizzas; a guy that I know, that's a friend of mine, is bringing them up from a place down on Peach Street. I said, 'Oh, really,' I say, Maybe I'll come around and get a piece. He says, No, it's for the guys. He says, You're going to have to go somewhere else to get your lunch today.

"He says, But I will catch you later, that's the phrase he always used, 'I'll catch you later,' [when] he was real friendly with his intimate friends, he'd say, 'I'll catch you later,' that was his way of saying goodbye, miss you, or something like that."[74]

Diehl-Armstrong's explanation stretched belief. Here was someone who, throughout her life, held herself out as superior to most everyone else, who prided herself in her independence and intelligence, and now she was testifying that she had no idea what Bill Rothstein was doing at the pay phone. By that logic, Diehl-Armstrong was admitting that, despite her stellar intellect and her assertiveness, she had allowed herself to be hoodwinked by a group of men headed by the likes of Bill Rothstein and Ken Barnes. She also strained credibility when she said she was not with Ken Barnes that day. In his testimony, Jerry Clark detailed how Diehl-Armstrong had shown him where she was when Wells was killed, and one of the spots was the parking lot of the Eat'n Park restaurant, where Barnes had said he and Diehl-Armstrong acted as lookouts. Clark also testified that he asked Diehl-Armstrong whether she had been driving with Barnes the wrong way on Interstate 79. Clark testified that Diehl-Armstrong "again denied being with Mr. Barnes that day. But [she] said her vision is not good, that someone possibly could have been with her in her vehicle without her knowing it."[75] Diehl-Armstrong's explanation, as Clark conveyed it, seemed ridiculous: She was saying she had no idea who was with her in a car because she could not see well enough. During her testimony, Diehl-Armstrong claimed that Clark was lying; she said most everyone else who testified against her lied as well.

Her garrulousness hurt her case. All the statements she gave to the FBI, before Tom Patton became her lawyer and quieted her, worked against Diehl-Armstrong. Her constant chattering—about egg timers, about Rothstein, about where she had been on August 28, 2003—strengthened the government's case. When she said she had placed her head in the lion's mouth by talking to Clark and Jason Wick and the other investigators, she was right. She could have said nothing, which would have made the government's job harder and would have given Sughrue more ways to maneuver at trial. Or she could have told Clark and Wick everything she knew, which could have led to a plea deal and created problems for Ken Barnes as her codefendant; maybe she would have been able to testify against him. Instead, Diehl-Armstrong chose to go only halfway in what she told the investigators. Once Barnes made his full confession, she was the sole target of the United States Attorney's Office. If she thought she could outwit the investigators by talking so much to them, she was mistaken. She had all but talked herself into a federal prosecution.

"I have a very uphill battle here," she once said of the Pizza Bomber case.[76]

The witnesses at trial were plentiful—thirty for the government and nine for the defense. Ken Barnes testified about Diehl-Armstrong's role.

His account fit what the female inmates—six in all—testified that Diehl-Armstrong told them, often in separate and isolated conversations. The UPS driver testified that he saw Rothstein and Diehl-Armstrong at the pay phone. Another witness said he saw Brian Wells drive away from the dirt road next to Rothstein's house the day before Wells was killed, which also supported Barnes's account that he, Diehl-Armstrong, Rothstein, and the others held a planning meeting with Wells the day before he robbed the bank. Floyd Stockton, Bill Rothstein's housemate, was scheduled to testify, but never came to court; he suffered a stroke just as the trial started. He recovered, but was unable to make the trip from Washington State, where he was living. Partly due to the lack of Stockton's testimony, many questions in the Pizza Bomber case were left unanswered: Who wrote the notes that Wells had with him? Whose idea was the scavenger hunt? Where was the bomb made? How close was Wells to the Fractured Intellectuals before he joined their strange plan?

Sughrue highlighted the gaps in the case in his closing argument. He also said that Diehl-Armstrong's mental state ruled out her knowing participation in the conspiracy. He referred to Diehl-Armstrong's lengthy testimony—she was on the stand for five hours and twenty minutes over a day and a half—and her penchant for shouting remarks from the defense table.

"Marjorie Diehl-Armstrong [is] vulnerable," Sughrue told the jury. "She's mentally ill, she told you she's diagnosed with bipolar. She told you that she has paranoid personality disorder. She said that she had narcissistic, and the government agrees she has grandiose tendencies.

"I'm not asking you to like Marjorie Diehl-Armstrong as she sits there, making these remarks and saying things about different witnesses and about the prosecution and the agents," Sughrue said. "Your job is not to like her, your job is not to invite her over for dinner or have a birthday party for her. Your job is to understand that once you are a collective jury and you go back there to decide the facts, to know that that oath you swore first starts out with the presumption of innocence."[77]

Sughrue blamed Rothstein for Diehl-Armstrong's indictment.

"There is a constant theme throughout this case, ladies and gentlemen, and that is Bill Rothstein and his ability to manipulate people," he said, "his ability to categorize people, and his ability to insulate people."[78]

In his closing argument, Marshall Piccinini characterized Diehl-Armstrong as shrewd and self-reliant. He said that no one took advantage of her. He said she was incapable of allowing anyone, including Bill Rothstein, to dupe her.

"She is not subject to manipulation," Piccinini told the jury. "Not subject to manipulation. Things need to go Marge Diehl-Armstrong's way. When you cross-examine her and ask her a question, things need to go her way. When her own attorney asked her a question, things need to go her way.

"When you saw her sitting here, it's all about her; nobody could ever manipulate her," Piccinini said. "She was not subject to manipulation. She was maniacal, devious, involved. She is not manipulated by Mr. Rothstein. They are both manipulators."[79]

Diehl-Armstrong was quiet when the jury delivered its guilty verdict on November 1, 2010. At the time when outbursts would be most expected, she said nothing. She instead flooded the courtroom with comments on February 28, 2011, when Judge McLaughlin sentenced her to life plus thirty years. She used that time to explain what had unfolded in her life over her sixty-two years; to proclaim her innocence; and to quote the Arkansas proverb about what doesn't come out in the wash will come out in the rinse. She spoke of how she was once a musical prodigy on her way to what she thought would be a long and distinguished career in education.

Diehl-Armstrong's remarks about her past reminded everyone in the courtroom that the Pizza Bomber case concerned much more than what she did in the course of a day in Erie, Pennsylvania, on August 28, 2003. The case also drew on psychiatric evidence that went back six decades—evidence that, taken together, presented a multilayered history of Diehl-Armstrong's mental illness, a detailed portrait of her mind.

Marjorie Diehl-Armstrong continued to have a different understanding of that history as she waited to hear the sentence. No matter what any psychiatrist or lawyer or judge had concluded about her over all those years, she said she still knew herself best. The person so many others had evaluated and assisted; the person who had been convicted in connection with the murders of two men and acquitted, by arguing self-defense, in the killing of a third; the person who had undergone years of competency reviews while in state and federal prisons—that person, Marjorie Diehl-Armstrong said, was not her.

She was different, she said.

She was better.

"I'm not a crazed killer that goes around here wanting to kill and injure people," Diehl-Armstrong said in some of her final remarks to the judge. "I am not that type of a woman. I never have been."[80]

Afterword

$\mathcal{I}$n the end, Marjorie Diehl-Armstrong was left without one of the things that she craved the most: money. Harold Diehl disinherited his only child.

He all but wrote Diehl-Armstrong out of his will in 2005, nine years before his death. Diehl-Armstrong learned of her disinheritance while her father was still alive and suffering from dementia. In 2010, while awaiting trial in the Pizza Bomber case, she petitioned a probate judge in Erie County to declare her father mentally incapacitated and unable to manage his financial affairs. The litigation revealed that Harold Diehl's assets, once estimated to be $1.8 million, had dropped to $185,000 by mid-2010,[1] mainly because he had given so much of his fortune away to his friends and neighbors—those good-hearted beneficiaries who he said truly cared for him but whom Diehl-Armstrong called "vultures." The litigation also revealed that Diehl had bequeathed Diehl-Armstrong $100,000 in a will in 2000, but wrote a new will in 2005 that left her only $2,000; he left the bulk of his estate to his friends. Diehl-Armstrong claimed another will, which she said was drafted in 2008, was the most accurate: that will named her the sole beneficiary of her father's estate. But a judge ruled the 2008 document was fraudulent. And the judge ruled the 2005 will—and its $2,000 legacy to Diehl-Armstrong—was valid.

The disinheritance was the result of the deteriorating relationship between Harold Diehl and his daughter. He changed the 2000 will after Diehl-Armstrong tried to get him removed as the administrator of his wife's estate that same year—the attempt in which Diehl-Armstrong, in court records, called her father an abusive alcoholic who all but killed her mother. Harold Diehl's anger at his only child, his estate lawyer said, "went beyond the fact" that she had pleaded guilty but mentally ill in one homicide and had been indicted in the Pizza Bomber case. The anger, the lawyer said, was rooted in

197

Diehl-Armstrong's unwarranted vitriol toward her father and the false claims she made against him in the fight over the administration of Agnes Diehl's estate.[2]

"It is an unusual circumstance where neighbors are favored over a child," the lawyer said, "but this is an unusual fact pattern."[3]

Harold Diehl, who had been Marjorie Diehl-Armstrong's closest living relative, died on January 8, 2014, at the Pennsylvania Soldiers' and Sailors' Home in Erie. He was ninety-five years old and died in debt. He had $118,000 in his estate, but it all went to pay medical bills.[4] Diehl-Armstrong did not even get the $2,000 he promised her.

Diehl-Armstrong said she was defrauded out of a fortune. She never stopped considering herself an heiress.

"God put me in this family," she said. "I have the birthright. I have the bloodline."[5]

She would never stop maintaining her innocence in the Pizza Bomber case, though she lost every appeal. The most significant post-verdict ruling came on November 15, 2012, when the United States Court of Appeals for the Third Circuit denied her direct appeal. In a unanimous decision, the Circuit Court turned away each of Diehl-Armstrong's contentions, which Doug Sughrue, her trial lawyer, filed on her behalf. Diehl-Armstrong claimed that Judge Sean J. McLaughlin erred by finding her competent to stand trial, by not suppressing some evidence, and by not postponing the trial to allow for Robert L. Sadoff to testify about how her mental illness, including her paranoia, would have prevented her from cooperating with Ken Barnes, Bill Rothstein, and the others in the plot that ended in Brian Wells's death. In each instance, the Circuit Court upheld McLaughlin's rulings and said he properly used his discretion. Regarding McLaughlin's finding that Diehl-Armstrong was competent to stand trial, the Circuit Court wrote, "Because the Court based its opinion on reasoned expert testimony and its own observations, we cannot say that its judgment was clearly wrong."[6]

Diehl-Armstrong unsuccessfully appealed to the United States Supreme Court, which refused to hear her case, and she then lost another federal appeal in which she claimed Sughrue was ineffective at trial. Diehl-Armstrong represented herself in that appeal. Some of the documents she submitted were handwritten. A judge dismissed all the claims and declined to issue a certificate that would have allowed Diehl-Armstrong to appeal further; he found that she had suffered no violation of her constitutional rights. The judge wrote: "The Court has endeavored to address all the arguments in Defendant's numerous submissions, which run the gamut in terms of legibility and coherency. After having done so, the Court concludes that there is no basis for providing her the relief she requested. Defendant's claims were either raised and rejected on direct appeal, procedurally defaulted because they could have been raised on direct appeal, or are completely lacking in merit."[7]

Diehl-Armstrong scored one post-verdict legal victory. The win was largely procedural, but she took pride in it. The Pennsylvania Board of Probation and Parole on October 16, 2014, granted Diehl-Armstrong parole in the state sentence of seven to twenty years that she had been serving since January 2005 for the murder of Jim Roden. She had to finish that sentence before she could start serving her federal sentence of life plus thirty years in the Pizza Bomber case. Diehl-Armstrong had been denied parole for years and had even sued the parole board in federal court, claiming the denials were unwarranted. It was in rejecting that appeal, in April 2014, that United States Magistrate Martin C. Carlson referred to Diehl-Armstrong as "a coldly calculated criminal recidivist and serial killer." The parole order of October 2014 released Diehl-Armstrong from state incarceration, but only so she could go to federal prison. She was transferred from Pennsylvania's State Correctional Institution at Muncy to her new permanent home: the Federal Medical Center in Carswell, in Texas, where years earlier she had undergone mental health treatment to determine her competency. Diehl-Armstrong said she realized that winning state parole would do nothing to reduce her lifelong federal incarceration. However, she said, in federal prison, "the law library is better."[8]

Ken Barnes fared somewhat better in federal prison. He got his forty-five-year sentence cut in half in June 2011. The United States Attorney's Office requested the reduction in light of Barnes's cooperation in the Pizza Bomber case. Even with the break, Barnes, who was fifty-seven years old in June 2011, risked dying in prison, given his poor health. He was last incarcerated at the low-security Federal Correctional Institution at Coleman, in central Florida. His sentence expires in 2027, when he will be seventy-four years old. Barnes has never publicly expressed regret about pleading guilty, testifying against Diehl-Armstrong, or getting such a lengthy sentence, even with the reduced time. He said he pleaded guilty "to be on the right side of God."[9]

Diehl-Armstrong has never wavered in her disgust of Barnes.

"He is a dirt bag," she said.[10]

Diehl-Armstrong continues to take no psychotropic drugs. The degree of her bipolar disorder is difficult to gauge absent personal observation, but it often seems less severe, based on her accounts. In telephone interviews, she still exhibits, at times, telltale symptoms of her manic-depression—her incessant talking and pressured speech, particularly when she is stressed. The rate of her speech nearly always speeds up when she is recounting the evidence in the Pizza Bomber case, and how she said she was framed. "It is an insane, stupid crime to begin with," she said in mid-2016. "To me, it's a stupid, asinine case. I will never take the blame for it because I never did it."[11]

Diehl-Armstrong said her cancer is in remission. She credited continued chemotherapy and divine intervention. She has far outlasted the minimum of three years that doctors said she had to live before the start of the Pizza Bomber trial, in 2010. She said she expects to live far longer than the seven-year maximum those doctors also gave her.

"I'm not yet dead by a long shot," she said in 2012, expressing a defiant attitude that continues to this day.[12]

"My health is a miracle," she said in September 2016, in one of the latest interviews she gave before the completion of this book. "I am feeling fantastic. I am happy and pleasant and thankful to God that I am doing so well. If you didn't tell me I had cancer, I wouldn't know."[13]

"My health is my number one priority," she said. "It is not me. It is from God. He's been better to me than anyone else has."[14]

Still doubtful is whether Diehl-Armstrong believes her enemies—those she said abused her, framed her, and refused to help her—also deserve such charity. She has never stopped talking about fate, and how she believes her foes will get what they deserve.

"I'm sitting back," she said, "waiting for karma to kick in."[15]

For her part, Diehl-Armstrong some time ago decided how she wants posterity to understand what happened to her, how she wants posterity to realize she suffered her many problems through no fault of her own. In 2008, a year after she was indicted in the Pizza Bomber case, and while serving a sentence for the second killing of a boyfriend, she explained that she had already chosen the phrase she wants carved on her gravestone.

"My epitaph," Marjorie Diehl-Armstrong said: "Death by legal system."[16]

Notes

INTRODUCTION

1. Report and Recommendation, April 17, 2014, at 7, *Marjorie Diehl-Armstrong v. Pennsylvania Board of Probation and Parole*, 1:13-CV-2302 (M.D. Pa.).

2. Transcript of record at 30, sentencing, February 28, 2011, *United States of America v. Marjorie Diehl-Armstrong*, United States District Court for the Western District of Pennsylvania, Crim. 07-26 Erie.

CHAPTER 1

1. Transcript of record at 20–21, sentencing, February 28, 2011, *United States of America v. Marjorie Diehl-Armstrong*, United States District Court for the Western District of Pennsylvania, Crim. 07-26 Erie.

2. Ibid., 22.

3. Ibid., 23.

4. Ibid., 27.

5. Ibid., 29.

6. Ibid.

7. Ibid., 30.

8. Ibid., 31.

9. Ibid.

10. Transcript of record at 23, January 27, 2005, *Commonwealth of Pennsylvania v. Marjorie E. Diehl-Armstrong*, Court of Common Pleas, Erie County, Pennsylvania, Criminal Division, No. 236 A & B of 2004.

11. Ibid.

12. Ibid.

13. Report and Recommendation, April 17, 2014, at 15, *Marjorie Diehl-Armstrong v. Pennsylvania Board of Probation and Parole*, 1:13-CV-2302 (M.D. Pa.).

14. Ibid., 7.

15. Ibid., 12.

16. Jim Martin, "Will History Repeat?" *Erie Times-News*, November 8, 2015.

17. Marjorie Diehl-Armstrong, telephone interview from prison with Ed Palattella, June 3, 2016.

18. "Paper Plant Closes," *Erie Times-News*, August 4, 2013.

19. "Miss Agnes Eleanor Wolfenden, Bride of Harold Albert Diehl," *Erie Daily Times*, August 26, 1942.

20. Transcript of record at 37, bond hearing, *Commonwealth of Pennsylvania v. Marjorie Diehl*, No. 1370 A & B of 1984.

21. Obituary, Harold A. Diehl, *Erie Times-News*, January 13, 2014.

22. Answer, New Matter and Counter Petition for Relief to Petition for Financial Guardianship, May 26, 2010, at 2, *In Re: Harold A. Diehl*, Court of Common Pleas, Erie County, Pennsylvania, Orphans' Court Division, 149 of 2010. See also Ed Palattella, "Father's Assets Quickly Being Drained," *Erie Times-News*, July 16, 2010.

23. Transcript of record at 130, October 26, 2010, *United States v. Marjorie Diehl-Armstrong*.

24. Ibid.

25. "John C. Diehl Is Dead at 87," *Erie Daily Times*, August 28, 1952.

26. Transcript of record at 134, October 26, 2010, *United States v. Marjorie Diehl-Armstrong*.

27. Ibid.

28. Ibid.

29. Diehl-Armstrong, telephone interview from prison with Palattella, May 6, 2009.

30. Ibid.

31. Transcript of record at 130, October 26, 2010, *United States v. Marjorie Diehl-Armstrong*.

32. Transcript of record at 5, bond hearing, August 23, 1984, *Commonwealth of Pennsylvania v. Marjorie Diehl*.

33. Transcript of record at 132, October 26, 2010, *United States v. Marjorie Diehl-Armstrong*.

34. Transcript of record at 5, bond hearing, August 23, 1984, *Commonwealth of Pennsylvania v. Marjorie Diehl.*

35. Transcript of record at 6, May 24, 1988, *Commonwealth of Pennsylvania v. Marjorie Diehl.*

36. Ibid.

37. Diehl-Armstrong, telephone interview from prison with Palattella, December 18, 2012.

38. Initial Evaluation sheet for Marjorie Diehl, August 1, 1972, 000827, included in packet of information from Hamot Community Mental Health, entered as evidence in *United States v. Marjorie Diehl-Armstrong.* Copy in authors' possession.

39. Gerald Cooke, PhD, to Leonard G. Ambrose III, Esquire, May 15, 1985, 3, entered as evidence in *United States v. Marjorie Diehl-Armstrong.* Copy in authors' possession.

40. Transcript of record at 133, October 26, 2010, *United States v. Marjorie Diehl-Armstrong.*

41. Diehl-Armstrong, telephone interview from prison with Palattella, September 24, 2009.

42. Ibid., February 9, 2016.

43. David B. Paul, MD, to the Honorable Roger M. Fischer, judge on the Court of Common Pleas, Erie County, Pennsylvania, August 1, 1985, 1, entered as evidence in *United States v. Marjorie Diehl-Armstrong.* Copy in authors' possession.

44. Transcript of record at 145, October 26, 2010, *United States v. Marjorie Diehl-Armstrong.*

45. Paul to Fischer, 1. Diehl-Armstrong also said she weighed as little as eighty-five pounds. See also Transcript of record at 179, October 26, 2010, *United States v. Marjorie Diehl-Armstrong.*

46. Paul to Fischer, 1.

47. Ibid., 2.

48. Ibid., 2.

49. Ibid., 1.

50. Ibid., 1.

51. Cooke to Ambrose, 3.

52. Ibid., 3.

53. Robert B. Callahan, MD, letter to Whom It May Concern, April 11, 1983, 1, entered as evidence in *United States v. Marjorie Diehl-Armstrong.* Copy in authors' possession.

54. Transcript of record at 179, October 26, 2010, *United States v. Marjorie Diehl-Armstrong.*

55. Ibid., 180. The pop singer and drummer Karen Carpenter, who had a string of hits in the early 1970s with her brother, died of anorexia in 1983, at age thirty-two. She was extremely thin throughout her career.

56. Transcript of record at 16–17, May 25, 1988, *Commonwealth of Pennsylvania v. Marjorie Diehl.*

57. Ibid.

58. Ibid., 138. See also Mayview State Hospital, psychological evaluation of Marjorie Diehl, September 22, 1987, entered as evidence in *United States v. Marjorie Diehl-Armstrong.* Copy in authors' possession.

59. Cooke to Ambrose, 8.

60. Ibid., 3.

61. Ibid.

62. Paul to Fischer, 3.

63. Cooke to Ambrose, 4.

64. Ibid.

65. Ibid., 2.

66. Transcript of record at 17, September 4, 1987, *Commonwealth of Pennsylvania v. Marjorie Diehl.*

67. Cooke to Ambrose, 4.

68. Initial Evaluation sheet for Marjorie Diehl at Hamot, 000827.

69. Transcript of record at 22–25, bond hearing, August 23, 1984, *Commonwealth of Pennsylvania v. Marjorie Diehl.* See also Palattella, "Cycle of Trouble," *Erie Times-News*, October 19, 2007.

70. Transcript of record at 20–21, sentencing, February 28, 2011, *United States v. Marjorie Diehl-Armstrong.*

CHAPTER 2

1. Marjorie Diehl-Armstrong, telephone interview from prison with Ed Palattella, May 6, 2009.

2. Ibid., February 11, 2008.

3. Ibid., April 1, 2008.

4. Ibid.

5. Diehl-Armstrong, telephone interview from prison with Palattella, February 2, 2008.

6. Ibid., November 19, 2014.

7. Federal Bureau of Investigation, *Serial Murder: Multi-Disciplinary Perspectives for Investigators* (2005), 2, https://www.fbi.gov/stats-services/publications/serial-murder.

8. Timothy Williams and Monica Davey, "U.S. Murders Surged in 2015, F.B.I. Finds," *New York Times*, September 26, 2016. The FBI does not keep specific statistics for serial murder.

9. Marissa A. Harrison, Erin A. Murphy, Lavina Y. Ho, Thomas G. Bowers, and Claire V. Flaherty, "Female Serial Killers in the United States: Means, Motives, and Makings," *Journal of Forensic Psychiatry & Psychology* 26, no. 3 (2015): 384.

10. Amanda L. Farrell, Robert D. Keppel, and Victoria B. Titterington, "Lethal Ladies: Revisiting What We Know about Female Serial Killers," *Homicide Studies* 15, no. 3 (2011): 228.

11. FBI, *Serial Murder*, 9.

12. Ibid.

13. Protection of Children from Predators Act of 1998, Pub. L. No. 105-314, 112 Stat. 2986 (1998).

14. Ibid., 2987.

15. FBI, *Serial Murder*, 8.

16. Eric W. Hickey, *Serial Murderers and Their Victims*, fifth edition (Belmont, CA: Wadsworth, 2010), 27.

17. Harrison et al., "Female Serial Killers in the United States," 388.

18. Farrell et al., "Lethal Ladies," 231.

19. Hickey, *Serial Murderers and Their Victims*, 3.

20. Vincent Canby, "Methods of Madness in *Silence of the Lambs*," *New York Times*, February 14, 1991.

21. Hickey, *Serial Murderers and Their Victims*, 255.

22. Eric W. Hickey, telephone interview with Ed Palattella, February 2, 2016.

23. Edith Hamilton, "The Quest of the Golden Fleece," *Mythology: Timeless Tales of Gods and Heroes* (New York: Grand Central Publishing, 2011), 160–80.

24. Charles McNulty, "A *Medea* for the Ages," *Los Angeles Times*, December 17, 2002.

25. Euripides, *Medea*, in *Greek Plays in Modern Translation*, ed. Dudley Fitts (New York: Dial Press, 1947), 207.

26. Peter Vronsky, *Female Serial Killers: How and Why Women Become Monsters* (New York: Berkley Books, 2007), 70–71.

27. Vronsky, *Female Serial Killers*, 72.

28. Cornelius Tacitus, *The Annals of Imperial Rome*, trans. Michael Grant (Harmondsworth, UK: Penguin Books, 1978), 282.

29. Ibid., 291.

30. *Dio's Rome, Volume V., Books 61–76 (A.D. 54–211) An Historical Narrative Originally Composed in Greek during the Reigns of Septimius Severus, Geta and Caracalla, Macrinus, Elagabalus and Alexander Severus: And Now Presented in English Form by Herbert Baldwin Foster* (1905; Project Gutenberg, 2014), 64:3, http://www.gutenberg.org/files/10890/10890-h/10890-h.htm.

31. Vronsky, *Female Serial Killers*, 78.

32. Ibid.

33. Vronsky, *Female Serial Killers*, 82.

34. Kimberly L. Craft, "About the Countess," in *Infamous Lady: The True Story of Countess Erzsébet Báthory*. Accessed February 29, 2016. http://infamous lady.com/about_the_author.html.

35. Vronsky, *Female Serial Killers*, 87.

36. Craft, "About the Countess."

37. Vronsky, *Female Serial Killers*, 93.

38. Craft, "About the Countess."

39. Vronsky, *Female Serial Killers*, 81.

40. Ibid., 97.

41. Ibid., 99.

42. Hickey, *Serial Murderers and Their Victims*, 268–69; Vronsky, *Female Serial Killers*, 107–8.

43. "Mary Ann Cotton," in *Murderpedia.org*, accessed February 29, 2016. http://murderpedia.org/female.C/c/cotton-mary-ann.htm. Marissa A. Harrison and colleagues are among the academic researchers who have vouched for the accuracy of Murderpedia.org, whose entries are based on numerous sources, such as newspaper articles. "Notably, we found the Murderpedia.org entries we used to be error-free (i.e., verifiable by legitimate sources 100% of the time in our sample)," Harrison et al. wrote in "Female Serial Killers in the United States" (398).

44. Ibid. Mary Ann Cotton is often also described as "Britain's first serial killer," though Vronsky's history of serial killers challenges that description.

45. Ibid.

46. Ibid.

47. "Lydia Sherman," *Murderpedia.org*, accessed February 29, 2016. http://murderpedia.org/female.S/s/sherman-lydia.htm.

48. "The Derby Poisoner," *New York Times*, January 11, 1873.

49. Ibid.

50. Hickey, *Serial Murderers and Their Victims*, 264.

51. Ibid.

52. Ibid.

53. Ibid.

54. Michael D. Kelleher and C. L. Kelleher, *Murder Most Rare: The Female Serial Killer* (Westport, CT: Praeger, 1998), 34.

55. Debbie Jackson and Hilary Pittman, "Throwback Tulsa: Charming, Friendly Nannie Doss Poisoned Four Husbands," *Tulsa World*, August 27, 2015, http://www.tulsaworld.com/blogs/news/throwbacktulsa/throwback -tulsa-charming-friendly-nannie-doss-poisoned-four-husbands/article_ c43b83ff-f12e-5952-a64b-21a1c0fbdcd4.html.

56. Vronsky, *Female Serial Killers*, 140.

57. Kelleher and Kelleher, *Murder Most Rare*, 76.

58. Hickey, *Serial Murderers and Their Victims*, 260–61; Kelleher and Kelleher, *Murder Most Rare*, 80–81.

59. Kelleher and Kelleher, *Murder Most Rare*, 82.

60. Ludmilla Lelis, "Kill Me Now, Wuornos Urges," *Orlando Sentinel*, July 21, 2001; Paul Pinkham, "'Damsel of Death' Aileen Wuornos Executed," *Florida Times-Union*, October 10, 2002.

61. Kelleher and Kelleher, *Murder Most Rare*, 82.

62. Lelis, "Kill Me Now, Wuornos Urges."

63. Jackie Hallifax, for the Associated Press, "Florida High Court Says Wuornos Can Fire Lawyers," *St. Augustine Record*, April 2, 2002.

64. Lise Fisher and Karen Voyles, "Serial Killer Wuornos Executed by Injection," *Gainesville Sun*, October 10, 2002.

65. Ibid.

CHAPTER 3

1. Carla Lucero, "Summary," *Wuornos*, accessed March 1, 2016, www. wuornos.org.

2. Ibid., main page.

3. Editorial, "Femme Fatale," *New York Times*, February 2, 1991.

4. Ibid.

5. Ibid.

6. Eric W. Hickey, telephone interview with Ed Palattella, February 2, 2016.

7. Emily Anthes, "Lady Killers," *New Yorker*, May 9, 2015, http://www .newyorker.com/tech/elements/female-serial-killers.

8. Marjorie Diehl-Armstrong, telephone interview from prison with Ed Palattella, July 26, 2012.

9. Ibid., March 25, 2016.

10. Ibid., July 26, 2012.

11. Amanda L. Farrell, Robert D. Keppel, and Victoria B. Titterington, "Lethal Ladies: Revisiting What We Know about Female Serial Killers," *Homicide Studies* 15, no. 3 (2011): 230. See also Scott Bonn, "5 Myths about Serial Killers and Why They Exist," *Scientific American*, October 24, 2014, https://www.scientificamerican.com/article/5-myths-about-serial-killers-and-why-they-persist-excerpt/.

12. Diehl-Armstrong, telephone interview from prison with Palattella, November 19, 2014.

13. Eric W. Hickey, *Serial Murderers and Their Victims*, fifth edition (Belmont, CA: Wadsworth, 2010), 256.

14. Ibid.

15. Anthes, "Lady Killers."

16. Marissa A. Harrison, Erin A. Murphy, Lavina Y. Ho, Thomas G. Bowers, and Claire V. Flaherty, "Female Serial Killers in the United States: Means, Motives, and Makings," *Journal of Forensic Psychiatry & Psychology* 26, no. 3 (2015): 385.

17. Farrell et al., "Lethal Ladies," 245.

18. Anthes, "Lady Killers."

19. "Dorothea Helen Puente," in *Murderpedia.org*, accessed February 29, 2016, http://murderpedia.org/female.P/p/puente-dorothea.htm.

20. Hickey, *Serial Murderers*, 26.

21. Farrell et al., "Lethal Ladies," 230.

22. Hickey, *Serial Murderers*, 242.

23. Harrison et al., "Female Serial Killers," 403.

24. Ibid., 389.

25. Ibid., 390.

26. Ibid., 392.

27. Ibid., 397.

28. Hickey, interview with Ed Palattella.

29. Harrison, "Female Serial Killers," 396.

30. Hickey, *Serial Murderers*, 267.

31. "Jane Toppan," in *Murderpedia.org*, accessed February 29, 2016, http://murderpedia.org/female.T/t/toppan-jane.htm.

32. Ibid.

33. Anthes, "Lady Killers."

34. Belea T. Keeney and Kathleen M. Heide, "Gender Differences in Serial Murderers: A Preliminary Analysis," *Journal of Interpersonal Violence* 9, no. 3 (1994): 396.

35. Harrison, "Female Serial Killers," 396–97.

36. Ibid., 397.

37. Hickey, *Serial Murderers*, 273.

38. Federal Bureau of Investigation, *Serial Murder: Multi-Disciplinary Perspectives for Investigators* (2005): 14, https://www.fbi.gov/stats-services/publications/serial-murder.

39. Ibid.

40. Scott A. Bonn, "How to Tell a Sociopath from a Psychopath," *Psychology Today*, January 22, 2014, https://www.psychologytoday.com/blog/wicked-deeds/201401/how-tell-sociopath-psychopath.

41. Ibid.

42. FBI, *Serial Murder*, 15.

43. Diehl-Armstrong, telephone interview from prison with Palattella, August 4, 2016.

44. Ibid., November 9, 2008.

45. Ibid., April 21, 2008.

46. Harrison et al., "Female Serial Killers," 395.

47. Hickey, *Serial Murderers*, 255.

48. Ibid., 256.

49. Hickey, interview with Ed Palattella.

50. Ibid.

CHAPTER 4

1. John Guerriero, "Witness: After Shooting Boyfriend, Diehl Acted 'Like a Beaten Puppy,'" Erie, PA, *Morning News*, August 17, 1984. See also Jerry Clark and Ed Palattella, *Pizza Bomber: The Untold Story of America's Most Shocking Bank Robbery* (New York: Berkley Books/Penguin, 2012), 41.

2. Erie police inventory for homicide case #140 of 1984, August 6, 1984, entered as evidence in *Commonwealth of Pennsylvania v. Marjorie Diehl*, Court of Common Pleas, Erie County, Pennsylvania, Criminal Division, No. 1370 A & B 1984. Copy in authors' possession.

3. Guerriero, "Witness: After Shooting Boyfriend, Diehl Acted 'Like a Beaten Puppy.'"

4. Ibid.

5. Ibid.

6. Transcript of record at 24, May 25, 1988, *Commonwealth of Pennsylvania v. Marjorie Diehl*.

7. Clark and Palattella, *Pizza Bomber*, 41.

8. Erie police inventory; Victoria Fabrizio, "Surplus Food Removed from Suspect's Home," *Erie Daily Times*, August 2, 1984.

9. Opinion, July 14, 1988, at 4, *County of Erie v. Marjorie Diehl*, Court of Common Pleas, Erie County, Pennsylvania, No. 2122-A-1988, Civil Division. Copy in authors' possession.

10. Ibid.

11. Associated Press, "Surplus Cheese Goes to Poor as President Signs Farm Bill," *New York Times*, December 23, 1981.

12. Ibid.

13. "County Values Cache of Food at $9,890," *Erie Daily Times*, August 24, 1984.

14. Erie County, Inventory of Removed Foodstuffs, entered as evidence in *Commonwealth of Pennsylvania v. Marjorie Diehl*. Copy in authors' possession. See also Fabrizio, "Surplus Food Removed from Suspect's Home."

15. Guerriero, "Witness: After Shooting Boyfriend, Diehl Acted 'Like a Beaten Puppy.'"

16. Fabrizio, "Surplus Food Removed from Suspect's Home."

17. Erie County, Inventory of Removed Foodstuffs.

18. Fabrizio, "Surplus Food Removed from Suspect's Home."

19. Jeff Pinski, "Cops Find Suspect's Home Filled with Surplus Food," Erie, PA, *Morning News*, August 1, 1984.

20. William A. Rothstein, videotaped interview with Erie police, September 22, 2003. Copy in authors' possession.

21. Transcript of record at 126–27, October 26, 1010, *United States of America v. Marjorie Diehl-Armstrong*, United States District Court for the Western District of Pennsylvania, Crim. 07-26 Erie.

22. Ibid., 127.

23. Ibid., 127–28.

24. Transcript of record at 131, May 24, 1988, *Commonwealth of Pennsylvania v. Marjorie Diehl*.

25. Ibid., 132.

26. Ibid., 131.

27. Ibid., 183–84.

28. Randy O. Frost and Gail Steketee, *Stuff: Compulsive Hoarding and the Meaning of Things* (Boston: Houghton Mifflin Harcourt, 2010), 12.

29. Ibid., 13.

30. Transcript of record at 152, October 26, 2010, *United States v. Marjorie Diehl-Armstrong*; Transcript of record at 65–66, 70, 159, October 27, 2010, *United States v. Marjorie Diehl-Armstrong*. In addition, Diehl-Armstrong has repeatedly brought up her teeth in interviews with Ed Palattella and Jerry Clark.

31. Transcript of record at 159, October 27, 2010, *United States v. Marjorie Diehl-Armstrong*.

32. Lillian L. Meyers, PhD, to the Honorable Roger M. Fischer, judge on the Court of Common Pleas, Erie County, Pennsylvania, November 9, 1987, 2, entered as evidence in *United States v. Marjorie Diehl-Armstrong*. Copy in authors' possession.

33. Frost and Steketee, *Stuff*, 22. They describe "goat paths" as "a phrase well known in the hoarding self-help world."

34. For a description of the paths in Diehl-Armstrong's house, see William A. Rothstein, interview with Pennsylvania State Police and other investigators, September 21, 2003, 19. Copy in authors' possession.

35. David B. Paul, MD, to the Honorable Roger M. Fischer, judge on the Court of Common Pleas, Erie County, Pennsylvania, September 3, 1987, 2, entered as evidence in *United States v. Marjorie Diehl-Armstrong*. Copy in authors' possession.

36. Ibid.

37. Transcript of record at 92, 95, competency hearing, September 4, 1987, *Commonwealth of Pennsylvania v. Marjorie Diehl*.

38. Transcript of record at 21, testimony of Robert L. Sadoff, MD, May 25, 1988, *Commonwealth of Pennsylvania v. Marjorie Diehl*.

39. Ibid., 23–24.

40. Ibid., 24

41. David F. Tolin, Randy O. Frost, and Gail Steketee, *Buried in Treasures: Help for Compulsive Acquiring, Saving, and Hoarding* (Oxford: Oxford University Press, 2007), 37–38. See also Frost and Steketee, *Stuff*, 15.

42. Frost and Steketee, *Stuff*, 15 (high intelligence of hoarders), 35–36 (anorexia).

43. Tolin, Frost, and Steketee, *Buried in Treasures*, 36 (emphasis in the original).

44. Transcript of record at 179, October 26, 2010, *United States v. Marjorie Diehl-Armstrong*.

45. Ibid., 180.

46. David B. Paul, MD, to the Honorable Roger M. Fischer, judge on the Court of Common Pleas, Erie County, Pennsylvania, August 1, 1985, 2, entered as evidence in *United States v. Marjorie Diehl-Armstrong*. Copy in authors' possession.

47. Transcript of record at 180, October 26, 2010, *United States v. Marjorie Diehl-Armstrong*.

48. Gerald Cooke, PhD, to Leonard G. Ambrose III, May 15, 1985, 3, entered as evidence in *United States v. Marjorie Diehl-Armstrong*. Copy in authors' possession.

49. Marjorie Diehl-Armstrong, telephone interview from prison with Ed Palattella, November 16, 2007.

50. Ibid., July 29, 2008.

51. Transcript of record at 6, May 23, 1988, *Commonwealth of Pennsylvania v. Marjorie Diehl*. See also Transcript of record at 169, October 26, 2010, *United States v. Marjorie Diehl-Armstrong*.

52. Transcript of record at 6, May 23, 1988, *Commonwealth of Pennsylvania v. Marjorie Diehl*.

53. Ibid.

54. Diehl-Armstrong, telephone interview from prison with Palattella, February 26, 2016.

55. Transcript of record at 71, testimony of Robert L. Sadoff, May 25, 1988, *Commonwealth of Pennsylvania v. Marjorie Diehl*.

56. Cooke to Ambrose III, 6.

57. Howard P. Friday, PhD, psychological evaluation of Marjorie Diehl, tested September 22, 1987, at Mayview State Hospital, Pennsylvania, 2, entered as evidence in *United States v. Marjorie Diehl-Armstrong*. Copy in authors' possession.

58. Cooke to Ambrose, 6.

59. Ibid.

60. Friday, psychological evaluation of Marjorie Diehl.

61. Transcript of record at 12, bond hearing, August 23, 1984, *Commonwealth of Pennsylvania v. Marjorie Diehl*.

62. Transcript of record at 127, May 24, 1988, *Commonwealth of Pennsylvania v. Marjorie Diehl*.

63. Transcript of record at 131, October 26, 2010, *United States v. Marjorie Diehl-Armstrong*.

64. Transcript of record at 18, testimony of Robert L. Sadoff, May 25, 1988, *Commonwealth of Pennsylvania v. Marjorie Diehl*.

65. Transcript of record at 9, May 23, 1988, *Commonwealth of Pennsylvania v. Marjorie Diehl*.

66. Transcript of record at 151, October 26, 2010, *United States v. Marjorie Diehl-Armstrong*.

67. Ibid., 152.

68. Ibid., 152–53.

69. Ibid., 153.

70. Diehl-Armstrong to Palattella, May 12, 2009.

71. Transcript of record at 10, bond hearing, August 23, 1984, *Commonwealth of Pennsylvania v. Marjorie Diehl*.

72. Ibid.

73. Transcript of record at 180, October 26, 2010, *United States v. Marjorie Diehl-Armstrong.*

74. Ibid., 161.

75. Ibid., 168.

76. For more details on the relationship between Diehl and Rothstein, see Clark and Palattella, *Pizza Bomber*, 112–17.

77. Transcript of record at 171, October 26, 2010, *United States v. Marjorie Diehl-Armstrong.*

78. Ibid.

79. Transcript of record at 34, bond hearing, February 12, 2004, *Commonwealth of Pennsylvania v. Marjorie E. Diehl-Armstrong*, Court of Common Pleas, Erie County, Pennsylvania, Criminal Division, No. 236 A & B of 2004.

80. Transcript of record at 180, October 26, 2010, *United States v. Marjorie Diehl-Armstrong.*

81. Transcript of record at 9, May 23, 1988, *Commonwealth of Pennsylvania v. Marjorie Diehl.*

82. Transcript of record at 58–59, testimony of Robert L. Sadoff, May 25, 1988, *Commonwealth of Pennsylvania v. Marjorie Diehl.*

83. Diehl in some of her testimony states that she first sought mental health treatment when she was twenty-one years old, and she also states that she first got treatment two years later, in 1972, when she was twenty-three. Her psychiatric records show that she first got treatment in 1972.

84. Transcript of record at 180, October 26, 2010, *United States v. Marjorie Diehl-Armstrong.*

85. Transcript of record at 11, May 23, 1988, *Commonwealth of Pennsylvania v. Marjorie Diehl.*

86. Transcript of record at 75, competency hearing, September 4, 1987, *Commonwealth of Pennsylvania v. Marjorie Diehl.*

87. Transcript of record 21, bond hearing, August 23, 1984, *Commonwealth of Pennsylvania v. Marjorie Diehl.*

88. Initial Evaluation sheet for Marjorie Diehl, August 1, 1972, 000826, included in packet of information from Hamot Community Mental Health, entered as evidence in *United States v. Marjorie Diehl-Armstrong.* Copy in authors' possession.

89. Ibid., 000827.

90. Federal Bureau of Prisons, Competency to Stand Trial Evaluation, Marjorie Diehl-Armstrong, April 15, 2008, 5, entered into evidence in *United States v. Marjorie Diehl-Armstrong.* Copy in authors' possession.

91. Ibid. See also Initial Evaluation Sheet for Marjorie Diehl, and Transcript of record at 75, competency hearing, September 4, 1987, *Commonwealth of Pennsylvania v. Marjorie Diehl*.

92. Transcript at 13, May 23, 1988, *Commonwealth of Pennsylvania v. Marjorie Diehl*.

93. Transcript of record at 13, bond hearing, August 23, 1984, *Commonwealth of Pennsylvania v. Marjorie Diehl*.

94. Ibid.

95. Ibid., 19.

96. Transcript of record at 25–26, October 26, 2010, *United States v. Marjorie Diehl-Armstrong*; Transcript of record at 14, May 23, 1988, *Commonwealth of Pennsylvania v. Marjorie Diehl*.

97. Ibid., 14–15. See also Transcript of record 19–20, bond hearing, August 23, 1984, *Commonwealth of Pennsylvania v. Marjorie Diehl*.

98. Kripa Singh, MD, Pennsylvania Bureau of Disability Determination, October 10, 1989, 2, entered into evidence in *United States v. Marjorie Diehl-Armstrong*. Copy in authors' possession.

99. Vocational report for Marjorie Diehl-Armstrong, circa 1975, entered into evidence in *United States v. Marjorie Diehl-Armstrong*. Copy in authors' possession.

100. Transcript of record at 16, May 23, 1988, *Commonwealth of Pennsylvania v. Marjorie Diehl*, trial.

101. Robert D. Callahan, MD, to To Whom It May Concern, December 7, 1981, entered into evidence in *United States v. Marjorie Diehl-Armstrong*. Copy in authors' possession.

102. Robert D. Callahan, MD, to To Whom It May Concern, April 11, 1983, 1, entered into evidence in *United States v. Marjorie Diehl-Armstrong*. Copy in authors' possession.

103. Ibid.

104. Ibid., 1–2.

105. Ibid., 3.

106. Lisa Thompson, "The $50,000 Question," *Erie Times-News*, September 29, 2003.

107. Criminal complaint and related records, *Commonwealth of Pennsylvania v. Marjorie Diehl*, Court of Common Pleas of Erie County, Pennsylvania, Criminal Division, No. 858 of 1980.

108. Transcript of record at 38, bond hearing, August 23, 1984, *Commonwealth of Pennsylvania v. Marjorie E. Diehl-Armstrong*.

109. Ibid.

110. Ibid., 43. See also "Murder Suspect's Background Examined," *Erie Daily Times*, August 24, 1984, which clarifies that Diehl-Armstrong said that male urine can test positive for pregnancy under certain conditions.

111. Transcript of record at 38, bond hearing, August 23, 1984, *Commonwealth of Pennsylvania v. Marjorie Diehl*.

112. Erica Erwin, "Defendant's Background Revealed in Testimony," *Erie Times-News*, September 22, 2003.

113. Case file, *Commonwealth of Pennsylvania v. Marjorie Diehl*, No. 858 of 1980.

114. Mary Ellen Camp, assistant director, Council on Volunteers for Erie County, to Roselle Walkiewicz, ARD Program, Erie County Courthouse, September 14, 1982. In case file of *Commonwealth of Pennsylvania v. Marjorie Diehl*, No. 858 of 1980. Copy in authors' possession.

115. Transcript of record at 18, May 23, 1988, *Commonwealth of Pennsylvania v. Marjorie Diehl*, No. 1370 A & B 1984.

116. Saint Vincent Health Center, Community Health Center Assessment for Marjorie Diehl, August 6, 1981, entered into evidence in *United States v. Marjorie Diehl-Armstrong*. Copy in authors' possession.

117. Saint Vincent Health Center, Community Health Center Assessment for Marjorie Diehl, undated, but believed to be from September 1981, based on the Community Health Center Assessment from August 6, 1981, entered into evidence in *United States v. Marjorie Diehl-Armstrong*. Copy in authors' possession.

118. Ibid.

119. Findings of Fact and Conclusions of Law, July 29, 2008, at 3, *United States v. Marjorie Diehl-Armstrong*.

120. Paul Francis, MD, evaluation of Marjorie Diehl, December 22, 1981, entered into evidence in *United States v. Marjorie Diehl-Armstrong*. Copy in authors' possession.

121. Ibid.

122. Findings of Fact and Conclusions of Law, at 4.

123. Ibid., 5.

124. Social Security Administration, Disability Determination and Transmittal for Marjorie Diehl, April 19, 1983, entered into evidence in *United States v. Marjorie Diehl-Armstrong*. Copy in authors' possession.

125. Ibid.

126. Ibid.

127. Saint Vincent Health Center, Community Health Center Assessment for Marjorie Diehl, May 27, 1983, entered into evidence in *United States v. Marjorie Diehl-Armstrong*. Copy in authors' possession. Information

on Diehl not taking Tofranil regularly is from an undated document in the same file and also in the authors' possession.

128. Decision in the Case of Marjorie E. Diehl, Department of Health and Human Services, Social Security Administration, January 31, 1984, 5, entered into evidence in *United States v. Marjorie Diehl-Armstrong.* Copy in authors' possession.

129. Ibid., 4.

130. Ibid.

131. Ibid.

132. Thompson, "The $50,000 Question."

133. Transcript of record at 18, May 23, 1988, *Commonwealth of Pennsylvania v. Marjorie Diehl.*

134. Ibid.

135. Ibid., 30.

136. "Diehl Didn't Consider Seeking Help," Erie, PA, *Morning News,* May 25, 1988.

137. Transcript of record at 32, May 23, 1988, *Commonwealth of Pennsylvania v. Marjorie Diehl.*

CHAPTER 5

1. Transcript of record at 5, May 25, 1988, *Commonwealth of Pennsylvania v. Marjorie Diehl,* Court of Common Pleas of Erie County, Pennsylvania, Criminal Division, No. 1370 A & B 1984.

2. Ibid., 5–7.

3. Ibid., 8–9.

4. Ibid., 14–15.

5. David Healy, *Mania: A Short History of Bipolar Disorder* (Baltimore: Johns Hopkins University Press, 2008), 5.

6. Andrew Solomon, *The Noonday Demon: An Atlas of Depression* (New York: Simon & Schuster, 2001), 286.

7. Ibid.

8. Ibid., 287.

9. Ibid., 288.

10. Ibid., 291.

11. Richard Knoll, *The Encyclopedia of Schizophrenia and Other Psychotic Disorders,* third edition (New York: Facts on File, 2007), x.

12. Ibid., xii.

13. Philippe Pinel, *A Treatise on Insanity*, quoted in E. Fuller Torrey and Michael B. Knable, *Surviving Manic Depression* (New York: Basic Books, 2002), frontispiece.

14. Ibid., xiii.

15. Gary Greenberg, *The Book of Woe: The DSM and the Unmaking of Psychiatry* (New York: Blue Rider Press, 2013), 12.

16. Benjamin Rush, *Medical Inquiries and Observations upon the Diseases of the Mind* (Philadelphia: Kimber & Richardson, 1812), 61, https://collections.nlm.nih.gov/bookviewer?PID=nlm:nlmuid-2569036R-bk.

17. Ibid., 33.

18. Ibid., 62.

19. Ibid., 41.

20. Leonard George, foreword to *The Encyclopedia of Schizophrenia and Other Psychotic Disorders*, third edition (New York: Facts on File, 2007), vi.

21. Greenberg, *The Book of Woe*, 61–62.

22. George, foreword to *The Encyclopedia of Schizophrenia and Other Psychotic Disorders*, vi.

23. Greenberg, *The Book of Woe*, 14.

24. Knoll, *The Encyclopedia of Schizophrenia and Other Psychotic Disorders*, xv.

25. Ibid., xvii.

26. Torrey and Knable, *Surviving Manic Depression*, xv.

27. Greenberg, *The Book of Woe*, 26.

28. Ibid.

29. American Medico-Psychological Association, *Statistical Manual for Use of the Institutions for the Insane* (New York: Bureau of Statistics, the National Committee for Mental Hygiene, 1918), 3, https://ia801405.us.archive.org/14/items/statisticalmanu00assogoog/statisticalmanu00assogoog.pdf.

30. Ibid., 18.

31. Ibid.

32. Ibid., 23–24 (emphasis in the original).

33. Ibid., 24.

34. Ibid.

35. Ibid., 23 (emphasis in the original).

36. Donald W. Black and Jon E. Grant, *DSM-5 Guidebook* (Washington, DC: American Psychiatric Publishing, 2014), xix.

37. Greenberg, *The Book of Woe*, 32.

38. Black and Grant, *DSM-5 Guidebook*, xix.

39. L. J. Davis, "The Encyclopedia of Insanity: A Psychiatric Handbook Lists a Madness for Everyone," *Harper's Magazine*, February 1997, 64.

40. Ibid.

41. Ibid., xx.

42. Ibid., xxi.

43. Ibid.

44. Ibid.

45. Greenberg, *The Book of Woe*, 35, 36. See also "The Issue Is Subtle, the Debate Is Still On," *New York Times*, December 23, 1973.

46. Benedict Carey, "Psychiatrists Revise the Book of Human Troubles," *New York Times*, December 17, 2008.

47. Ibid.

48. Henry Alford, "Endpaper: You Could Look It Up," *New York Times Magazine*, April 3, 1994.

49. Davis, "The Encyclopedia of Insanity," 61–62.

50. American Psychiatric Association, *Diagnostic and Statistical Manual of Mental Disorders*, fourth edition: *DSM-IV* (Washington, DC: American Psychiatric Publishing, 1994), xvi.

51. Ibid., xv.

52. Black and Grant, *DSM-5 Guidebook*, xvii. See also, Ibid., 4, for why, starting with the fifth edition of the *Diagnostic and Statistical Manual of Mental Illness*, the American Psychiatric Association started using Arabic numerals rather than Roman numerals in the manual's title. The APA believed Roman numerals "too limiting" for future text revisions. "For simplicity, future changes prior to the manual's next complete revision can be designated as DSM-5.1, DSM-5.2, and so forth."

CHAPTER 6

1. Transcript of record at 106, May 24, 1988, *Commonwealth of Pennsylvania v. Marjorie Diehl*, Court of Common Pleas, Erie County, Pennsylvania, Criminal Division, No. 1370 A & B 1984.

2. Ibid., 107.

3. Jeff Pinski, "Woman Charged with Murder," Erie, PA, *Morning News*, July 31, 1984.

4. John Guerriero, "Witness: After Shooting Boyfriend, Diehl Acted 'Like a Beaten Puppy,'" Erie, PA, *Morning News*, August 17, 1984. Donna Mikolajczyk died on December 18, 2010, in Erie. She was seventy-six years old.

5. Erie police inventory for evidence tagged 32900, July 31, 1984, entered into evidence in *Commonwealth of Pennsylvania v. Marjorie Diehl*. Copy in authors' possession.

6. Erie police inventory for evidence tagged 32899, July 31, 1984, entered into evidence in *Commonwealth of Pennsylvania v. Marjorie Diehl;* copy in authors' possession.

7. Pinski, "Woman Charged with Murder."

8. Information in this section taken from police reports and supplemental police reports in the case of *Commonwealth of Pennsylvania v. Marjorie Diehl.* Copies in authors' possession.

9. Transcript of record at 101, May 24, 1988, *Commonwealth of Pennsylvania v. Marjorie Diehl.*

10. Ibid., 102–3.

11. Ibid., 167. Diehl had four lawsuits pending in the Erie County Court of Common Pleas when she was arrested for Thomas's death. One was over foot surgery, and the other three were related to two auto accidents, one in 1978 and the other in May 1982. In the 1982 case, Diehl claimed the car in which she was riding was rear-ended in Erie. Edwin Carey, Diehl's landlord and erstwhile boyfriend, was driving the car. Diehl said she suffered neck and back injuries, and claimed she risked arthritis because of the accident as well. See Victoria Fabrizio, "Source of $18,000 Subject of Hearing," *Erie Daily Times*, August 7, 1984.

12. The murkiness surrounding the origins of the cash fit a theme that would recur in Diehl's other criminal cases—prosecutors repeatedly hinted that Diehl, however she got all the cash, was committing fraud by failing to let the government know she had other income while she was receiving Social Security disability benefits. The defense in each case sought to keep testimony about the cash to a minimum, though certainly any reasonable juror would wonder how Diehl came to possess so much money and why she could continue to receive disability payments. "The source of the funds, as well as the issue of whether the Defendant was receiving welfare and/or disability benefits at the time she had the funds, is not only irrelevant but extremely prejudicial," her lawyers wrote in a pretrial motion in the Thomas case. "Whether the Defendant accepted welfare and/or disability benefits without telling the paying department and/or agency that she had cash on hand is irrelevant and immaterial to whether the cash on hand was used on the morning of July 30, 1984, to solicit Donna Mikolajczyk to help her remove the body." Defense motion in limine, May 28, 1988, at 4, *Commonwealth v. Diehl.* Copy in authors' possession.

13. "Fischer Rules Diehl Entitled to Part of $18,000 Seized," *Erie Daily Times*, July 15, 1988.

14. Police inventory of items taken from Diehl's shopping bags, filed as evidence in *Commonwealth of Pennsylvania v. Marjorie Diehl.* Copy in

authors' possession. See also Transcript of record at 104, May 24, 1988, *Commonwealth of Pennsylvania v. Marjorie Diehl.*

15. Ibid., 105–6.

16. Ibid., 109.

17. Pinski, "Woman Charged with Murder."

18. Ibid.

19. Ibid.

20. Guerriero, "Witness: After Shooting Boyfriend, Diehl Acted 'Like a Beaten Puppy.'"

21. Susan Lasky, statement to Erie police, July 30, 1984, entered as evidence in *Commonwealth v. Marjorie Diehl.* Copy in authors' possession.

22. Ibid.

23. Ibid.

24. Marjorie Diehl, statement to Erie police Detective Thomas Nelson, July 30, 1984, entered as evidence in *Commonwealth v. Diehl.* Copy in authors' possession.

25. Diehl, statements to Erie police, July 30, 1984, contained in police supplemental reports, entered as evidence in *Commonwealth v. Marjorie Diehl.* Copy in authors' possession.

26. Ibid.

27. Erie County coroner's report for Robert David Thomas, July 30, 1984, entered as evidence in *Commonwealth of Pennsylvania v. Marjorie Diehl.* Copy in authors' possession.

28. Ibid.

29. Ibid.

30. "Diehl Might Use Insanity Defense," Erie (PA) *Morning News,* November 3, 1984.

31. Transcript of record at 24, competency hearing, September 4, 1987, *Commonwealth of Pennsylvania v. Marjorie Diehl.*

32. Marjorie Diehl to Honorable Roger M. Fischer, judge on the Court of Common Pleas, Erie County, Pennsylvania, March 11, 1986, entered as evidence in *Commonwealth of Pennsylvania v. Diehl.* Copy in authors' possession.

33. Transcript of record at 7, bond hearing, August 23, 1984, *Commonwealth of Pennsylvania v. Marjorie Diehl.* See also "Murder Suspect's Background Examined," *Erie Daily Times,* August 24, 1984.

34. Victoria Fabrizio, "Veshecco Reveals Murder Plot Probe," *Erie Daily Times,* December 5, 1984.

35. "Witness Claims He Forgot Information Related to Diehl Case," *Erie Daily Times,* December 21, 1984.

36. "Diehl's Attorney Questions Witness' Conflicting Stories," *Erie Daily Times*, December 14, 1984.

37. Jim Thompson, "Diehl's Parents Paid $60,000 for Defense," *Erie Daily Times*, June 15, 1988.

38. Erie County coroner's report for Edwin A. Carey, April 4, 1985. Copy in authors' possession.

39. Ibid.

40. Ibid.

41. Gerald Cooke, PhD, to Leonard G. Ambrose III, May 15, 1985, 5, entered as evidence in *United States v. Marjorie Diehl-Armstrong*, United States District Court for the Western District of Pennsylvania, Crim. 07-26 Erie. Copy in authors' possession.

42. Transcript of record at 150, October 26, 2010, *United States v. Marjorie Diehl-Armstrong*.

43. Marjorie Diehl-Armstrong, telephone interview from prison with Ed Palattella, August 16, 2016.

44. Leonard G. Ambrose III to the Honorable Roger M. Fischer, judge on the Court of Common Pleas, Erie County, Pennsylvania, June 13, 1985, 1, entered as evidence in *United States v. Marjorie Diehl-Armstrong*. Copy in authors' possession.

45. Ibid., 2.

46. Robert L. Sadoff, MD, to Leonard G. Ambrose III, June 7, 1985, 2, entered as evidence in *United States v. Marjorie Diehl-Armstrong*. Copy in authors' possession.

47. Cooke to Ambrose, 1.

48. Ibid., 7.

49. Marjorie Diehl to the Honorable Roger M. Fischer, June 16, 1987, entered as evidence in *United States v. Marjorie Diehl-Armstrong*. Copy in authors' possession.

50. Ibid. See also Transcript of record at 82, competency hearing, September 4, 1987, *Commonwealth of Pennsylvania v. Marjorie Diehl*.

51. Assistant Erie County District Attorney Timothy J. Lucas to Leonard G. Ambrose III, October 31, 1986, entered in evidence in *Commonwealth of Pennsylvania v. Marjorie Diehl*. Copy in authors' possession.

52. Diehl to Fischer.

53. Ted S. Urban, psychological report on Marjorie Diehl, August 8, 1987, 4, entered as evidence in *United States v. Marjorie Diehl-Armstrong*; copy in authors' possession.

54. Ibid., 3.

55. Ibid.

56. Ibid.

57. Ibid., 5.

58. David B. Paul, MD, to Erie County Judge Roger M. Fischer, September 3, 1987, 3, entered as evidence in *United States v. Marjorie Diehl-Armstrong*. Copy in authors' possession.

59. Ibid., 3–4.

60. Transcript of record at 31, 37, competency hearing, September 4, 1987, *Commonwealth of Pennsylvania v. Marjorie Diehl*, transcript.

61. Ibid., 78.

62. Ibid., 84.

63. Paul to Fischer, 1.

64. Transcript of record at 36, competency hearing, September 4, 1987, *Commonwealth of Pennsylvania v. Marjorie Diehl*, transcript.

65. Ibid.

66. Ibid., 80.

67. Howard P. Friday, PhD, psychological evaluation of Marjorie Diehl, September 22, 1987, 1, entered as evidence in *United States v. Marjorie Diehl-Armstrong*. Copy in authors' possession.

68. Lillian M. Meyers, PhD, to Erie County Judge Roger M. Fischer, November 9, 1987, 1, entered as evidence in *United States v. Marjorie Diehl-Armstrong*. Copy in authors' possession.

69. Duncan Campbell, MD, and Howard P. Friday, PhD, Summary and Evaluation for Court, January 29, 1988, 2, entered as evidence in *United States v. Marjorie Diehl-Armstrong*. Copy in authors' possession.

70. Ibid.

71. Campbell, Summary and Evaluation for Court, 2.

72. Meyers to Fischer, 1.

73. Ibid.

74. Campbell, Summary and Evaluation for Court, 2.

75. Transcript of record at 38, competency hearing, September 4, 1987, *Commonwealth of Pennsylvania v. Marjorie Diehl*.

76. Campbell, Summary and Evaluation for Court, 2.

77. Ibid., 3.

78. Ibid.

79. Leonard G. Ambrose III to the Honorable Roger M. Fischer, February 16, 1988, 3, entered as evidence in *Commonwealth of Pennsylvania v. Marjorie Diehl*. Copy in authors' possession.

80. Campbell, Summary and Evaluation for Court, 3.

81. Ibid.

82. Ibid.

83. Ibid.
84. Ambrose to Fischer, 2.

CHAPTER 7

1. Patricia E. Erickson and Steven K. Erickson, *Crime, Punishment, and Mental Illness: Law and the Behavioral Sciences in Conflict* (New Brunswick, NJ: Rutgers University Press, 2008), 2.
2. Ibid., 14–17.
3. Jillian K. Peterson, Patrick Kennealy, Jennifer Skeem, Beth Bray, and Andrea Zvonkovic, "How Often and How Consistently Do Symptoms Directly Precede Criminal Behavior among Offenders with Mental Illness?" *Law and Human Behavior* 38, no. 5 (2014): 439–49. Published by the American Psychological Association.
4. Ibid.
5. Erickson and Erickson, *Crime, Punishment, and Mental Illness*, 58.
6. Ibid., 56.
7. Ibid., 59.
8. Ibid.
9. Michael L. Perlin, *The Jurisprudence of the Insanity Defense* (Durham, NC: Carolina Academic Press, 1994), 74.
10. Rita J. Simon and Heather Ahn-Redding, *The Insanity Defense, the World Over* (Lanham, MD: Lexington Books, 2006), 4–5.
11. Ibid., 4.
12. Ibid.
13. Anthony Platt and Bernard L. Diamond, "The Origins of the Right and Wrong Test of Criminal Responsibility and Its Subsequent Development in the United States: An Historical Survey," *California Law Review* 54, no. 3 (1966): 1229.
14. Aristotle, *The Nicomachean Ethics*, in Ibid., n12.
15. R. D. Melville, *A Manual of the Principles of Roman Law* (Edinburgh: W. Green & Son, 1915), 89.
16. Eugene J. Chesney, "Concept of Mens Rea in the Criminal Law," *Journal of Criminal Law and Criminology* 29, no. 5 (1939): 630.
17. Justinian I, *The Digest of Justinian, Volume I*, trans. Charles Henry Munro (Cambridge: Cambridge University Press, 1904), 59–60.
18. Homer D. Crotty, "History of Insanity as a Defence to Crime in English Criminal Law," *California Law Review* 12, no. 2 (1924): 107.
19. Norman J. Finkel, *Insanity on Trial* (New York: Plenum Press, 1988), 8.

20. Crotty, "History of Insanity as a Defence to Crime in English Criminal Law," 109.

21. Ibid., 108–9.

22. William Lambarde, *Archeion; or, A Discourse upon the High Courts of Justice in England*, in Valerie P. Hans and Neil Vidmar, *Judging the Jury* (Cambridge, MA: Perseus Publishing, 1986), 187.

23. Finkel, *Insanity on Trial*, 12.

24. Ibid., 13. For further discussion, see Rita James Simon, *The Jury and the Defense of Insanity* (Boston: Little, Brown and Company, 1967), 17.

25. Simon, *The Jury and the Defense of Insanity*, 17–18.

26. Finkel, *Insanity on Trial*, 12.

27. Perlin, *The Jurisprudence of the Insanity Defense*, 79.

28. Finkel, *Insanity on Trial*, 17.

29. Simon, *The Jury and the Defense of Insanity*, 20. See also John P. Martin, "The Insanity Defense: A Closer Look," *Washington Post*, February 27, 1998.

30. Finkel, *Insanity on Trial*, 18–19.

31. Simon, *The Jury and Defense of Insanity*, 20–21.

32. Finkel, *Insanity on Trial*, 21.

33. Perlin, *The Jurisprudence of the Insanity Defense*, 80–81.

34. Henry J. Steadman, Margaret A. McGreevy, Joseph P. Morrisey, Lisa A. Callahan, Pamela Clark Robbins, and Carmine Cirincione, *Before and after Hinckley: Evaluating Defense Reform* (New York: The Guilford Press, 1993), 46.

35. Richard C. Allen, "The Brawner Rule—New Lyrics for an Old Tune," *Washington University Law Review* 1 (1973), 68.

36. Perlin, *The Jurisprudence of the Insanity Defense*, 84.

37. Simon, *The Jury and the Defense of Insanity*, 31.

38. Perlin, *The Jurisprudence of the Insanity Defense*, 86.

39. Ibid., 87.

40. *United States v. Brawner*, 471 F.2d 969, syllabus (D.C. Cir. 1972).

41. Vincent J. Fuller, "United States v. John W. Hinckley Jr. (1982)," *Loyola of Los Angeles Law Review* 33, no. 2: 700.

42. Gardiner Harris, "Reagan's Assailant Is Ordered Released," *New York Times*, July 28, 2106. See also Ben Nuckols, Associated Press, "Judge: Hinckley Can Leave Hospital," *Erie Times-News*, July 28, 2016.

43. Steadman et al., *Before and after Hinckley*, 2.

44. Stuart Taylor Jr., "Hinckley Hails 'Historical' Shooting to Win Love," *New York Times*, July 9, 1982.

45. Ibid.

46. "A Crime of Insanity," *Frontline*, Public Broadcasting System, 2002, accessed May 14, 2016, http://www.pbs.org/wgbh/pages/frontline/shows/crime/trial/history.htm.
47. Insanity Defense Reform Act of 1984, Pub. L. No. 98-473, 98 Stat. 2057 (1984).
48. Steadman et al., *Before and after Hinckley*, 38.
49. Ibid., 39.
50. Pennsylvania Consolidated Statutes Title 18 § 314 (passed December 15, 1982).

CHAPTER 8

1. Lenore E. Walker, "Battered Woman Syndrome," *Psychiatric Times*, July 7, 2009, http://www.psychiatrictimes.com/trauma-and-violence/battered-woman-syndrome.
2. Erie County District Attorney's motion in limine, April 26, 1988, at 1, *Commonwealth v. Marjorie Diehl*, Court of Common Pleas, Erie County, Pennsylvania, No. 1370 A & B of 1984. Copy in authors' possession.
3. *Commonwealth v. Stonehouse*, 521 PA 41 (1989) 555 A.2d 772.
4. Transcript of record at 76, testimony of Robert L. Sadoff, MD, May 25, 1988, *Commonwealth of Pennsylvania v. Marjorie Diehl*.
5. Victoria Fabrizio, "Diehl's Murder Trial Begins," *Erie Daily Times*, May 19, 1988.
6. *Commonwealth of Pennsylvania v. Marjorie Diehl*, trial transcript, May 23, 1988, 96.
7. Ibid., May 24, 1988, 69.
8. Ibid., 70.
9. Ibid., 188–89.
10. Ibid., 33. Court records show that Thomas received a year of probation, thus he was not on parole. See *Commonwealth of Pennsylvania v. Robert D. Thomas*, Court of Common Pleas, Erie County, Pennsylvania, No. 994 of 1983. Copies of records in authors' possession.
11. Ibid., 9–10.
12. Ibid., 64.
13. Ibid.
14. Ibid.
15. Ibid., 65.
16. Erie police continuation report, July 30, 1984, entered as evidence in *Commonwealth of Pennsylvania v. Marjorie Diehl*. Copy in authors' possession.

17. Transcript of record at 66, May 24, 1988, *Commonwealth of Pennsylvania v. Marjorie Diehl.*

18. Ibid.

19. Ibid., 67.

20. Ibid.

21. Ibid., 82.

22. Ibid.

23. Ibid., 84.

24. Ibid., 85.

25. Ibid., 77.

26. Ibid., 78–79.

27. Ibid., 88.

28. Ibid., 91.

29. Ibid., 94.

30. Ibid., 97–98.

31. Ibid., 98.

32. Ibid., 98–99.

33. "Diehl Didn't Consider Seeking Help," Erie, PA, *Morning News*, May 25, 1988.

34. "Photographs Taken of Diehl's Bruises," *Erie Daily Times*, May 27, 1988.

35. "Physician, Criminologist Quizzed in Murder Trial," *Erie Daily Times*, May 23, 1988.

36. Jim Thompson, "Diehl Bursts into Tears upon Her Acquittal," *Erie Daily Times*, June 2, 1988.

37. Jim Thompson, "Expert Uses Props to Re-enact Shooting," *Erie Daily Times*, May 26, 1988.

38. Ibid.

39. Transcript of record at 47, testimony of Sadoff, May 25, 1988, *Commonwealth of Pennsylvania v. Marjorie Diehl.*

40. Ibid., 55.

41. Ibid., 57.

42. Ibid., 58–59.

43. Ibid., 40.

44. Ibid., 34.

45. Ibid., 54.

46. Ibid., 53.

47. Ibid., 54.

48. Ibid., 44.

49. Ibid., 163.

50. Transcript of record at 25, testimony of Sadoff, May 25, 1988, *Commonwealth of Pennsylvania v. Marjorie Diehl.*
51. Ibid., 75–76.
52. Transcript of record at 25, closing argument of Leonard G. Ambrose III, May 31, 1988, *Commonwealth of Pennsylvania v. Marjorie Diehl.*
53. Jim Thompson, "Diehl Jury Still Out," *Erie Daily Times*, June 1, 1988.
54. Ibid.
55. Ibid.
56. Ibid.
57. Ibid.
58. Thompson, "Diehl Bursts into Tears upon Her Acquittal."
59. John Guerriero, "Jury Acquits Diehl; Says She Fired in Self-Defense," Erie, PA, *Morning News*, June 2, 1988.
60. Jerry Clark and Ed Palattella, *Pizza Bomber: The Untold Story of America's Most Shocking Bank Robbery* (New York: Berkley Books/Penguin, 2012), 344.
61. Ibid.
62. Ibid.
63. Ibid. See also Guerriero, "Jury Acquits Diehl; Says She Fired in Self-Defense."
64. Guerriero, "Jury Acquits Diehl; Says She Fired in Self-Defense."
65. Ibid.
66. Jim Thompson, "Judge Sentences Marjorie Diehl to Probation on Firearms Charge," *Erie Times-News*, July 8, 1988.
67. Ibid.
68. "Diehl Gets Probation for Firearm Charge," Erie, PA, *Morning News*, July 8, 1988.

CHAPTER 9

1. Frederick K. Goodwin and Kay Redfield Jamison, *Manic-Depressive Illness* (New York: Oxford University Press, 1990), 56.
2. National Institute of Mental Health, *Bipolar Disorder among Adults*, accessed June 21, 2016, http://www.nimh.nih.gov/health/statistics/prevalence/bipolar-disorder-among-adults.shtml.
3. Alan C. Swann, Marijn Lijffijt, Scott D. Lane, Kimberly J. Kjome, Joel L. Steinberg, and F. Gerard Moeller, "Criminal Conviction, Impulsivity, and Course of Illness in Bipolar Disorder," *Bipolar Disorders* 13, no. 2 (2011): 173–81, http://www.ncbi.nlm.nih.gov/pmc/articles/PMC3151155.

4. Ed Palattella, telephone interview from prison with Marjorie Diehl-Armstrong, February 11, 2008.

5. Ibid., April 29, 2009.

6. E. Fuller Torrey and Michael B. Knable, *Surviving Manic Depression* (New York: Basic Books, 2002), 21.

7. Goodwin and Jamison, *Manic-Depressive Illness*, 57.

8. David Healy, *Mania: A Short History of Bipolar Disorder* (Baltimore: Johns Hopkins University Press, 2008), 9.

9. As quoted in Goodwin and Jamison, *Manic-Depressive Illness*, 58.

10. Torrey and Knable, *Surviving Manic Depression*, 19.

11. Goodwin and Jamison, *Manic-Depressive Illness*, 59.

12. Ibid., 60.

13. Torrey and Knable, *Surviving Manic Depression*, 12.

14. Healy, *Mania*, 72.

15. Torrey and Knable, *Surviving Manic Depression*, 21.

16. Ibid., 19–20.

17. Ibid., 25.

18. Ibid.

19. Ibid., 30.

20. Goodwin and Jamison, *Manic-Depressive Illness*, 36.

21. Ibid., 37.

22. Wes Burgess, *The Bipolar Handbook* (New York: Avery/Penguin, 2006), 28.

23. Torrey and Knable, *Surviving Manic Depression*, 39–40.

24. Ibid., 41.

25. David B. Paul, MD, to the Honorable Roger M. Fischer, judge of the Court of Common Pleas, Erie County, Pennsylvania, August 1, 1985, 2, entered into evidence in *Commonwealth of Pennsylvania v. Marjorie Diehl*, No. 1370 A & B of 1984. Copy in authors' possession.

26. American Psychiatric Association, *Diagnostic and Statistical Manual of Mental Disorders*, fifth edition: *DSM-5* (Washington, DC, American Psychiatric Publishing, 2013), 123.

27. Ibid.

28. Ibid.

29. National Institute of Mental Health, "Bipolar Disorder," accessed June 21, 2016, http://www.nimh.nih.gov/health/topics/bipolar-disorder/index.shtml.

30. American Psychiatric Association, *DSM-5*, 123.

31. National Institute of Mental Health, "Bipolar Disorder."

32. American Psychiatric Association, *DSM-5*, 810.

33. Ibid.

34. Torrey and Knable, *Surviving Manic Depression*, 39.

35. Ibid., xvii.

36. Ibid., 108.

37. Ibid., 268.

38. Burgess, *The Bipolar Handbook*, 41.

39. Transcript of record at 183, October 26, 2010, *United States v. Marjorie Diehl-Armstrong*, United States District Court for the Western District of Pennsylvania, Crim. 07-26 Erie.

40. Ibid.

41. Ibid., 185.

42. Ibid., 186.

CHAPTER 10

1. Marjorie Diehl-Armstrong, telephone interview from prison with Ed Palattella, August 18, 2016.

2. Transcript of record at 14, October 20, 2003, *United States of America v. Marjorie Diehl-Armstrong*, United States District Court for the Western District of Pennsylvania, Crim. 07-26 Erie.

3. Ibid.

4. Ibid.

5. Report of Paul H. Soloff, MD, to MacDonald, Illig, Jones & Britton law firm, February 19, 1997, 1, attached to Pretrial Narrative Filed on Behalf of A. K. Mitra, MD, May 4, 1998, *Marjorie Armstrong v. Saint Vincent Health Center*, Court of Common Pleas, Erie County, Pennsylvania, No. 14316-1994. Copy in authors' possession.

6. Plaintiff's Pretrial Statement, January 23, 1987, attached report, *Armstrong v. Saint Vincent Health Center*. Copy in authors' possession.

7. Ibid.

8. Soloff to MacDonald, Illig, Jones & Britton, 1.

9. Diehl-Armstrong, telephone interview from prison with Palattella, August 18, 2016.

10. Ibid.

11. Ibid.

12. Ibid. See also Plaintiff's Pretrial Statement, *Armstrong v. Saint Vincent Health Center*.

13. Diehl-Armstrong, telephone interview from prison with Palattella, August 18, 2016.

14. Soloff to MacDonald, Illig, Jones & Britton, 1–2.

15. Ibid.

16. Arrest and court records, *Commonwealth of Pennsylvania v. Richard Armstrong*, Court of Common Pleas, Erie County, Pennsylvania, No. 1550 of 1989. Copies in authors' possession.

17. Ibid.

18. Arrest and court records, *Commonwealth of Pennsylvania v. Richard Armstrong*. Copies in authors' possession.

19. Ibid.

20. Douglas L. Deitrich, senior malpractice claim specialist, Phico Insurance, to Susan A. Thomas, senior claim representative, full formal report, December 15, 1984, 1, attached to Motion for Leave to Take Depositions, and Motion to Compel and for Sanctions, April 2, 1997, *Marjorie Armstrong v. Saint Vincent Health Center*. Copy in authors' possession. No marriage license exists in Erie County, Pennsylvania, for Marjorie Diehl and Richard Armstrong. Also, Diehl-Armstrong told Ed Palattella on March 8, 2017, that she and Armstrong were married in Crawford County, Pennsylvania, immediately south of Erie County. But the clerk of courts for Crawford County, Patricia Wetherbee, told Palattella that no marriage license was on file there for Marjorie Diehl and Richard Armstrong.

21. K. Singh, MD, mental health progress notes for Marjorie Diehl, January 28, 1991, 1. Entered into evidence in *United States v. Marjorie Diehl-Armstrong*. Copy in authors' possession.

22. Ibid., 1–2.

23. Soloff to MacDonald, Illig, Jones & Britton.

24. Ibid.

25. Ibid.

26. Singh, mental health progress notes for Marjorie Diehl, July 31, 1991. Entered into evidence in *United States v. Marjorie Diehl-Armstrong*. Copy in authors' possession.

27. Singh, mental health progress notes for Marjorie Diehl, November 7, 1991, 1, entered into evidence in *United States v. Marjorie Diehl-Armstrong*. Copy in authors' possession.

28. *In Re: Marjorie E. Diehl, debtor*, Chapter 13 plan, October 7, 1991, United States Bankruptcy Court for the Western District of Pennsylvania, No. 91-00697E. Copy in authors' possession.

29. Singh, mental health progress notes for Marjorie Diehl, January 21, 1991, entered into evidence in *United States v. Marjorie Diehl-Armstrong*. Copy in authors' possession.

30. Ibid.

31. Ibid.

32. Soloff to MacDonald, Illig, Jones & Britton, 1–2.

33. Ibid.

34. Paul M. Paris, MD, to Marcia Haller, August 28, 1997, 1, attached to Pretrial Narrative Filed on Behalf of A. K. Mitra, MD, May 4, 1998, *Marjorie Armstrong v. Saint Vincent Health Center*. Copy in authors' possession.

35. Ibid., 2.

36. Transcript of record at 147, October 26, 2003, *United States v. Marjorie Diehl-Armstrong*.

37. Diehl-Armstrong's civil suit states that Armstrong called for an ambulance: Second Amended Complaint, March 10, 1995, at 6, *Armstrong v. Saint Vincent Health Center*. But Diehl-Armstrong testified at the Pizza Bomber trial that she called the ambulance: Transcript of record at 147, October 26, 2003, *United States v. Marjorie Diehl-Armstrong*.

38. Peter E. Sheptak, MD, to Marcia Haller, February 25, 1998, 1–2, attached to Pretrial Narrative Filed on Behalf of A. K. Mitra, May 4, 1998, *Armstrong v. Saint Vincent Health Center*. Copy in authors' possession.

39. Paris and Sheptak. See also Pretrial Narrative of Defendant A. K. Mitra, MD, at 1–2, in *Armstrong v. Saint Vincent Health Center*.

40. Ibid., including Pretrial Narrative of Mitra.

41. Ibid.

42. Second Amended Complaint, *Armstrong v. Saint Vincent Health Center*. See also Pretrial Narrative of Mitra, *Armstrong v. Saint Vincent Health Center*.

43. Deitrich to Thomas, 1–3.

44. Ibid. See also Second Amended Complaint, *Armstrong v. Saint Vincent Health Center*.

45. Deitrich to Thomas, 1–3.

46. Ibid.

47. Ibid.

48. Plaintiff's Pretrial Statement, *Armstrong v. Saint Vincent Health Center*.

49. Transcript of record at 150, October 26, 2003, *United States v. Marjorie Diehl-Armstrong*.

50. Ibid., 146.

51. Singh, mental health progress notes for Marjorie Diehl, January 28, 1993, entered into evidence in *United States v. Marjorie Diehl-Armstrong*. Copy in authors' possession.

52. Ibid.

53. Ibid.

54. Ibid.

55. Transcript of record at 151, October 26, 2003, *United States v. Marjorie Diehl-Armstrong*.

56. Ibid.

57. Ibid., 151.

58. Ibid., 155.

59. Ibid., 157.

60. Ibid., 161.

61. Ed Palattella and Kevin Flowers, "Defendant Had Violent History with Victim," *Erie Times-News*, September 22, 2003.

62. Ibid.

63. Ibid.

64. Ibid.

65. Transcript of record at 122, October 21, 2003, *United States v. Marjorie Diehl-Armstrong*.

66. Motion for Destruction of Perishable Items and/or Trash, September 24, 2003, at 1–2, and Exhibit A, *Commonwealth of Pennsylvania vs. Marjorie Diehl-Armstrong*, Court of Common Pleas, Erie County, Pennsylvania, CR-374-03. Copy in authors' possession.

67. Tim Hahn and Erica Erwin, "Rothstein Melted Shotgun: Police Start Cleaning Out Home Where Man Died," *Erie Times-News*, September 25, 2003.

68. Ibid.

69. Diehl-Armstrong, telephone interview from prison with Palattella, January 15, 2010.

70. Ibid.

71. Singh, mental health progress notes for Marjorie Diehl, January 26, 1996, entered into evidence in *United States v. Marjorie Diehl-Armstrong*. Copy in authors' possession.

72. Ibid., July 19, 1993.

73. Ibid., January 10, 1995.

74. Asha S. Deshpande, MD, mental health progress notes for Marjorie Diehl, October 18, 1999, 1–2, entered into evidence in *United States v. Marjorie Diehl-Armstrong*. Copy in authors' possession.

75. Ibid.

76. Ibid., November 15, 1999.

77. Ibid., April 17, 2000.

78. Ibid., May 3, 2000.

79. Ibid., November 15, 2000.

80. Erie County coroner's report, Agnes Diehl, July 16, 2000. Copy in authors' possession.

81. Formal Amended Caveat, September 18, 2000, at 2, *In Re: In the Estate of Agnes E. Diehl*, Court of Common Pleas, Erie County, Pennsylvania, Orphans' Court Division, No. 318-2000. Copy in authors' possession.

82. Ibid.

83. Records in the estate of Agnes E. Diehl, Register of Wills, Erie County, Pennsylvania, No. 2001-134.

84. Answer, New Matter and Counter Petition for Relief to Petition for Financial Guardianship, May 25, 2010, at 2, *In Re: Harold A. Diehl*, Court of Common Pleas, Erie County, Pennsylvania, Orphans' Court Division, No. 149 of 2010. Copies of court records in authors' possession. See also Ed Palattella, "Diehl-Armstrong Loses Estate Fight, Again," *Erie Times-News*, March 19, 2015.

85. Formal Amended Caveat, at 4, *In Re: In the Estate of Agnes E. Diehl*.

86. Deshpande, November 15, 2000.

87. Marjorie Diehl-Armstrong to Pennsylvania Department of Revenue, September 6, 2000, 3, included in *In Re: In the Estate of Agnes E. Diehl*. Copy in authors' possession.

88. Transcript of record at 161, October 26, 2003, *United States v. Marjorie Diehl-Armstrong*.

89. Ibid., 175.

90. Ibid., Transcript of record at 121–22, October 21, 2003.

91. Ibid., 122.

92. Erie police investigative report on suspected burglary at Marjorie Diehl-Armstrong's house on May 30, 2003, case No. 2003-00024697. Copy in authors' possession.

93. Diehl-Armstrong, interview from prison with Palattella, November 11, 2007.

94. Erie police investigative report on suspected burglary at Marjorie Diehl-Armstrong's house on May 30, 2003, case No. 2003-00024697.

95. Transcript of record at 29, bond hearing, February 12, 2004, *Commonwealth of Pennsylvania v. Marjorie E. Diehl-Armstrong*, No. 236 A & B of 2004.

96. Memorandum in Support of Defendant's Motion to Set Bond/Motion for Return of Property, February 17, 2004, at 2–3, *Commonwealth of Pennsylvania v. Marjorie E. Diehl-Armstrong*. Copy in authors' possession.

97. Transcript of record at 124, October 26, 2003, *United States v. Marjorie Diehl-Armstrong*. Transcript of record at 30, bond hearing, February 12, 2004, *Commonwealth of Pennsylvania v. Marjorie E. Diehl-Armstrong*.

98. Deshpande, mental health progress notes for Marjorie Diehl, June 26, 2001, entered into evidence in *United States v. Marjorie Diehl-Armstrong*. Copy in authors' possession.

99. Deshpande, August 1, 2001.

100. Deshpande, April 23, 2003.

101. Ibid.

102. Ibid.

103. Transcript of record at 9, October 27, 2003, *United States v. Marjorie Diehl-Armstrong*.

104. Deshpande, May 21, 2003.

105. Transcript of record at 123, October 21, 2003, *United States v. Marjorie Diehl-Armstrong*.

106. Ibid., 123.

107. Ibid.

108. Ibid., 125.

109. Ibid., 126.

110. Transcript of record at 12, 15, 17, preliminary hearing, January 20, 2004, *Commonwealth of Pennsylvania v. Marjorie E. Diehl-Armstrong*.

111. Ibid., 17.

112. Transcript of record at 9, October 27, 2003, *United States v. Marjorie Diehl-Armstrong*.

113. Ibid., transcript of record at 8. See also, Erie police investigative report on suspected burglary at Marjorie Diehl-Armstrong's house on May 30, 2003.

114. Transcript of record at 16, preliminary hearing, January 20, 2004, *Commonwealth of Pennsylvania v. Marjorie E. Diehl-Armstrong*.

115. Ibid.

116. Erie police investigative report into the death of Jim Roden, case No. 2003-00047574. Copy in authors' possession.

117. Jerry Clark and Ed Palattella, *Pizza Bomber: The Untold Story of America's Most Shocking Bank Robbery* (New York: Berkley Books/Penguin, 2012), 141–42.

118. Ibid., 57.

119. Kara Rhodes, "Rothstein Was Sub in Erie Schools," *Erie Times-News*, October 2, 2003.

120. Clark and Palattella, *Pizza Bomber*, 58.

121. Diehl-Armstrong, telephone interview from prison with Palattella, May 20, 2008.

122. Ibid., November 6, 2007.

123. Ibid., November 30, 2007.

124. Transcript of record at 43, preliminary hearing, January 20, 2004, *Commonwealth of Pennsylvania v. Marjorie E. Diehl-Armstrong*.

125. Ibid., 49.

126. Transcript of record at 35, bond hearing, February 12, 2004, *Commonwealth of Pennsylvania v. Marjorie E. Diehl-Armstrong.*

127. Ibid., 36.

128. Ibid., 30.

129. Clark and Palattella, *Pizza Bomber*, 60–61.

130. Transcript of record at 90, bond hearing, February 12, 2004, *Commonwealth of Pennsylvania v. Marjorie E. Diehl-Armstrong.*

131. Ibid., 96.

132. Receipt and other records included in file of *Commonwealth of Pennsylvania v. Marjorie E. Diehl-Armstrong.*

133. Transcript of recording of 911 call Bill Rothstein made to Pennsylvania State Police at 8:15 p.m. on September 20, 2003. Copy in authors' possession.

134. Ibid.

135. Lisa Thompson, "The $50,000 Question," *Erie Times-News*, September 29, 2003.

136. Clark and Palattella, *Pizza Bomber*, 128.

137. Federal Bureau of Prisons, competency to stand trial evaluation for Marjorie Diehl-Armstrong, April 25, 2008. Entered into evidence in *United States v. Marjorie Diehl-Armstrong.* Copy in authors' possession.

138. Transcript of record at 107, preliminary hearing, January 20, 2004, *Commonwealth of Pennsylvania v. Marjorie E. Diehl-Armstrong.*

139. Transcript of record at 14, October 20, 2003, *United States v. Marjorie Diehl-Armstrong.*

140. Transcript of record at 62, preliminary hearing, January 20, 2004, *Commonwealth of Pennsylvania v. Marjorie E. Diehl-Armstrong.*

141. Clark and Palattella, *Pizza Bomber*, 175.

142. Tim Hahn, "Police Search Diehl-Armstrong's Cottage," *Erie Times-News*, October 3, 2003.

143. Tim Hahn, "Fire Destroys Cottage," *Erie Times-News*, January 10, 2004.

144. Transcript of record at 33, 130, October 26, 2003, *United States v. Marjorie Diehl-Armstrong.*

145. Transcript of record at 36, 46, 6, bond hearing February 12, 2004, *Commonwealth of Pennsylvania v. Marjorie E. Diehl-Armstrong.*

146. Ibid., 31.

147. Laszlo Petras, MD, and LuAnn Cochenour, Mayview State Hospital summary concerning Marjorie Diehl-Armstrong, August 19, 2004, entered into evidence in *Commonwealth of Pennsylvania v. Marjorie E. Diehl-Armstrong.* Copy in authors' possession.

148. Ibid.
149. Ibid.
150. Ibid.
151. Ibid.
152. Ibid.
153. Transcript of record at 28, plea and sentencing, January 7, 2005, *Commonwealth of Pennsylvania v. Marjorie E. Diehl-Armstrong*; Transcript of record at 28, bond hearing, February 12, 2004., Ibid.
154. Ibid., 22.
155. Ibid., 28–29.
156. Ibid., 23.
157. Ibid.
158. Ibid., 25.
159. Ibid., 26–27.

CHAPTER 11

1. Transcript of record at 89, October 28, 2003, *United States of America v. Marjorie Diehl-Armstrong*, United States District Court for the Western District of Pennsylvania, Crim. 07-26 Erie.
2. Ibid., 127.
3. Ibid., 21.
4. Ibid., 23.
5. Marjorie Diehl-Armstrong, telephone interview from prison with Ed Palattella, January 18, 2008.
6. Ibid., July 29, 2008.
7. Ibid., November 8, 2007.
8. For a more detailed account of Brian Wells's last moments, see Jerry Clark and Ed Palattella, *Pizza Bomber: The Untold Story of America's Most Shocking Bank Robbery* (New York: Berkley Books/Penguin, 2012), 1–29.
9. Ibid. See also WJET-TV Erie broadcast of Pizza Bomber case, August 28, 2003.
10. Transcript of record at 125, October 15, 2003, *United States v. Marjorie Diehl-Armstrong*.
11. Bill Rothstein's suicide note, September 21, 2003, entered into evidence in *Commonwealth of Pennsylvania v. Marjorie E. Diehl-Armstrong*, No. 236 A & B of 2004. Copy in authors' possession.
12. Tim Hahn, "Handyman-Wells Link? Rothstein Wrote Suicide Note Proclaiming Innocence in Pizza Deliveryman's Killing," *Erie Times-News*, September 27, 2003.

13. Clark and Palattella, *Pizza Bomber*, 155. See also videotaped police interview with Bill Rothstein during the tour of his house, September 22, 2003. Copy in authors' possession.

14. Clark and Palattella, *Pizza Bomber*, 188. Also, Palattella and Tim Hahn interview with Bill Rothstein, July 30, 2004.

15. Competency order, July 29, 2008, *United States v. Marjorie Diehl-Armstrong*.

16. Clark and Palattella, *Pizza Bomber*, 202. See also FBI 302 notes of interview with Marjorie Diehl Armstrong, April 27, 2005. Copy in authors' possession.

17. Clark and Palattella, *Pizza Bomber*, 203. See also FBI 302 notes of interview with Marjorie Diehl Armstrong, April 27, 2005. Copy in authors' possession.

18. Clark and Palattella, *Pizza Bomber*, 216. See also FBI 302 notes of interview with Marjorie Diehl Armstrong, July 5, 2005. Copy in authors' possession.

19. Clark and Palattella, *Pizza Bomber*, 201–11. See also Transcript of record at 130, October 20, 2003, *United States v. Marjorie Diehl-Armstrong*.

20. Ibid., 16.

21. Ibid.

22. Transcript of record at 140–41, October 21, 2003, *United States v. Marjorie Diehl-Armstrong*.

23. Ibid., 203.

24. FBI 302 notes of interview with Ken Barnes, December 9, 2005. Copy in authors' possession.

25. Clark and Palattella, *Pizza Bomber*, 82, which refers to the coroner's report on Robert Pinetti's death.

26. Transcript of record at 123, October 21, 2003, *United States of America v. Marjorie Diehl-Armstrong*.

27. Clark and Palattella, *Pizza Bomber*, 16. Copy of notes also in authors' possession.

28. Ibid., 91. Copy of statement in authors' possession.

29. Ibid., 281. See also FBI 302 notes of interview with Marjorie Diehl-Armstrong on May 10, 2006. Copy in authors' possession.

30. Transcript of record at 53–73, October 18, 2003, *United States v. Marjorie Diehl-Armstrong*.

31. Diehl-Armstrong, telephone interview from prison with Palattella, August 21, 2008.

32. Ibid.

33. Transcript of record at 5, July 12, 2007, *United States of America v. Marjorie Diehl-Armstrong*.

34. Ramit Plushnick Masti, "Robbery-Plot Suspect's Father Not Surprised," *Philly.com*, July 13, 2007, http://www.philly.com/philly/news/penn sylvania/20070713_Suspects_father_not_surprised.html.

35. Ibid.

36. Ed Palattella, Kara Rhodes, Steven M. Sweeney, and Lisa Thompson, "Plot Unfolds," *Erie Times-News*, July 12, 2007.

CHAPTER 12

1. Robert L. Sadoff, MD, to Thomas Patton, January 15, 2008, 4, entered as evidence in *United States of America v. Marjorie Diehl-Armstrong*, United States District Court for the Western District of Pennsylvania, Crim. 07-26 Erie. Copy in authors' possession.

2. Order, May 31, 2005, *Commonwealth of Pennsylvania v. Marjorie E. Diehl-Armstrong*, No. 236 A & B of 2004. The final distributed amount was $73,429.34.

3. Marjorie Diehl-Armstrong, telephone interview from prison with Ed Palattella, November 7, 2007.

4. Ibid.

5. Ibid.

6. Diehl-Armstrong, telephone interview from prison with Palattella, November 14, 2007.

7. Ibid.

8. Competency to Stand Trial Evaluation for Marjorie-Armstrong, April 15, 2008, entered into evidence in *United States v. Marjorie Diehl-Armstrong*. Copy in authors' possession.

9. Government's Proposed Findings of Fact and Conclusions of Law Regarding Competency Hearing for Marjorie Diehl Armstrong, June 23, 2008, at 16, Ibid.

10. Ibid.

11. Competency to Stand Trial Evaluation for Marjorie Diehl-Armstrong, April 15, 2008, entered into evidence in *United States v. Marjorie Diehl-Armstrong*.

12. Ibid.

13. Ibid.

14. Ibid.

15. Ibid.

16. Ibid.

17. Ed Palattella, "Competency Hearing Ends," *Erie Times-News*, May 23, 2008.

18. Ed Palattella, "Mental State: Experts Disagree," *Erie Times-News*, May 22, 2008.

19. Ibid.

20. Ibid.

21. Ibid.

22. Ed Palattella, "Fit to Be Tried," *Erie Times-News*, May 21, 2008.

23. Ibid.

24. Ibid.

25. Ibid.

26. Ibid.

27. Findings of Fact and Conclusions of Law, July 29, 2008, at 45, *United States v. Diehl-Armstrong*.

28. Palattella, "Competency Hearing Ends."

29. Diehl-Armstrong, telephone interview from prison with Palattella, May 22, 2008.

30. Ibid.

31. Ibid, May 28, 2008.

32. Ibid.

33. Findings of Fact and Conclusions of Law, at 47–48, *United States v. Diehl-Armstrong*.

34. Diehl-Armstrong, telephone interview from prison with Palattella, September 3, 2008.

35. Ed Palattella, "Barnes Gets 45 Years," *Erie Times-News*, December 4, 2008.

36. Ibid.

37. Ibid.

38. Findings of Fact and Conclusions of Law, September 8, 2009, at 10, *United States v. Diehl-Armstrong*.

39. Ibid.

40. Ibid.

41. Ibid., 27.

42. Ibid., 18.

43. Ibid., 63.

44. Ibid., 63–64.

45. Jerry Clark and Ed Palattella, *Pizza Bomber: The Untold Story of America's Most Shocking Bank Robbery* (New York: Berkley Books/Penguin, 2012), 357.

46. Ibid., 356.

47. Findings of Fact and Conclusions of Law, September 8, 2009, at 59, *United States v. Marjorie Diehl-Armstrong*.

48. Ed Palattella, "Case to Get New Lawyer," *Erie Times-News*, September 8, 2009.

49. Ibid.

50. Ibid.

51. Ed Palattella, "Request for New Lawyer Denied," *Erie Times-News*, June 5, 2010.

52. Ed Palattella, notes from hearing in United States District Court in Erie, Pennsylvania, in *United States v. Diehl-Armstrong*, October 12, 2010.

53. Ed Palattella, "Nonlocal Jurors Sought," *Erie Times-News*, August 28, 2010.

54. Diehl-Armstrong, telephone interview from prison with Palattella, October 13, 2010.

55. Palattella, "Nonlocal Jurors Sought."

56. Ibid., April 7, 2010.

57. Ibid.

58. Ibid.

59. Ibid., April 9, 2010.

60. Ibid., December 21, 2009.

61. Ed Palattella, "Killer Maintains Contact with Reporter," *Erie Times-News*, August 25, 2013.

62. Ibid., May 12, 2009.

63. Ibid., April 9, 2010.

64. Palattella, "Killer Maintains Contact with Reporter."

65. Ibid., March 2, 2010.

66. Findings of Fact and Conclusions of Law, September 8, 2009, at 13, *United States v. Diehl-Armstrong*.

67. Diehl-Armstrong, telephone interview from prison with Palattella, May 6, 2008.

68. Competency to Stand Trial Evaluation for Marjorie Diehl-Armstrong, April 15, 2008, entered into evidence in *United States v. Marjorie Diehl-Armstrong*.

69. Robert L. Sadoff to Douglas Sughrue, September 13, 2010, 3, entered into evidence in *United States v. Diehl-Armstrong*. Copy in authors' possession.

70. Ibid., 4.

71. Ibid.

72. Ibid., 4–5.

73. Ed Palattella, "Accused Plotter to Take Witness Stand," *Erie Times-News*, October 26, 2010.

74. Transcript of record at 76–77, October 27, 2003, *United States v. Diehl-Armstrong*. Copy in authors' possession.

75. Transcript of record, 83, October 22, 2010; Ibid.

76. Diehl-Armstrong, telephone interview from prison with Palattella, May 1, 2008.

77. Transcript of record at 85, October 28, 2010, *United States v. Diehl-Armstrong*.

78. Ibid., 79.

79. Ibid., 131.

80. Ibid., 19.

AFTERWORD

1. Ed Palattella, "Father's Assets Quickly Being Drained," *Erie Times-News*, July 16, 2010.

2. Answer, New Matter and Counter Petition for Relief to Petition for Financial Guardianship, May 25, 2010, at 5, *In Re: Harold A. Diehl*, Court of Common Pleas, Erie County, Pennsylvania, Orphans' Court Division, No. 149 of 2010. Copies of court records in authors' possession.

3. Palattella, "Father's Assets Quickly Being Drained."

4. Ed Palattella, "No Inheritance Left," *Erie Times-News*, February 23, 2014.

5. Ed Palattella, "Bomb Suspect Seeks Ruling on Dad," *Erie Times-News*, May 17, 2010.

6. *United States of America v. Marjorie Diehl-Armstrong*, No. 11-1601 (3rd Cir. 2012), at 7.

7. Memorandum Opinion, December 28, 2015, at 17, *United States of America v. Marjorie Diehl-Armstrong*, United States District Court for the Western District of Pennsylvania, Crim. 07-26 Erie.

8. Ed Palattella, "Diehl-Armstrong Wins Parole, but Gets No Relief in Pizza Bomber Case," *Erie Times-News*, November 10, 2014.

9. Ed Palattella, "Barnes' Pizza Bomber Sentence Halved," June 7, 2011, *Erie Times-News*.

10. Marjorie Diehl-Armstrong, telephone interview from prison with Ed Palattella, July 29, 2008.

11. Ibid., August 4, 2016.

12. Ibid., September 27, 2012.

13. Ibid., September 17, 2016.

14. Ibid.

15. Ibid., June 3, 2016.

16. Ibid., October 3, 2008.

Selected Bibliography

American Medico-Psychological Association. *Statistical Manual for Use of the Institutions for the Insane.* New York: Bureau of Statistics, the National Committee for Mental Hygiene, 1918. https://ia801405.us.archive.org/14/items/statisticalmanu00assogoog/statisticalmanu00assogoog.pdf

American Psychiatric Association. *Diagnostic and Statistical Manual of Mental Disorders,* fourth edition: *DSM-IV.* Washington, DC: American Psychiatric Publishing, 1994.

American Psychiatric Association. *Diagnostic and Statistical Manual of Mental Disorders,* fifth edition: *DSM-5.* Washington, DC: American Psychiatric Publishing, 2013.

Bailey, Frankie Y., and Donna C. Hale. *Blood on Her Hands: Women Who Murder.* Belmont, CA: Wadsworth, 2004.

Black, Donald W., and Jon E. Grant. *DSM-5 Guidebook.* Washington, DC: American Psychiatric Publishing, 2014.

Burgess, Wes. *The Bipolar Handbook.* New York: Avery/Penguin, 2006.

Clark, Jerry, and Ed Palattella. *Pizza Bomber: The Untold Story of America's Most Shocking Bank Robbery.* New York: Berkley Books/Penguin, 2012.

Cleckley, Hervey M. *The Mask of Sanity: An Attempt to Clarify Some Issues about the So-called Psychopathic Personality.* St. Louis, MO: C. V. Mosby Co., 1964.

Erickson, Patricia E., and Steven K. Erickson. *Crime, Punishment, and Mental Illness.* New Brunswick, NJ: Rutgers University Press, 2008.

Farrell, Amanda L., Robert D. Keppel, and Victoria B. Titterington. "Lethal Ladies: Revisiting What We Know about Female Serial Killers." *Homicide Studies* 15, no. 3 (2011): 228–52.

Federal Bureau of Investigation. *Serial Murder: Multi-Disciplinary Perspectives for Investigators* (2005): https://www.fbi.gov/stats-services/publications/serial-murder.

Finkel, Norman J. *Insanity on Trial.* New York: Plenum Press, 1988.

Frost, Randy O., and Gail Steketee, *Stuff: Compulsive Hoarding and the Meaning of Things.* Boston, MA: Houghton Mifflin Harcourt, 2010.

George, Leonard. Foreword to *The Encyclopedia of Schizophrenia and Other Psychotic Disorders*, third edition. New York: Facts on File, 2007.

Giannangelo, Stephen J. *The Psychopathology of Serial Murder: A Theory of Violence.* Westport, CT: Praeger, 1996.

Goodwin, Frederick K., and Kay Redfield Jamison. *Manic-Depressive Illness.* New York: Oxford University Press, 1990.

Greenberg, Gary. *The Book of Woe: The DSM and the Unmaking of Psychiatry.* New York: Penguin/Blue Rider Press, 2013.

Harrison, Marissa A., Erin A. Murphy, Lavina Y. Ho, Thomas G. Bowers, and Claire V. Flaherty. "Female Serial Killers in the United States: Means, Motives, and Makings." *Journal of Forensic Psychiatry & Psychology* 26, no. 3 (2015): 383–406.

Healy, David. *Mania: A Short History of Bipolar Disorder.* Baltimore, MD: Johns Hopkins University Press, 2008.

Hermsen, Lisa M. *Manic Hands: Mania's Mad History and Its Neuro-Future.* New Brunswick, NJ: Rutgers University Press, 2011.

Hickey, Eric W. *Serial Murderers and Their Victims*, fifth edition. Belmont, CA: Wadsworth, 2010.

Holmes, Ronald M., and Stephen T. Holmes, eds. *Contemporary Perspectives on Serial Murder.* Thousand Oaks, CA: Sage, 1998.

Jones, Ann. *Women Who Kill.* New York: Holt, Rinehart and Winston, 1980.

Keeney Belea T., and Kathleen M. Heide. "Gender Differences in Serial Murderers: A Preliminary Analysis." *Journal of Interpersonal Violence* 9, no. 3 (1994): 383–98.

Kelleher, Michael D., and C. L. Kelleher. *Murder Most Rare: The Female Serial Killer.* Westport, CT: Praeger, 1998.

Knoll, Richard. *The Encyclopedia of Schizophrenia and Other Psychotic Disorders*, third edition. New York: Facts on File, 2007.

Leyton, Elliott H., ed. *Serial Murder: Modern Scientific Perspectives.* Burlington, VT: Ashgate Publishing Co., 2000.

Mann, Coramae Richey. *When Women Kill.* Albany: State University of New York Press, 1996.

Melville, R. D. *A Manual of the Principles of Roman Law.* Edinburgh: W. Green & Son, 1915.

Norris, Joel. *Serial Killers*. New York: Anchor Books/Doubleday, 1988.

Perlin, Michael. *The Jurisprudence of the Insanity Defense*. Durham, NC: Carolina Academic Press, 1994.

Ramsland, Katherine. *The Human Predator: A Historical Chronicle of Serial Murder and Forensic Investigation*. New York: Berkley Books: 2005.

———. *Inside the Minds of Mass Murderers: Why They Kill*. Westport, CT: Praeger, 2005.

Ressler, Robert A., and Tom Shactman. *I Have Lived in the Monster: A Report from the Abyss*. New York: St. Martin's Press, 1997.

Rush, Benjamin. *Medical Inquiries and Observations upon the Diseases of the Mind*. Philadelphia: Kimber & Richardson, 1812. https://collections.nlm. nih.gov/bookviewer?PID=nlm:nlmuid-2569036R-bk

Schouten, Ronald, and James Silver. *Almost a Psychopath*. Center City, MN: Hazelden, 2012.

Schurman-Kauflin, Deborah. *The New Predator: Women Who Kill*. New York: Algora Publishing, 2000.

Scott, Charles, ed. *DSM-5 and the Law*. New York: Oxford University Press, 2015.

Simon, Rita J. *The Jury and the Defense of Insanity*. Boston, MA: Little, Brown and Company, 1967.

Simon, Rita J., and Heather Ahn-Redding. *The Insanity Defense, the World Over*. Lanham, MD: Lexington, 2006.

Solomon, Andrew. *The Noonday Demon: An Atlas of Depression*. New York: Touchstone/Simon & Schuster, 2001.

Steadman, Henry J., Margaret A. McGreevy, Joseph P. Morrisey, Lisa A. Callahan, Pamela Clark Robbins, and Carmine Cirincione. *Before and after Hinckley: Evaluating Defense Reform*. New York: The Guilford Press, 1993.

Tolin, David F., Randy O. Frost, and Gail Steketee. *Buried in Treasures: Help for Compulsive Acquiring, Saving, and Hoarding*. Oxford: Oxford University Press, 2007.

Torrey, E. Fuller, and Michael B. Knable. *Surviving Manic Depression*. New York: Basic Books, 2002.

Vronsky, Peter. *Female Serial Killers: How and Why Women Become Monsters*. New York: Berkley Books, 2007.

Index

About the Authors

Jerry Clark retired as a special agent with the Federal Bureau of Investigation in 2011 after twenty-seven years in law enforcement, including careers as a special agent with the Drug Enforcement Administration and the Naval Criminal Investigative Service. He received a PhD in public service leadership from Capella University, an MA in forensic psychology from the City University of New York John Jay College of Criminal Justice, and a BA in psychology from Edinboro University of Pennsylvania. Clark is an assistant professor of criminal justice at Gannon University in Erie, Pennsylvania, where he is also co-owner of Clark & Wick Investigations LLC. He lives with his wife and two children in Erie.

Ed Palattella joined the *Erie Times-News*, in Erie, Pennsylvania, in 1990. He has won a number of awards, including for his investigative work and coverage of crime. He arrived in Erie after reporting for the *Point Reyes Light* in Marin County, California. Palattella received an MA in journalism from Stanford University and a BA in English literature from Washington University in St. Louis. He lives with his wife and two children in Erie.

Clark and Palattella are the coauthors of *Pizza Bomber: The Untold Story of America's Most Shocking Bank Robbery*, and *A History of Heists: Bank Robbery in America*. As a special agent with the FBI, Clark led the investigation of the Pizza Bomber case in Erie, Pennsylvania, which was FBI Major Case 203. Palattella covered the case as a reporter for the *Erie Times-News*. He continued to hear regularly, by phone, from the incarcerated Marjorie Diehl-Armstrong until shortly before her death in April 2017.